THE

ELEMENTS

OF

JOURNALISM

THE
ELEMENTS
OF
JOURNALISM

REVISED AND UPDATED THIRD EDITION

What Newspeople Should Know
and the Public Should Expect

Bill Kovach & Tom Rosenstiel

 THREE RIVERS PRESS • NEW YORK

Published in the United States by Three Rivers Press, an imprint of the Crown
Publishing Group, a division of Random House LLC, a Penguin Random House
Company, New York.

www.crownpublishing.com

Three Rivers Press and the Tugboat design are registered trademarks of
Random House LLC.

Grateful acknowledgment is made to Cable News Network, Inc. (CNN) for
permission to reprint a text excerpt from the show *Crossfire* (October 15, 2004).
Reprinted by permission of Cable News Network, Inc. (CNN).

Originally published in hardcover in the United States by Crown Publishers, an
imprint of the Crown Publishing Group, a division of Random House LLC, New
York, in 2001 and subsequently revised and published in paperback by Three
Rivers Press, an imprint of the Crown Publishing Group, a division of Random
House LLC, New York, in 2007.

Library of Congress Cataloging-in-Publication data is available upon request.

ISBN 978-0-8041-3678-5

eBook ISBN 978-0-8041-3679-2

Printed in the United States of America

Book design by Maria Elias

10   9   8

Revised Edition

For Lynne
&
For Beth and Karina

CONTENTS

When we first wrote this book in 2001, our purpose was different than it is now.

Our intention then was to identify common principles shared by people who called themselves journalists working in different mediums and traditions. Even then, these shared ideas and theories of journalism were not as well understood or articulated as many might have supposed, including by those in news. People in different media tended to use different vocabularies. Many often mistook their practices—the techniques they used every day at their jobs—for fundamental principles of purpose. (The concept that journalists should get at the truth of events is a principle. The use of the inverted pyramid structure for writing news stories is a practice.) Most journalists, trained in an apprenticeship model that emphasized craft, tended to dismiss as too theoretical such abstract questions as trying to define the role of journalists in society. There was also a growing culture war in news companies at the time between business and editorial people as they eyed the growing pressures caused by the coming digital revolution. The reason we wrote this book, in part, was that this vagueness about journalism's underlying principles and values had left journalists vulnerable—first to a counting house mentality that discouraged investing in innovation, then to an epochal digital disruption that demanded journalism rethink how it fulfilled its fundamental purpose on behalf of citizens.

But back then, the values we unearthed that made up the elements of journalism were largely the domain of professionals—a loosely organized group who practiced journalism for a living and who called themselves journalists.

Now, a dozen years later, our goal in this new edition is different in one important respect. Our purpose is to identify the core principles that underlie the production of responsible journalism in which anyone in the world might be staff.

Journalism and the elements of journalism should concern all citizens today even more than they once did precisely because the distinctions between citizen and journalist, reporter and editor, audience and producer are not vanishing but blurring. Journalism isn't dying. It is becoming more of a collaboration. And journalists are not being replaced or becoming irrelevant. Their role has become more complex and more critical.

This transformation has been particularly profound since the second edition of this book was published in 2007. Media brand names that dominated the twentieth century, such as *Newsweek* magazine and the Times Mirror and Knight Ridder newspaper companies, are gone. Network TV newsrooms have shrunk by more than half, newspaper newsrooms by more nearly a third, and newspaper industry revenues by even more. To a significant degree, in less than half a decade, digital disruption has overturned the economic model that sustained news reporting and presentation for more than a century.

In the face of this, we are increasingly asked the same question: *To what extent do the principles that guided journalism in the nineteenth and twentieth centuries still apply? Indeed, are there any principles at all?*

As the contours of the digital revolution have grown clearer, we have grown even more confident that not only do the elements of journalism endure–but in an age when anyone may produce and distribute news, they matter even more.

What has been transformed–profoundly–is how those who produce news fulfill those principles.

The reason the core elements of journalism endure is simple: They never came from journalists in the first place. They flowed from the public's need for news that was credible and useful. The elements of journalism are the ingredients that allow people to know the facts and context of events, to understand how they should react to that information, and to work on compromises and solutions that make their communities better. Journalists didn't create these needs–they simply developed a series of concepts and methods for meeting them.

Today, these principles are more important precisely because whether a work of journalism comes from a trusted brand name is no longer the only clue to its value. In an age when journalism may come from many sources, we must all learn to navigate with a more discerning eye to know which content is credible and which is suspect.

The elements of journalism, in other words, always belonged to the public. To survive as citizens today, we must understand them, own them, and apply them as never before.

Whether a news report is produced by a citizen eyewitness, funded by a grant from an advocacy nonprofit, or delivered by a conventional news source, for instance, we still need it to be truthful. But in an age when false rumors may be tweeted in real time, how someone reporting the news fulfills the principle of truthfulness has changed substantially. A reporter cannot ignore what is already public or has been reported elsewhere. He or she must note the false rumor's presence, track its impact, and show why it should be disbelieved or what would need to be established for it to be proved true.

Saying that the principles of journalism endure should not be mistaken for an argument in favor of nostalgia and resistance to innovation. To the contrary, it is a call for a deeper and broader application of journalism's purpose–adapted to the new ways that news is gathered and delivered.

In the first edition of *The Elements of Journalism*, published in 2001, we argued that the goal of journalism, its value and purpose, was to help citizens gain the knowledge they needed to self-govern and navigate their lives. The principles of journalism that we outlined in the first edition formed something that many journalists could not articulate but that was consistent throughout different styles of and approaches to news. We described what news was for, its value, why it was created, and thus what kind of news should be made public.

In the time since the first two editions of this book were published, journalism has become a collaborative exercise, an ongoing participatory conversation among those who produce news and those who consume it. In this new edition, we will describe the contours of that collaboration and new concepts necessary for journalism to be reliable, useful, and worthy of the public service mission to which it aspires—and which in America is afforded constitutional protection.

This purpose is not easily fulfilled. Many of the changes of the last decade at first glance may seem to stand in the way of journalistic resurgence. The collapse of the advertising-based revenue model has shrunken the size of most organized newsrooms. At the same time, a new wave of social media has emerged, built around brevity, networking, and ease of use, led by YouTube, Facebook, Twitter, Pinterest, Storify, Instagram, and others. These new platforms began to fulfill the promise that we are all producers as well as consumers in a way that the first wave of social media—blogging—had only hinted at.

The crisis facing organized journalism in the wake of these changes is not primarily an audience problem. Particularly at the local level, audiences in the digital space still get their news from trusted and familiar brands, although they come by those brands through the use of many different delivery systems. The crisis facing organized journalism is more fundamentally a revenue problem. Though the audience has migrated to news publishers online, revenue has not.

At the same time, the technology that has devastated the economic structure of news has also created powerful new tools to make the news we get better. Journalism can be more accurate, more informative, more engaging, by being produced in collaboration with the intelligence of the community once imagined to be merely an audience and by employing the machinery of the network to also make it more empirical.

The openness of the network also represents similar pulls in opposing directions when it comes to freedom. Citizens who want to resist authoritarian regimes have more tools to do so. Yet the network is equally open to anyone who wants to manipulate the public—from propagandists to commercialists to governments.

Thus more responsibility falls on all of us as citizens and as journalists to grasp the fundamentals of journalism and to protect them. Journalism is the literature of civic life. When the whole world is its staff, understanding the elements of journalism is everyone's responsibility.

Readers familiar with this book's previous editions will find changes throughout this new one. Many of the examples illustrating the ideas we are conveying have been replaced by newer ones. In some cases, newer developments have been added to the existing incidents because they build on one another and together tell a more complex story. The new edition deals with the role of aggregators, social media, the shift toward more collaboration with community, or what some call "open journalism,"[1] more extensively than did earlier editions. At the same time, it grapples with a new wave of concentration in media that has occurred following the Great Recession, after which more media companies came under the ownership of hedge funds and others for whom journalism is not a central activity. Much of the revenue surrounding journalism now flows to companies such as Google that are engaged in its distribution but not its creation and, thus, its values.[2]

Among the changes, the chapter on journalism's allegiance to citizens has been reimagined to accommodate the fact that journalism now is often produced in venues such as think tanks, corporations, and advocacy groups. By what standards does the public decide whether work produced by organizations like these is credible? The second edition of this book talked about the rising influence of the accounting mentality in news companies and the failure of a host of mergers after 2001. This third edition includes discussion of new stresses placed on journalism's values as companies grapple with the failure of online display advertising to bring in revenue commensurate with the size of its audience on that platform.

In the first edition, we argued that the real meaning of objectivity had more to do with transparency than the absence of bias–an argument that was challenging and controversial when we introduced it then. Today, it is accepted and widely echoed. We argued a decade ago that a transparent method of verification was the most important tool for professional journalists trying to answer doubts the public had about their work. Now it is also a way to invite the public into the production of the news, to create a collaborative journalism that is better than either journalists or citizens could produce alone.

In the chapter on journalism as a public forum, the nature of that forum has expanded dramatically with innovations in social media. In the second edition, we talked about how what linguist Deborah Tannen dubbed the "Argument Culture," in which media staged polarizing debates in order to attract an audience, was giving way to something new: media that offered affirmation and reassurance rather than pyrotechnic debate. We called this a new Journalism of Affirmation because it built an audience around partisan reassurance, and this neo-partisan journalism has grown in popularity since 2007. At the same time, the move from blogs to social media forums–in which everyone is a participant and commentator–has made the Web the new setting for the Argument Culture.

In the chapter on making the news comprehensive and proportional, the age of mixing news and entertainment (which came to be known as "infotainment") has given way to a new form of tabloidization, in which publishers chase maximum page views and raw numbers with material that often is at odds with long-term growth based on depth and quality. That chapter contains a new approach for news publishers to do research and use metrics in the digital age.

In chapter 10, we examine how conscience in the news has expanded from being principally a matter of how to exercise sound judgment in large institutional news settings to being a matter of exercising it in settings where the underwriter or owner is financing the activity not only for commercial reasons, but sometimes also for political ones.

Recent and ongoing disruptions in news have heightened many tensions in the last six years: tensions between champions of technology and those who feel threatened by it, between advocates of user-generated content and those who place more value on professionalism, between those who worry about the shrinking role of professional news gatherers and those who think traditional media's flaws were so great that its diminishing influence should be welcomed.

These stresses will prove healthy, once they are ultimately resolved. The same technology that has devastated the economic model of news has also provided an extraordinary set of new means for gathering and delivering it. The journalism of the twenty-first century has the potential to be more engaging, more valuable, and more informative than the journalism of the twentieth.

But in the meantime, some of these tensions have proven counterproductive. The arguments between advocates of the new and defenders of the old often fail to grasp that the two sides need each other more than they realize. This interdependence is not nearly as new as it seems. What may seem today to be inadequate examples of transparency and listening to the audience—such as letters to the editors, op-ed pages, guest columns, corrections, or even datelines and bylines—were born from the same spirit of connectedness that advocates of networked journalism champion today.

The future of news, in other words, is more firmly rooted in its history, and its enduring values, than many recognize. But whether that future is characterized by a new age of enlightenment or one of manipulation will depend more now on both what the public demands of the news and the degree to which it participates in its responsible production.

This new, third edition of *The Elements of Journalism* has been revised and modernized to help the public and the journalists who serve them in that journey.

Bill Kovach and Tom Rosenstiel, January 2014

THE

ELEMENTS

OF

JOURNALISM

INTRODUCTION

W hen anthropologists began to compare notes on the nature of communication in the world's few remaining primitive cultures, they discovered something unexpected. From the most isolated tribal societies in Africa to the most distant islands in the Pacific, people shared an essentially similar definition of news. They shared gossip. They talked about their leaders. They even looked for the same qualities in the messengers they picked to gather and deliver their news: people who could run swiftly, gather accurate information, and retell it in an engaging way. While tastes have ebbed and flowed and news has been at times more and less serious, historians have discovered that the basic news values have remained relatively constant throughout time. "Humans have exchanged a similar mix of news . . . throughout history and across cultures," historian Mitchell Stephens has written.[1]

How do we explain this rough continuity and consistency? The answer, historians and sociologists have concluded, is that news satisfies a basic human impulse. People have an intrinsic need–an instinct–to know what is occurring beyond their own experience, the events over the next hill.[2] Being aware of events we cannot see for ourselves engenders a sense of security, control, and confidence. One writer has called it "a hunger for awareness."[3]

One of the first things people do when meeting a friend or acquaintance is to share information. "Have you heard about . . . ?" We want to know if they've heard what we have, and if they heard it the same way. There is a thrill in a shared sense of discovery. We form relationships, choose friends, and make character judgments based partly on whether someone reacts to information the same way as we do.

When the flow of news is obstructed, "a darkness falls" and anxiety grows.[4] The world, in effect, becomes too quiet. We feel alone. John McCain, the U.S. senator from Arizona and former presidential candidate, wrote that in his five and a half years as a prisoner of war in Hanoi, what he missed most was not comfort, food, freedom, or even his family and friends. "The thing I missed most was information—free uncensored, undistorted, abundant information."[5] In classes on news at SUNY Stony Brook, students are put through news blackouts in which they are cut off from all media. During these blackouts they begin to wear clothes not suited to the weather, carry umbrellas unnecessarily, and become anxious.[6]

Call it the Awareness Instinct.

We need news to live our lives, protect ourselves, bond with each other, and identify friends and enemies. What we came to call journalism is simply the system societies generate to supply this information about what is and what's to come. That is why we care about the character of the news and journalism we get: News influences the quality of our lives, our thoughts, and our culture. News from its beginning created what technologists today call the "social flow" of information. Writer Thomas Cahill, the author of several popular books on the history of religion, has put it this way: You can tell "the worldview of a people ... the invisible fears and desires ... in a culture's stories."[7]

At a moment of revolution in communications, what do the stories we tell say about our worldview—our fears, desires, and values?

On the eve of the digital revolution, on a rainy Saturday in June 1997, twenty-five journalists gathered at the Harvard Faculty Club. Around the long table sat editors of several of the nation's top newspapers, as well as some of the most influential names in television and radio, several of the top journalism educators, and some of the country's most prominent authors. We were among those gathered.

The digital age was only beginning, but the journalists gathered that day already thought something was seriously wrong with their profession. They barely recognized what they considered journalism in much of their colleagues' work. Instead of serving a larger public interest, they feared, their profession was damaging it.

The public, in turn, had already started to distrust journalists, even hate them. And it would only get worse. In 1999, less than half of Americans (45 percent) believed the press protected democracy, nearly ten points lower than in 1985.[8] By 2011, as many people would feel the press hurt democracy as helped it, 42 percent. And just 15 percent would think the press was independent, less than half the number (37 percent) in 1985.[9]

The problem is not just public perception. By the late 1990s, many journalists were beginning to share the public's growing skepticism about the press. "In the newsroom we no longer talk about journalism," said Maxwell King, the editor of the *Philadelphia Inquirer*, that day in Cambridge. Another editor agreed: "We are consumed with business pressure and the bottom line." The concern wasn't that the values of news had deteriorated. It was that news companies had begun to operate in a way that suggested they no longer believed in those values.

News was becoming entertainment, and entertainment news. Journalists' bonuses were increasingly tied to profit margins, not to the quality of their work. As the discussion drew to a close, Columbia University professor James Carey offered what many recalled as a summation: "The problem is that you see journalism disappearing inside the larger world of communications. What you yearn to do is recover journalism from that larger world."

Digital technology had not yet eroded the advertising revenue model that financed journalism, or diminished journalists' ability to verify the news before the public saw it. Newspaper revenue, for instance, would continue to grow for seven more years, peaking in 2005. What worried some of the leaders of America's journalistic and educational institutions was commercialization—the sense that the leaders of their companies had become more concerned with growing profits to please investors and had lost confidence that investing in better, more innovative journalism could help them engage new audiences.

Already, largely because of the corporate structure of the news industry, newsroom leaders were worried about an important existential question. If journalism—the system by which citizens get news—was being subsumed by commercialization, what would replace it? Advertising? Entertainment? E-commerce? Propaganda? Ideological news? Fragmentation? And what would the consequence be? The idea of user-generated content, news in which everyone participated, was not yet a topic of serious discussion beyond a few digital pioneers.

Most of the people in that room had seen the industry undergo enormous changes throughout their careers. For a century prior to the Internet, disruptive technologies and new formats emerged roughly every fifteen to twenty years. Radio had come in the 1920s, followed by television in the 1950s (delayed by World War II), cable television, and then the deregulation of electronic media in the 1980s that helped give way to the new era of partisanship on radio and TV. With each new technology, new forms of entertainment emerged to compete for people's attention. The incumbent media would change, shove over, lose some hold on the audience, and then adapt as a smaller entity.

At its best, journalism survived because it provided something unique to a culture: independent, reliable, accurate, and comprehensive information that citizens require in order to make sense of the world around them. A journalism that provides something other than that subverts democratic culture. This is what happens when governments control the news, as it did in Nazi Germany or the Soviet Union. We see this today in places like Singapore, where news is controlled to encourage capitalism but discourage participation in public life.

The public's growing discontent with journalism that began in the 1980s is not a rejection of journalism's values. It is a result of journalists' failure to live up to those values. Look closely at the data on trust, for instance, and you will see that even today the public has not given up its expectation that the news will be independent and reliable, or that news be produced by people who are operating in the public interest. Data from the Pew Research Center shows that a clear majority–64 percent–of the public prefers getting news from sources that have no political point of view–and those numbers have barely budged over the course of two decades.[10] The number is even more pronounced (74 percent) when people are asked about online news content.[11] The public largely still expects the news to be produced by skilled professionals; what disappoints them is that the news has not lived up to those promises.

On one level, the credibility crisis is ironic. Many news companies had tried to adapt to a changing marketplace by delivering what they thought the public wanted, trying to make the news more like entertainment. Television news in particular had leaned toward celebrity scandal and true crime to lure viewers back–and had done so unsuccessfully. The number one topic on nightly news in the 1990s was crime, during a decade when crime was dropping. While stories such as the O. J. Simpson trial and the murder of a child named Jon-Benet Ramsey would buoy ratings briefly, audiences began to sense they were being exploited. The credibility research found the public decried media sensationalism–a fact some in the news business dismissed as public hypocrisy.

Distracted by the myopia of trying to keep audiences interested in old platforms and managing costs to protect profits, news companies missed something essential: People were not abandoning news. They simply were abandoning traditional formats in favor of new ones that were more convenient. First, twenty-four-hour cable news was an easier way to check out headlines than waiting for the evening newscast at 6:30, even if the later evening newscast might be a better product. Soon enough, the Web would prove to be profoundly more convenient, deeper, and eventually, more portable.

Journalists were culpable in their own way for the growing discontent and migration of the public. They staked too much faith in traditional definitions of quality news and failed to study the changing news audience. They saw the Internet as a threat to what they knew and failed to recognize it as an opportunity to reach new audiences in new ways with new forms of content. The gathering in Cambridge in 1997 was a signal that, even before the digital disruption, many journalists sensed their industry had lost focus on the public and in a journalism that served its needs.

In short, the collective failure of the news industry to adapt to the digital revolution was rooted in a crisis of confidence about news that had been sounding alarms a decade earlier.

In the years since then, one group of oligarchies has been replaced by another. Media companies that produced news and subsidized its creation largely by selling advertising have been replaced by an even smaller group of technology firms that control access to the Internet by making devices, producing operating systems, selling apps, organizing content, and selling products online. Brands such as *Newsweek* and *U.S. News & World Report* are gone. Google and Facebook have a share of the public's attention that those old media empires could never have imagined.

In both scenarios, the same question pertains: As citizens, do we have access to independent, accurate information that makes it possible for us to govern ourselves?

The group of journalists in Cambridge that day in 1997 decided on a plan: engage journalists and the public in a careful examination of what journalism was supposed to be. As a group, we set out to answer two questions: If newspeople thought journalism was somehow different from other forms of communication, how was it different? And if they thought journalism needed to change but that some core principles couldn't be sacrificed, what were those principles?

Over the next two years, the group, calling itself the Committee of Concerned Journalists, organized the most comprehensive and systematic examination ever conducted by journalists of newsgathering and its responsibilities. We held twenty-one public forums, which were attended by three thousand people and involved testimony from more than three hundred journalists. We partnered with a team of university researchers who conducted more than one hundred three-and-a-half-hour interviews with journalists about their values. We produced two surveys of journalists about their principles. We held a summit of First Amendment and journalism scholars. With the Project for Excellence in Journalism, we produced nearly a dozen content studies of news reporting. We studied the history of the journalists who came before us, and we conducted training in newsrooms nationwide.

The ideas in this book began as the fruit of that examination, and they have grown with years of study since. What you read here is not an argument about what journalism should be. Rather, it is a distillation of how those engaged in creating journalism interpret what citizens think journalism is for and how, in turn, journalists should deliver it. It is predicated on the belief that the history and values by which journalism evolved should inform the journalism of our new century. There is no reason for the new journalism to be a repudiation of the best of the old, for journalism has always been a living thing. Every generation, building on what came before, has created it anew.

As such, we offer here a set of principles for anyone who might produce news in the twenty-first century, whether they be a professional in a newsroom, a citizen eyewitness posting pictures on a photo-sharing platform, or someone trying to distill the reports and conversation from social media and turn them into news. It also offers a guide to what values consumers should look for in the news they encounter.

The first edition, published in 2001, was a description of the theory and culture of journalism at the end of the twentieth century. The second edition, in 2007, began to account for the arrival of the digital age in a more sustained way. This new edition explores the relevance of journalism's core values in the face of the collapsed economic model that has shrunk most organized newsrooms, and the rise of social media that has transformed news into a broader and more pluralistic process.

Some of the language we use has taken on a different connotation in the time since the last edition of this book. While once, as we said in the preface, the word *journalist* described a group of organized professionals—working in what C. W. Anderson, Clay Shirky, and Emily Bell have called Industrial Journalism—now it describes anyone who might find him or herself producing news and who aspires to do it ethically and responsibly.[12]

This is an important change, but in many ways a less fundamental one than some imagine. We have always argued here that the question has never been who is or isn't a journalist. It is whether the work produced lives up to the character of what we would call journalism. That is still true.

Even before the epochal changes brought by the digital age, the roots of what has occurred were firmly planted. While most journalists could not easily articulate a theory of journalism (or even agree if they were engaged in a profession with shared principles), most people in society expected journalists to operate according to professional theory.

To add to the confusion, our educational system expects students to graduate high school and college with literacy in concepts of algebra, geometry, foreign language, and literature. Yet there is little serious demand or coherent effort to teach young citizens to comprehend what we think should be considered, as we said in the preface, the literature of civic life—the news.

This lack of clarity, for both citizens and newspeople, has weakened our journalism. If one accepts the tenet that democracy and journalism rise and fall together, it also likely has contributed to the polarization of American politics and the failure of the country to address the economic crisis that has beset the United States and the world since 2008. A lack of clarity about what journalism should be, and how to intelligently consume the news, has left both journalists and citizens less equipped to cope with the effects of the digital transformation, which demand more clarity of purpose from those who produce the news and greater awareness from those who consume it.

Unless we can grasp and reclaim the theory and practice of a free press, we risk allowing our first constitutional right to disappear. The quality of the journalism we consume now is far more a matter of what the public demands than simply what publishers want or can afford to provide. And a free press is distinct from free speech. The acts of reporting and commenting on the day's events relate to each other, but they are not synonymous. The quality of our democratic life depends, in short, on the public having the facts and being able to make sense of them. And that, even in a networked age, requires journalists. Whether we have them increasingly will depend on whether citizens can recognize the difference between propaganda and news—and whether they care.

For all the changes, there remain clear principles we require of our journalism, principles that citizens have a right to expect. The principles have ebbed and flowed over time, but they have survived because they provide things that citizens need from the news in order to adjust to the demands of life in an increasingly complex world. These are the principles, in other words, that have helped both journalists and the people even as journalism has changed with technology and new social demands. They are the elements of journalism: The first among them is that the purpose of journalism is to provide people with the information they need to be free and self-governing.

To fulfill this task:

1. Journalism's first obligation is to the truth.
2. Its first loyalty is to citizens.
3. Its essence is a discipline of verification.
4. Its practitioners must maintain an independence from those they cover.
5. It must serve as a monitor of power.
6. It must provide a forum for public criticism and compromise.
7. It must strive to make the significant interesting and relevant.
8. It must present the news in a way that is comprehensive and proportional.
9. Its practitioners have an obligation to exercise their personal conscience.
10. Citizens have rights and responsibilities when it comes to the news as well—even more so as they become producers and editors themselves.

Why these ten? Some readers may think items are missing here. Where is fairness? Where is balance? As we researched journalism's past and looked toward its future, it became clear that a number of familiar and even useful ideas associated with news were too vague to rise to the level of essential principles of journalism. Fairness, for instance, is so subjective a concept that it offered little guidance on how to operate. Balance, on the other hand, was an operational method that was so limited it often distorted the truth.

Another myth was that independence required journalists to be neutral. This confusion arose when the concept of objectivity became so mangled it began to be used to describe the very problem it was conceived to correct. If our work here does nothing else, we want to recapture the original meaning of objectivity intended when the concept migrated from social science to journalism early in the twentieth century. Objectivity was not meant to suggest that journalists were without bias. To the contrary, precisely because journalists could never be objective, their methods had to be. In the recognition that everyone is biased, in other words, the news, like science, should flow from a process for reporting that is defensible, rigorous, and transparent—and this process is even more critical in a networked age. Today, when content comes from so many sources, this concept of objectivity of method transparently conveyed—rather than personal objectivity—is more vital than ever.

In the new open ecosystem of news and information, the role of professional journalists is also smaller, and the role of citizens is larger—but not all voices are equal. Those with the means to prevail in an open marketplace—money, organized strategies for dissemination, and carefully designed networks to magnify a message's reach—have an advantage. If the "industrial" or professional press of the twentieth century constituted a fourth estate, and the new open system of citizens as producers and witnesses now constitutes a fifth estate, it is important to recognize that this new group also includes the institutions and actors journalists once covered—newsmakers who want to influence the public for commercial and political purpose. Yet it is an oversimplification to imagine that more sources simply means more truth. For all of the utopian enthusiasm, if we lose sight of the principles that make news trustworthy, the contributions of a smaller fourth estate and the new contributions of a fifth together will add up to something less than what society needs. We will lose the press as an independent institution, free to systematically monitor the other powerful forces and institutions in society.

In the new century, one of the most profound questions for a democratic society is whether news can survive as a source of independent and trustworthy information, or whether it will give way to a system of self-interested propaganda, of citizens consuming information in narrow channels or "filter bubbles," in which all claims are un-refereed and the loudest win. The answer will depend not just on the availability of reliable news but also on whether citizens learn to recognize which news is reliable; on what we demand of the news and those who produce it; whether we have the clarity and conviction to articulate what an independent press means and whether, as citizens, we care.

Some may ask whether there is a specific program laid out here to do that, to "fix" journalism's problems. Our answer to that comes in two parts.

The first part of the answer is that the yearning for a formulaic solution, a single defining moment, or a bold action does not reflect how change occurs.

The second part of the answer—the reason one will not find here a five- or ten-point program to solve the problems of journalism's role in society—is that our collective experience of more than seventy years in this business suggests a clearer lesson on how to find that solution.

The answer will be found when those who produce the news master the principles of journalism and rigorously apply them to the way they work and think every day. And it will be found in citizens recognizing good work, creating their own, and thereby generating more demand for it. The solution will be found the same way that athletes perfect performance: in the repetition of doing, until these elements become second nature. This is what will breed clarity of purpose, confidence of execution, and public respect.

The key to this, first, is to distinguish between the principles that guide journalism's purpose and not confuse them with the more ephemeral techniques that one generation develops in a specific medium to fulfill those principles. Only by recognizing the primacy of principles, and not confusing them with practices, can journalism evolve in a new century, with new technology, in a way that it can ethically fulfill the same democratic purpose it has in the past and create a new journalism that produces reliable information for the wired citizen.

1

What Is
Journalism For?

On a gray December morning in 1981, Anna
Semborska woke up and flipped on the radio
to hear her favorite program, *Sixty Minutes
Per Hour (60MPH)*. Semborska, who was seventeen, loved the way
the comedy revue pushed the boundaries of what people in Poland
could say out loud under Communist rule. Although it had been on
the air for some years, *60MPH* had become much bolder with the
rise of the labor union Solidarity. Sketches like one about a dim-
witted Communist doctor looking vainly to find a cure for extremism were an inspiration to Anna and her teenage friends in Warsaw.
The program showed her that other people felt about the world the
way she did but had never dared express. "We felt that if things like
these can be said on the radio then we are free," she would remember nearly twenty years later.[1]

But when Anna ran to the radio to tune in the show on December 13, 1981, she heard only static. She tried another station, then
another. Nothing. She tried to call a friend and found no dial tone.
Her mother called her to the window. Tanks were rolling by. The
Polish military government had declared martial law, outlawed Solidarity, and put the clamps back on the media and on speech. The
Polish experiment with liberalization was over.

Within hours, Anna and her friends began to hear stories that suggested something about this crackdown was different. One story involved the dogwalkers in a little town called Świdnik, near the Czech border. Every night at seven-thirty, when the state-run television news came on, nearly everyone in Świdnik went out and walked his or her dog in a little park in the center of town. It became a daily silent act of protest and solidarity. We refuse to watch, the people were saying in deed if not word. We reject your version of truth.

In Gdansk, there were the black TV screens. People there began moving their television sets to the windows—with the screens pointed out to the street. They were sending a sign to one another, and to the government. We, too, refuse to watch. We also reject your version of truth.

An underground press began to grow, on ancient hand-crank equipment. People began carrying video cameras and making private documentaries, which they showed secretly in church basements. Soon, Poland's leaders acknowledged that they were facing a new phenomenon, something they had to go west to name: the rise of Polish public opinion. In 1983, the government created the first of several institutes to study public opinion. Similar institutes would soon sprout up throughout Eastern Europe. But public opinion was something totalitarian officials could not dictate. At best, they could try to understand it and then manipulate it, not unlike Western democratic politicians. But they would not succeed.

After the Soviet bloc collapsed, leaders of the movement toward freedom would look back and think that the end of Communism owed a good deal to the coming of the new information technology and the effect it had on human souls. In the winter of 1989, Lech Walesa, the man who shortly would be elected Poland's new president, visited journalists in Washington. "Is it possible for a new Stalin to appear today who could murder people?" Walesa asked rhetorically. No, he answered himself, in the age of computers, satellites, faxes, VCRs, "it's impossible." Technology now made information available to too many people, too quickly. And information created democracy.[2]

In retrospect, looking at the evolution of democracy in Russia or China or genocidal regimes in Africa, we may wonder if Walesa was caught up in the euphoria of the moment. But his sentiment was less a reflection of naïveté than a burst of optimism coming from a part of the world that was just discovering technology and its power to do good and inspire people to fight for their freedom. And in six years, the Internet would be fully converted from a scientific and governmental system to a commercial one, available for everyday use.

What is journalism for? For the Poles and others in the emerging democracies of Eastern Europe, the question was answered with action. Journalism was for building a sense of community that the government could not control. Journalism was for citizenship. Journalism was for democracy. And as Czech president Václav Havel told a group of journalists gathered in Prague in 1991, journalism was for taking back the language from a government that had subverted it with propaganda that undermined freedom of thought itself. Millions of people, empowered by a free flow of information, became directly involved in creating a new government and new rules for the political, social, and economic life of their country. Is that always journalism's purpose? Or was that true for one moment, in one place?

Today, the question "What is journalism for?" is the implicit subject of much of the discourse found online about technology and news, and in a seemingly endless series of physical gatherings to discuss the same topics. While that discourse often has the political and theological tones of a revolutionary movement, it is far healthier than the lack of reflection about journalism's purpose that tended to dominate the twentieth century.

In the United States, during much of the last century, journalism was something of a tautology. If you owned a printing press or a broadcasting license, journalism was whatever you said it was. When we began our journey to identify the core principles that underlie reliable news some sixteen years ago, Maxwell King, then editor of the *Philadelphia Inquirer*, summarized this lack of reflection by offering the answer journalists of the time were likely to provide: "We let our work speak for itself." Or, when pressed to account for why the public could trust them, journalists confused their good intentions with good practice. They took it as a given that because newsrooms were insulated from commercial concerns they were working in the public interest.[3]

These simplistic answers were more harmful than journalists recognized. They invited skepticism from the public. And as the public's ability to comment openly in a worldwide interactive space grew, that skepticism became more focused and impassioned. If those who produce the news could not explain themselves, it was not illogical to think that maybe journalists' motives weren't that virtuous in the first place. By their silence, newspeople led people on the business side to believe their newsrooms were filled with smug, moralistic idealists. Journalists failed to think critically about why they did what they did, because they imagined their motives were so virtuous.

Now, in an open and competitive marketplace, the simplistic refrain that "journalism is a public service that speaks for itself" is exposed for its vacuity. Now that anyone with a computer can claim to be "doing journalism," technology has created a new economic organization of journalism in which the norms of the profession are being pulled and redefined, and sometimes abandoned altogether.

Perhaps, some suggest, the definition of journalism has been expanded by technology so that now anything can be seen as journalism. On closer examination, as the people of Poland and other nations that have escaped government control have demonstrated, the purpose of journalism is defined not by technology, nor by journalists or the techniques they employ, but by something more basic: the function news plays in the lives of people.

For all that has changed about journalism, its purpose has remained remarkably constant, if not always well served, since the notion of "a press" first evolved more than three hundred years ago. And for all that the speed, techniques, and character of news delivery have changed, and are likely to continue to change ever more rapidly, there exists a clear theory and philosophy of journalism that flows out of the function of news that has remained consistent and enduring.

The primary purpose of journalism is to provide citizens with the information they need to be free and self-governing.

As we have listened to citizens and journalists and watched the impact of technological disruption, it has become clear that the news' function encompasses several elements. The news helps us define our communities. It also helps us create a common language and common knowledge rooted in reality. Journalism also helps identify a community's goals, heroes, and villains. "We proceed best as a society if we have a common base of information," former NBC anchorman Tom Brokaw told the team of academic research partners who helped us identify the principles of journalism.[4] The news media serve as a watchdog, push people beyond complacency, and offer a voice to the forgotten. "I want to give voices to people who need the voice ... people who are powerless," said Yuen Ying Chan, a former reporter for the *New York Daily News* who created a journalism training program in Hong Kong.[5] The late James Carey, one of the most innovative thinkers about news, put it this way decades ago: "Perhaps in the end journalism simply means carrying on and amplifying the conversation of people themselves."[6] The rise of the Internet, blogs, social media, and mobile devices provides space for citizens to create their own journalism and obviously make this vision more relevant and contemporary than ever.

This definition has held so consistent through history, and proven so deeply ingrained in the thinking of those who produce news through the ages, that it constitutes a foundation for imagining journalism in the future. It is difficult, looking back, to separate the concept of journalism from the concept of creating community and later democracy. Journalism is so fundamental to that purpose that, as we will see, societies that want to suppress freedom must first suppress the press. They do not, interestingly, need to suppress capitalism. At its best, as we will also show, journalism helps us understand how citizens behave.

This definition of journalism as social connection and information flow also unlocks a wider and more innovative picture of journalism moving forward. It reveals that journalism has always been more of a service—a means for providing social connection and knowledge—than a fixed product—an outlet's stories or advertising.

Today, ironically, the long-standing theory and purpose of journalism are being challenged as if they were at odds with the conversation of people. We think that is both ahistorical and self-destructive.

Among some in the digital space, there is a tendency to dismiss journalistic values as if they were self-serving for journalists and disconnected from the public. At the same time, information companies are being created on the Web that provide social connection (restaurant reviews, entertainment updates, information about local goods and services) but create no journalism, and have little or no connection to the civic good that journalism provides. Some of these companies offer gathering places where journalism is present, but it is simply another commodity flowing through them, to which no particular special value is assigned.

There has been a shift in the relationship with government in this transition as well. The threat from government is no longer simply censorship—withholding information that is in the public interest. Using new technology, government has more and more tools to subvert the press by trying to supplant it with its own content while also censoring. That list of tools includes creating pseudojournalism in the form of faux news websites, video news releases, subsidies to "media personalities" willing to accept money to promote policy, and more. Government office holders, from the President to members of the local city council, now maintain their own direct channels to engage with the public, including offering the video feeds that generate the impression many official events don't need to be "covered" by the press because they are already "public." The Obama administration, in addition, has used technology to cast a wide net to try to identify, prosecute, and intimidate government employees who might talk to the press.

Taken together, these forces amount to a growing risk that journalism as an independent source in society for monitoring power, spotting abuse, alerting the public to problems, and creating social connection may be washed away in the flood of communication by commercial, political, and government sources. Perhaps for the first time in history, the real meaning of the First Amendment–protecting a free press as an independent institution–is threatened with the government not acting primarily as censor but instead offering a competing view of reality.

There are some who will listen to this discussion and contend that it's dangerous, or even antiquated, to attempt to define journalism. To define journalism, they argue, is to limit it. Maybe doing so violates the spirit of the First Amendment: "Congress shall make no law . . . abridging the freedom of speech or of the press." This is why journalists have avoided licensing in the manner of doctors and lawyers, they note. They also worry that defining journalism will only make it resistant to changing with the times, which probably will run it out of business.

Actually, the resistance to a definition of journalism is not a deeply held principle but a relatively recent and largely commercial impulse. At a more innovative point in journalism's history, publishers a century ago routinely championed their news values in front-page editorials, opinion pages, and company slogans, and just as often publicly assailed the journalistic values of their rivals. This was marketing. Citizens chose which publications to read based on their styles and their approaches to news. It was only as the press began to assume a more corporate, more homogeneous and monopolistic form that it became more reticent. Lawyers advised news companies against codifying their principles in writing for fear that they would be used against them in court. Thus, avoiding definition was a commercial strategy, not a principle born of First Amendment freedoms.

On the other side, some will argue that not only should journalism's purpose be unchanging–its form should be constant as well. They see changes in the way journalism looks from when they were young, and they fear that, in the memorable phrase of Neil Postman, we are "amusing ourselves to death." These critics miss another fact. Every generation creates its own journalism largely in reaction to technological advances that allow production and/or distribution of content more effectively. But the purpose and the underlying elements of journalism, we have found, have proven remarkably constant, just as we have discovered since we first wrote this book that there are strong consistencies in the essential values of journalists across countries, cultures, and political systems, despite many superficial differences.

Although professional journalists historically have been uncomfortable defining what they do, they have fundamentally agreed on their purpose. When we set out to chart the common ground of newspeople, this was the first answer we heard: "The central purpose of journalism is to tell the truth so that people will have the information that they need to be sovereign." It came from Jack Fuller, an author, novelist, lawyer, and then president of the Tribune Publishing Company, which produced the *Chicago Tribune*.[7]

Just as intriguing, when new entrants begin to produce news and information—even those initially who would never call themselves journalists—they often adhere to the same concepts of purpose that Fuller described. Omar Wasow, founder of a website called New York Online and one of the earliest of the self-described "garage entrepreneurs," wanted to help create citizens who are "consumers, devourers and debunkers of media . . . an audience who have engaged with the product and can respond carefully."[8] Almost a decade later, in 2006, Shawn Williams created DallasSouthBlog.com to focus on issues of concern to African-Americans in South Dallas and the rest of the country. By 2013, the blog was called DallasSouthNews and described itself as "a non-profit news organization utilizing technology, social media and journalistic principles to empower and inform underserved communities." Williams, who says he never imagined himself to be engaged in journalism, also sat on the National Advisory Board of the Poynter Institute, one of the country's most-esteemed journalism training organizations.

We wanted to make sure these ideas weren't just the random views of a few people, so in collaboration with the Pew Research Center for the People & the Press, we asked journalists what they considered the distinguishing feature of journalism. Those working in news volunteered this democratic function by nearly two to one over any other answer.[9] We also collaborated with developmental psychologists at Stanford, Harvard, and the University of Chicago, whose open-ended, in-depth interviews with a hundred more journalists revealed the same conclusion. "News professionals at every level . . . express an adamant allegiance to a set of core standards that are striking in their commonality and in their linkage to the public information mission," they wrote.[10]

Ethics codes and journalism mission statements bear the same witness. The goal is "to serve the general welfare by informing the people," says the code of the American Society of News Editors, the largest association of newsroom managers in North America. "Give light and the people will find their own way," reads the masthead of Scripps Company newspapers. It is no less true of outlets formed in the twenty-first century. "To practice and promote investigative journalism in the public interest," declares ProPublica's mission statement. Committed to "improving the conversation of our democracy in an increasingly interconnected world," reads that of GlobalPost.[11]

Those outside news, too, have understood that journalism has broader social and moral obligations. Listen to Pope John Paul II in June 2000: "With its vast and direct influence on public opinion, journalism cannot be guided only by economic forces, profit, and special interest. It must instead be felt as a mission in a certain sense sacred, carried out in the knowledge that the powerful means of communication have been entrusted to you for the good of all."[12]

This democratic mission is not just a modern idea. The concept of creating sovereignty has run through every major statement and argument about the press for centuries, not only from journalists but also from the revolutionaries who fought for democratic principles, both in America and in virtually every developing democracy since.

THE AWARENESS INSTINCT

Historian Mitchell Stephens studied how news has functioned in people's lives throughout history, and he found a remarkable consistency. "The basic topics with which . . . news accounts have been concerned, and the basic standards by which they evaluate newsworthiness, seem to have varied very little," he wrote. "Humans have exchanged a similar mix of news with a consistency throughout history and cultures that makes interest in this news seem inevitable, if not innate."[13] Various scholars have identified the reason for this. People crave news out of basic instinct—what we call the Awareness Instinct. They need to be aware of events beyond their direct experience. Knowledge of the unknown gives them security; it allows them to plan and negotiate their lives. Exchanging this information becomes the basis for creating community and making human connections.

News is that part of communication that keeps us informed of the changing events, issues, and characters in the world outside. In time, historians have suggested, rulers used news to hold their societies together. It provided a sense of unity and shared purpose. It even helped tyrannical rulers control their people by binding them together around a common threat.

History reveals one other important trend. The more democratic the society, the more news and information it tends to have. As societies first became more democratic, they tended toward a kind of pre-journalism. The earliest democracy, ancient Greece, relied on an oral journalism in the Athens marketplace in which "nearly everything important about the public's business was in the open," journalism educator John Hohenberg wrote.[14] The Romans developed a daily account of the Roman Senate and political and social life, called the *acta diurna*, transcribed on papyrus and posted in public places.[15] As European societies became more authoritarian and violent in the Middle Ages, communication waned and written news essentially disappeared.

THE BIRTH OF JOURNALISM

As the Middle Ages ended, news came in the form of song and story, in news ballads sung by wandering minstrels.

What we might consider modern journalism began to emerge, in the early seventeenth century, literally out of conversation, especially in public places. In England, the first newspapers grew out of coffeehouses—numerous enough for some to be known for special-izing in certain kinds of information. They became so popular that scholars complained that "nothing but news and the affairs of Christendom is discussed."

Later, in America, journalism grew out of pubs, or publick houses. Here, the bar owners, called publicans, hosted spirited conversations about information from travelers who often recorded what they had seen and heard in logbooks kept at the end of the bar. The first newspapers evolved out of these coffeehouses when enterprising printers began to collect the shipping news, tales from abroad and more gossip, and political arguments from the coffeehouses and to print them on paper.

With the evolution of the first newspapers, English politicians began to talk about a new phenomenon, which they called public opinion. By the beginning of the eighteenth century, journalists/printers had begun to formulate a theory of free speech and free press. In 1720, two London newspapermen, writing under the pen name "Cato," introduced the idea that truth should be a defense against libel. At the time, English common law had ruled the reverse: not only that any criticism of government was a crime but that "the greater the truth, the greater the libel," since truth did more harm.[16]

Cato's argument had a profound influence in the American colonies, where discontent against the English Crown was growing. A rising young printer named Benjamin Franklin was among those who republished Cato's writings. When a fellow printer named John Peter Zenger went on trial in 1735 for criticizing the royal governor of New York, Cato's ideas became the basis for his defense. People had "a right ... both of exposing and opposing arbitrary power ... by speaking and writing the truth," argued Zenger's lawyer, who was paid by Franklin, among others. The jury acquitted Zenger, shocking the colonial legal community, and the meaning of a free press in America began to take formal shape.

The concept became rooted in the thinking of the Founders, finding its way into the Virginia Declaration of Rights (written partly by James Madison), the Massachusetts constitution (written by John Adams), and most of the new colonial statements of rights. "No government ought to be without censors & where the press is free, no one ever will," Thomas Jefferson would tell George Washington.[17] Neither Franklin nor Madison thought such language was necessary in the federal Constitution, but two delegates, George Mason of Virginia and Elbridge Gerry of Massachusetts, walked out of the convention, and with men like Thomas Paine and Samuel Adams, they agitated the public to demand a written bill of rights as a condition of approving the Constitution. A free press thus became the people's first claim on their government.

Over the next two hundred years the notion of the press as a bulwark of liberty became embedded in American legal doctrine. "In the First Amendment," the Supreme Court ruled in upholding the *New York Times*' right in 1971 to publish the secret government documents called the Pentagon Papers, "the Founding Fathers gave the free press the protection it must have to fulfill its essential role in our democracy. The press was to serve the governed, not the governors."[18] The idea that was affirmed over and over by the courts, First Amendment scholar Lee Bollinger, then president of the University of Michigan, told us at one of our gatherings for this book, is a simple one: Out of a diversity of voices the people are more likely to know the truth and thus be able to self-govern.[19]

Even when journalism was in the hands of the yellow-press mavens at the eve of the twentieth century, or the tabloid sheets of the 1920s, building community and promoting democracy remained a core value. At their worst moments, Joseph Pulitzer and William Randolph Hearst appealed to both the sensational tastes and the patriotic impulses of their audiences. Pulitzer used his front page to lure his readers in, but he used his editorial pages to teach them how to be American citizens. On election nights he and Hearst would vie to outdo each other, one renting Madison Square Garden for a free party, the other illuminating campaign results on the side of his newspaper's skyscraper.

Whether one looks back over three hundred years, or even three thousand years, it is impossible to separate news from community and, over time, even more specifically from democratic community.

A FREE PRESS IN A NETWORK-CONNECTED AGE

Today, information is so free that the notion of journalism as a homogeneous entity might seem quaint in a world in which everyone may at some point produce it. Perhaps the First Amendment itself is an artifact of a more restricted and elitist era.

Certainly, the notion of the press as a gatekeeper–deciding what information the public should know and what it should not–no longer defines journalism's role. If the *New York Times* decides not to publish something, one of countless other websites, talk radio hosts, social media networks, blogs, or partisans will. The rise of Facebook and Twitter, not to mention organizations such as WikiLeaks, has transformed the essential equation of news–how information becomes public–from "one to many" to "many to many." Countless book titles of the last decade have made this point, from Dan Gillmor's *We the Media* to Clay Shirky's *Here Comes Everybody*.

These changes have profoundly altered the information life of everyone, even those who do not tweet, post on social networks, or offer comments online. As we search through Google for information, graze across a seemingly infinite array of outlets, share stories or links with friends, like things on Facebook pages, we become our own editors, researchers, and even news gatherers. What used to be called journalism is now only one part of the mix, and its role as intermediary and verifier, like the roles of other civic institutions, is a relatively smaller and thus weaker influence on the whole. We are witnessing the rise of a new and more active kind of American citizenship–with new responsibilities that are only beginning to be considered. The journalism of the twenty-first century must recognize this, and journalists must organize their work in a way that helps arm the public with the tools it needs to perform this more active form of citizenship.

In the gatekeeper metaphor, the press stood by an imagined village guardhouse and determined which facts were publicly significant and sufficiently vetted to be made public. In a networked world, the organized press plays that guardhouse role over a far more limited sphere of information–those stories over which they have exclusive, or practically exclusive, access, including their own enterprise reporting and some range of local information. In the age of police Twitter feeds and webcast government meetings, even this domain is rapidly shrinking.

For some, the end of the gatekeeper metaphor might suggest the end of journalism. Here comes everybody. Who needs paid observers?

We arrive at a different conclusion. We believe the end of the press's monopoly over mediating information to the public offers the opportunity to elevate the quality of journalism we receive, not weaken it. For that to happen, however, those who produce journalism must acquire a better understanding of what citizens need from their news, what citizens and the machinery of the digital network can contribute to that, and a more rigorous grasp of the tasks necessary for trained journalists to organize, verify, and add to these contributions.

What do we mean by a more rigorous understanding of the tasks of journalism? John Seely Brown, the former director of Xerox PARC, the legendary think tank in Silicon Valley, saw early on that rather than rendering the democratic public service notion of journalism moot, technology had instead changed how journalists fulfill it. "What we need in the new economy and the new communications culture is sense making. We have a desperate need to get some stable points in an increasingly crazy world." This means, Brown explained, that journalists need "the ability to look at things from multiple points of view and the ability to get to the core" of matters.[20] Futurist Paul Saffo described this task as applying journalistic inquiry and judgment "to come to conclusions in uncertain environments."[21]

Thus the new journalist is no longer deciding *what* the public should know—the classic role of gatekeeper—but working with audiences and technology to make order out of it, make it useful, take action on it. This does not mean simply adding interpretation or analysis to news reporting. It involves instead performing a series of different and more discrete tasks that, if understood more carefully, news producers should begin to perform better than they have before.

In our 2010 book, *Blur: How to Know What's True in the Age of*

Information Overload, we argued that the gatekeeper metaphor masked behind one phrase what were really various different functions that the public required from journalism. We argued there that if those specific needs were recognized and understood more clearly, journalists were more likely to perform them more effectively, including understanding how better to collaborate with citizens and employ technology to create a better journalism.

One primary task of the new journalist, as with the old, is to verify what information is reliable, to play the role of *Authenticator*. In the networked world, audiences may have heard differing assertions about an event before they encounter a formal journalistic account. Thus the role of the new journalist, more than the old, is to work with audiences to sort through these different accounts, to know which of the facts they may have encountered they should believe and which to discount.

A second task of anyone trying to report and present news is to be a *Sense Maker*, to put events in context in a way that turns information into knowledge. One value of making these tasks more distinct is that the responsibilities and the presentation will shift subtly when the task changes. It is important for those who report news and information, for instance, to know when they have moved from authenticating facts to synthesizing and contextualizing them. The analysis of events crosses into another level of subjectivity, and it requires making that shift clear by sharing different evidence for why this interpretation is likely the best one.

A third task is to *Bear Witness* to events. This occurs when the person functioning as journalist is the sole observer of an event. Recognizing this as a distinct journalistic role, even in a world in which journalists no longer so regularly play the role of the gatekeeper, is useful. Those engaged in journalism are not simply interpreters who comment. Being monitors, sentinels who ask questions and dig, remains vital. Valuing being a witness bearer also means that an effort is made to cover events that no one else is covering—so that there *is* a witness—and then to convey to readers why the event matters. It implies that institutional news organizations not deploy their resources only where there is already a crowd, and already an interest.

Doing so makes a publisher less useful, even if it is the easiest way to generate traffic. For a citizen who finds him- or herself at an event that citizen considers important, and where no press appear to be present, it may mean suddenly deciding to act journalistically, to tweet or take pictures or video–so there is a record.

A fourth task, closely related to witness bearer but also different, is *Watchdog*. This is the classic role of investigative reporting, uncovering wrongdoing. But it is sufficiently different in practice and organization from the more common but often undervalued role of witness bearing that it is important they are distinguished from each other. The more routine monitoring of witness bearing may be the spark that leads to the watchdog investigation. But they are not the same.

In addition to the four roles listed above that were buried within the gatekeeper concept, there are at least five other distinct functions that the public requires of journalism. Readers of this list may well conceive more–and that will only help. The key here is to isolate the functions we need from news to help our lives. Here are the other five functions citizens require of news that we identify:

- *Intelligent Aggregator (or Curator)*: Picking the best of other accounts, perhaps comparing the conflicting ones, recommending them to your audience–playing editor, in effect, of the rest of the information available.
- *Forum Leader*: Organizing public discussion in a way that reflects your journalistic values.
- *Empowerer*: Providing audiences tools and information so that they can act for themselves. This involves making information interactive, providing dates when action needs to be taken, explaining how to get more involved. It may go even further and involve organizing events that bring the community together to solve problems.
- *Role Model*: In a networked news environment, journalism is an even more public act than before. How one gathers the news, one's conduct and decision making are being

watched. That behavior must be exemplary, for it is, in a more explicit way than was once true, part of the brand.

- *Community Builder*: In older models of journalism, the news spoke for itself, and what citizens did with that news and information was beyond the sphere of the news provider. That is no longer the case. The purpose of news is to help people self-govern, but that only begins with giving them the information they need to do so. News must also be about solving the problems that confront individuals and the community. There are lines between news and advocacy, but helping solve problems is different from advocacy.

JOURNALISM AS ORGANIZED COLLABORATIVE INTELLIGENCE

Some advocates of the digital disruption believe that since no one controls information anymore, professional journalists in organized settings have become largely unnecessary or their role can be reduced to a narrower zone of activity far less focused than in the past on reporting and establishing facts. Since the information in the crowd is wider and deeper than whatever could be haphazardly collected by a few journalists, it will be closer to real truth anyway. Blogger Jonathan Stray in a post for Harvard's Nieman Journalism Lab epitomized the argument: "The Internet has solved the basic distribution of event-based facts in a variety of ways; no one needs a news organization to know what the White House is saying when all the press briefings are posted on YouTube. What we do need is someone to tell us what it means."[22]

Stray was building on arguments of a host of writers who form what has been dubbed the Future of News Movement. Perhaps no clearer expression of the ideas of the group has been put down than in the "manifesto" authored under the title *Post-Industrial Journalism* by three academics, C. W. Anderson, Emily Bell, and Clay Shirky. They articulated something similar if slightly broader than Stray: "The journalist has not been replaced but displaced, moved higher up the editorial chain from the production of initial observations to a role that emphasizes verification and interpretation, bringing sense to the streams of text, audio, photos and video produced by the public."[23]

The arguments that journalism can largely move beyond fact gathering and toward synthesis and interpretation might be called the Displacement Theory of News.

On the other hand, some have tilted too far the other way, viewing the benefits citizens and technology bring with excessive suspicion and tending to romanticize old methods. "The civic labour performed by journalists on the ground cannot be replicated by legions of bloggers sitting hunched over their computer screens," Bill Keller, then the executive editor of the *New York Times*, said in a 2007 public lecture in London.[24]

Both views go too far.

Citizens and machines should not try to "replicate" the role of professional journalists.

At the same time, and in much the same way, the notion that the public and machines can "displace" the fact-finding role of professional journalists in this collaboration is too constricted. We need journalists to do more than bring sense to the streams produced by the public. This idea of displacement or implied obsolescence or movement away from essential fact finding does not grasp the reality of how powerful institutions work or how to cover them. In the end, the notion that journalists as fact finders have been displaced is too theoretical, even dangerous. It leaves far too much power to the government, corporations, and other institutions to control the supply of public facts. The fact that the White House now has a YouTube channel, Twitter feed, and tumblr account should not be mistaken for an administration being open or transparent. Nor is journalism enhanced if journalists begin to limit themselves largely to material officially released rather than going out and digging for a more complete version of the truth. The Web may have given everyone publishing tools, but it does not enforce distribution of all facts that matter or structure them in a way that citizens can use.

Perhaps even more important, technology has not "solved" the problem of knowing the essential facts of events. The facts of most events that affect the public do not occur in public. Even the decisions revealed at most public meetings are made, more often than they should be, away from public view, in executive session or in even smaller more private meetings. Far too little of what we need to know is on YouTube. Yet if more of our civic proceedings moved there (which we support), there is no doubt much of the real decision making of news would then move further behind closed doors. C-SPAN did not magically make Congress work better. And the events in Afghanistan, or the impact of major health care legislation, require far more shoe leather and access than "bringing sense to the streams ... produced by the public." We cannot assume, in other words, the facts of civic life to be a commodity, the gathering and submission of which are taken care of by the network.

For most stories, learning the facts of an event is a multidimensional process of discovery—an official action, event, or revelation, followed by inquiry, reaction, and observation, new questions, then more inquiry—a process that repeats itself and involves shoe leather as well as making sense of the streams produced by officials and the public.

The discussion about technology and the network displacing factual reporting also tends to focus on a limited range of topics, often just national affairs. "Not all journalism matters," Anderson, Bell, and Shirky wrote in their manifesto, suggesting that a broad range of arts, sports, lifestyle reporting, and more did not. "Much of what is produced today is simply entertainment or diversion." They are wrong. As we will describe in detail in the chapter on comprehensiveness and proportion, the reporting of culture, social events, trends, sports, and much more form a vital part of how we come to understand community and civil society and how, as citizens, we navigate our lives. Journalism that narrows itself to accountability of government agencies will limit its value, its engagement, and its chance to sustain itself.

We see the future of news in the middle, between the skeptics and the utopians. Rather than displacing journalists, the network and citizens make possible a new and enriched kind of journalism in which citizens, technology, and professional journalists work together to create a public intelligence that is deeper and wider than any one of these could produce alone.

Machines bring the capacity to count beyond anything previously imaginable–to make the news more empirical and more accurate.

Citizens bring expertise, experience, and the ability to observe events from more vantage points–knowledge and expertise that are deeper than can be found in any newsroom or in a traditional reporter's "Rolodex" of sources.

Journalists bring access, the ability to interrogate people in power, to dig, to translate and triangulate and verify incoming information, and, more important, a traditional discipline of open-minded inquiry.

Working in concert, these three contributors can create a new kind of journalism, one that might best be understood as an organized collaborative intelligence.

We need journalists of the future, in other words, to embrace the potential of the network and to vet and organize its input, while also providing the elements that skilled journalists at any given moment are best disposed to offer. This is the way to a deeper and wider foundation of facts and community understanding.

Journalists in this vision will do much more now than produce narrative stories and the graphics that illustrate them. Instead, they will help gather and organize and structure this community intelligence, combining the technology of the machine network with the knowledge and input of the broader citizens and other sources, and adding the reportorial, evidentiary, and vetting skills they possess as journalists. This view of journalism is much more than a static product. It is, as we said, a kind of organized community intelligence.

But this better journalism, one that fulfills the promise of creating community and improving the lives of citizens, does not reside in an either/or view of journalism and technology. In this view, journalists are not displaced, replicated, confined, or elevated to synthesizers of meaning. This view does not denigrate the power of narrative, or the significance of witness-bearing reporting, or the importance of simply finding out what happened. It is a vision of journalism's future that doesn't denigrate its past.

Instead, this new vision of a new journalism depends on the networked media culture committing itself, as the old system did, to establishing verified and truthful information, and building out from that foundation of facts toward meaning. The driving force of the Age of Enlightenment, out of which grew the notion of individual worth and a public press, was the search for truthful information. This information freed the public from the control of centralized dictatorial or dogmatic power. We see parallels to that kind of control today forming in new places, corporate and governmental rather than monarchical or religious. If the journalism of verification is to survive in the new age, then it must become a force in empowering citizens with the information they need to effectively take part in self-government.

THE JOURNALIST'S THEORY OF DEMOCRACY

The question of what people need and want to know has always been critical. If the public is uninformed, the press has a responsibility to figure out why and what to do about it. But it has become more of a challenge in recent years for journalists to fulfill this responsibility.

Historically, most journalists, having no challenge to their role as mediators over information or to the profitability of their companies, were content to remain insulated from commercial pressure. They were content to let something called "news judgment," a subjective and wildly unscientific notion, dictate their decisions, the saving grace of which was that those judgments were independent from commercial pressure.

There was always reason to be concerned about how well this trust in subjective news judgment worked. We may have had the freest press imaginable, yet over the last thirty years the number of Americans who could even name their congressman was as low as three out of ten.[25] Little more than half of the American electorate votes in presidential elections–fewer than in countries without a First Amendment.[26] More than any other source, people get news from local television, a medium that largely ignores the process of how the government works.[27] In other surveys only 29 percent of respondents said they read a daily newspaper the day before, and people appear to be no more informed about the outside world than they were fifty years ago.[28] There is no evidence that with the arrival of the Internet those knowledge numbers have changed substantially.[29] Maybe, when you look hard, the idea that the press provides the information necessary for people to self-govern is revealed to be an illusion. Maybe people don't care. Maybe we don't, in reality, actually self-govern at all. The government operates, and the rest of us are largely bystanders.

This argument flared briefly in the 1920s in a debate of ideas between journalist Walter Lippmann and philosopher John Dewey. It was a time of pessimism about democracy. Democratic governments in Germany and Italy had collapsed. The Bolshevik revolution loomed over the West. There was a growing fear that police states were employing new technology and the new science of propaganda to control public will.

Lippmann, already one of the nation's most famous journalists, argued in a best-selling book called *Public Opinion* that democracy was fundamentally flawed. People, he said, mostly know the world only indirectly, through "pictures they make up in their heads." And they receive these mental pictures largely through the media. The problem, Lippmann argued, is that the pictures people have in their heads are hopelessly distorted and incomplete, marred by the irredeemable weaknesses of the press. Just as bad, even if the truth were to reach the public, the public's ability to comprehend the truth is undermined by human bias, stereotype, inattentiveness, and ignorance. In the end, Lippmann thought citizens are like theatergoers who "arrive in the middle of the third act and leave before the last curtain, staying just long enough to decide who is the hero and who is the villain."[30]

Public Opinion was an enormous success and gave birth, according to many, to the modern study of communications.[31] It also deeply moved the nation's most famous philosopher, Columbia professor

John Dewey, who called Lippmann's analysis about the limits of human perception "the most effective indictment of democracy . . . ever penned."[32]

But Dewey, who later expanded his critique in his own book *The Public and Its Problems*, said Lippmann's definition of democracy was fundamentally flawed. The goal of democracy, Dewey said, was not to manage public affairs efficiently. It was to help people develop to their fullest potential. Democracy, in other words, was the end, not the means. It was true that the public could only be an "umpire of last resort" over government, usually just setting the broad outlines of debate. That, however, was all the Founders ever intended, Dewey argued, for democratic life encompassed so much more than efficient government. Its real purpose was human freedom. The solution to democracy's problems was not to give up on it but to try to improve the skills of the press and the education of the public.

Dewey sensed something that is easier to grasp in today's networked news culture, when citizens are producers, critics, consumers, and editors as well as audience. He believed that if people were allowed to communicate freely with one another, democracy was the natural outgrowth of the human interaction. It was not a stratagem for making government better.

Ninety years later, the Lippmann-Dewey debates still constitute the essential arguments over the viability of a free press in democratic society. For all that the world has changed, Lippmann's skepticism and Dewey's optimism are echoed in the almost theological disputes today between those worried about the demise of the professional press and those who see something superior in the wisdom of the crowd.

For all that citizens can decide—what they want to know and when, for instance—the role of journalists as agenda setters—trying to signal to the audience what news is important, the top stories—has not disappeared. Those who cover the news professionally still have to decide how to deploy resources, which stories to cover, which to cover at length, which to handle in brief, and a thousand more decisions every day.

Today, however, those judgments about journalistic choices are made publicly and in real time—and can be measured in the analytics about what is read, viewed, shared, commented on, liked, and tweeted. The agenda itself has become a dialogue, and a healthy one.

For journalists, the challenge is how to respond so that they continue to play a constructive agenda-setting role that helps their community, and their different publics, and makes the journalism they produce useful to their fellow citizens. How, for instance, do news publishers use metrics thoughtfully, rather than employing them self-destructively, shallowing their content in an effort to maximize page views with slide shows and quick posts about celebrities? How do they use metrics to understand the public while adding a sense of significance to the news, to indicate to citizens, "this story matters; you should pay attention"? (We will discuss this at length in the chapter on comprehensiveness and proportionality.)

Journalists have always been engaged in something more important than merely the production of news. Whenever editors lay out a page or website, or reporters decide what angle or element of an event or issue to emphasize and explore, they are guessing at what readers want or need to know based on their personal interaction in daily life. As they do so, they are, however unconsciously, operating by some theory of democracy—some theory of what drives politics, citizenship, and how people make judgments.

Our purpose here is to lay out a theory that we think lies implicit, and often unrecognized, in the journalism that serves us best as citizens.

A number of critics argued that Lippmann's view dominated too much of how journalists operated over the next ninety years.[33] Studies show that newspapers and TV aimed their coverage at target markets that were designed to sell advertising rather than trying to inform a broad citizenry. Some publications, particularly newspapers, were tailored to elite demographics that were most attractive to some kinds of advertisers. Other publishers, such as local TV newscasts, were aimed at wide audiences that bought cars and beer but did little to offer civic news.[34] Policy and ideas were ignored or presented as sport, or were couched in the context of how a certain policy position is calculated to gain someone power over a rival.[35] Even the practice of interviewing voters in political campaigns, reporters admit, became a vanishing art, replaced by the perceived science of public opinion polling in which the public was merely a responder to questions invented by media. Even the representation of the public was incomplete, as surveys often screened out nonvoters, leaving results that gave no voice to an important segment of the population. As he saw the rise of polling, scholar James Carey wrote that we had developed "a journalism that justifies itself in the public's name but in which the public plays no role, except as an audience."[36] Citizens have become an abstraction, something the press talks about but not to.

No doubt the rise of citizen media and the empowering of consumers have helped address the problem of the public becoming an abstract construct in our public debates. The public is forcing itself into the conversation. It makes sense that those with their own political agendas are more likely to be exposed. Traditional journalism was always better at covering official debate that occurred in public spaces than at covering real public debate that occurred around the kitchen table.

The journalists who claim to know what citizens care about through today's discourse in social media will quickly find out they are equally as wrong.

Yet this does not solve for journalists the problem of discerning what it is citizens want and what they need. It calls instead for an even clearer theory of democracy and citizenship for the press.

As we examine the interactive relationship between journalists and citizens in the new public and networked sphere online, we see a more complicated and fluid vision of the public than the traditional debates usually offer. We think this vision holds a key to how both citizens and many journalists really operate.

THE THEORY OF THE INTERLOCKING PUBLIC

Dave Burgin, a newspaper editor who worked in venues from Florida to California, had a theory about news audiences that he passed on to young staffers when he taught them the art of page layout. Imagine, he would say, that no more than roughly 15 percent of your readers would want to read any one story on the page (for Burgin, who worked in newspapers, this meant a printed page). Your job was to make sure each page had a sufficient variety of stories so that every member of the audience would want to read at least one of them.[37]

Implicit in Burgin's theory of a diversified menu of news on each page is the idea that everyone is interested and even expert in something. The notion that some people are simply ignorant, or that other people are interested in everything, is a myth. As we listened to journalists and citizens talk, we realized that Burgin's theory was a more realistic description of how people interact with the news to form a public.

We call this the Theory of the Interlocking Public.

For the sake of argument, let's say there are three broad levels of public engagement on every issue, each with even subtler gradations. There is an involved public, with a personal stake in an issue and a strong understanding. There is an interested public, with no direct role in the issue but that is affected and responds with some firsthand experience. And there is an uninterested public, which pays little attention and will join, if at all, after the contours of the discourse have been laid out by others. In the interlocking public, we are all members of all three groups, depending on the issue.

An autoworker in suburban Detroit, for instance, may care little about agriculture policy or foreign affairs, and may only sporadically buy a newspaper or watch TV news. But he will have lived through many collective bargaining debates and know a good deal about corporate bureaucracy and workplace safety. He may have kids in local schools and friends on welfare, and know how pollution has affected the rivers where he fishes. To these and all other concerns he brings a range of knowledge and experience. On some matters he is the involved public; on others, the interested; and on still others, remote, unknowledgeable, and unengaged.

A partner in a Washington law firm will similarly defy generalization. She is a grandmother, avid gardener, and news junkie who looks from a distance like a classic member of the involved "elite." A leading expert on constitutional law who is quoted often in the press, she is also fearful of technology and bored by and ignorant of investing and business. Her children grown, she no longer pays attention to news about local schools or even local government.

Or imagine a stay-at-home mom in California with a high school education, who considers her husband's career her own. Her volunteer work at children's schools gives her keen ideas about why the local paper is wrong in its education coverage, and from her own life she has an intuitive sense about people.

These sketches are obviously made up, but they bring the complex notion of the public down to earth. The sheer magnitude and diversity of the people are the public's strengths. The involved expert on one issue is the ignorant and unconcerned citizen on another. The three groups—which themselves are only crude generalizations—work as a check on one another so that no debate becomes merely a fevered exchange between active interest groups. What's more, this mix of publics is usually much wiser than the involved public alone.

Listen to some journalists talk about the audience they imagine as they work, and you will hear a sense of the interlocking public. When Byron Calame was public editor of the *New York Times*, he heard it when he interviewed colleagues. "Several editors, including Suzanne Daley, who just became national editor after a stint as education editor, noted that they must keep two kinds of readers in mind. 'One is an expert on whatever subject we are writing about, someone who will read this story no matter what, but who will be highly judgmental. . . . The other is your basically curious person, but without a lot of time, who is, in my mind, the real challenge. He or she might read the story. But it has to hook them. The game in my head is: Okay, how do we write this so that it is accurate and has weight, but is still fun to read for someone who really doesn't care much about say, college dorms or tutoring?' "[38]

CUNY professor C. W. Anderson, in his writings about the fragmenting effect of the Web on audiences, has thought about a complex series of publics in ways that connect with our ideas here. He has suggested that different publics form around different issues and concerns that are more nuanced than people have generally suggested and that the Web lets us see these and connect with them. But he also has noted that the public does not form itself into a representative whole on the Web. It is more random parts. "Online, all publics appear fragmentary. There is always an element of the public that cannot be networked. There is always a fraction of this uncaptured public only a mouse click away."[39]

Our concept of the Interlocking Public and Anderson's idea of multiple publics are closely related, although what Anderson sees as fragmentary we would describe as pluralistic. Seen as blocks of people that intersect, and which benefit from the diversity of more intense and less intense interest, we think the public is far more able than Lippmann dreamed, and the press does not have the daunting job of delivering "truth" to a passive public as he imagined.

What is required from the news media—one that is now more a network of professionals and citizens together—is that they provide this more complex and dynamic public what it needs to sort out the truth for itself over time.

This more complex understanding of the public carries with it an indictment of the modern professional press. A journalism that focuses on the expert elite—the special interests—may be in part responsible for public disillusionment. Such a press does not reflect the world as most people live and experience it. Similarly, political coverage that focuses on tactical considerations for the political junkie and leaves the merely interested and the uninterested behind is failing in the responsibilities of journalism. On the other side of the scale, a journalism that leaves out important issues in favor of only featuring things that will generate the largest conceivable audience—all stories that could go viral all the time—actually leaves most of the audience behind.

In short, this more pluralistic vision of the interlocking public suggests that our news media should still try to serve the interests of the widest community possible. Even media that is niche in its interests has a community. One way to do that is to imagine and serve gradations of interest and knowledge in covering events. At the same time, trends developing in our new century make it clear that recognizing the needs of the more complex interlocking public will be more difficult than ever. The networked media of the digital age, for instance, has struggled to understand or create a coherent narrative for the fault lines in the American electorate, other than to label the country as "polarized." The press largely failed to see the conservative wave of the first two elections of the twenty-first century, as well as to anticipate or understand the rise of the Tea Party movement. The press similarly failed to anticipate the counter-movements, the election of Obama in 2008 and, with a handful of exceptions, his relatively easy reelection in 2012, fueled by what the media would almost instantly label as the inevitable result of changing demographics.

The failure of both the establishment press and our new more networked media to anticipate or explain these shifting patterns not only reveals how complex the interlocking public really is but also suggests that part of the problem is the way both the old media and the new frame issues. The country dismissed as polarized in 2013, for instance, contains a broad majority (73 percent) of people who support more background checks on gun buying, but Congress is still unable to pass such legislation.[40]

In an increasingly crowded media environment, the most precious commodity of all becomes attention. To gain it, and hold it, some publishers have resorted to the political version of sensationalism: to fear monger, to employ stereotypes and labels that marginalize and demean one's antagonists. Often in coverage of the great social issues of the latter half of the twentieth century—civil rights, the sexual revolutions, anti–Vietnam War sentiment, immigration, and globalization—traditional media employed such generalizations and pigeonholing and depended on spokespeople for the extremes. These stereotypes and labels became the lingua franca of the public debate and pulled the news media away from stopping to ask to what extent these positions were widely held, or even what they meant. In the open culture of the Web, where the most passionate and organized interests can marshal voices that look like "the public," the tendency toward extremism and polarization may have only increased. The mistake we often make is imagining that discourse in social media is somehow more real, or closer to the true public, because it is unmediated. It is an illusion, and not just because only a fraction of Americans are active in social media (only 18 percent of Americans with Internet access used Twitter in 2013). The conversation in social media is also unrepresentative. When the Pew Research Center monitored the discourse on Twitter over the course of a year and compared it to scientific samples of the public answering survey questions on the same issues, it found little correlation. The sentiment in social media, rather, tended to be dominated by whatever side was outraged at a given moment.[41]

That poses a whole new set of challenges for understanding the public, as Anderson has said. And it raises the responsibility. If our new journalism is to work for citizens of a democratic society, then it must begin to facilitate the understanding that allows the sort of compromise on which governance of a complex interlocking public depends.

The Theory of the Interlocking Public also casts a shadow over the concept of niche marketing in a media landscape where more voices are vying for attention. Many of the niches created by the new information delivery platforms are much harder to define than the artificial categories identified by marketing research may imply. Television aimed at women ages eighteen to thirty-four (or Generation X, or soccer moms, or football fans) is likely to alienate larger numbers than anticipated of the very group at which it is aimed. People are simply more complex than the categories and stereotypes we've created for them.

THE NEW CHALLENGE

If the Theory of the Interlocking Public reinforces the notion that news should enhance democratic freedom, journalism may face its greatest threat yet in the early decades of the Web.

At the beginning of the Internet age, more traditional media companies saw the future in terms of size. That led to a wave of consolidations and mergers—and nearly all of these concentrations failed. As these companies consolidated, however, they began to move their interests further away from journalism and further toward commercial gain—away, in a sense, from mission and toward profit as a reason for being.

When his company won television rights for Singapore, media baron Rupert Murdoch praised the country for being undemocratic:

> Singapore is not liberal, but it's clean and free of drug addicts. Not so long ago it was an impoverished, exploited colony with famines, diseases, and other problems. Now people find themselves in three-room apartments with jobs and clean streets. Material incentives create business and the free market economy. If politicians try it the other way around with democracy, the Russian model is the result. Ninety percent of the Chinese are interested more in a better material life than in the right to vote.[42]

Never before had a modern publisher advocated capitalism without democracy in this way. Yet, following Murdoch's pronouncement, other examples would follow of ownership that subordinated journalism to other commercial interests.

In the second decade of the twenty-first century, the word *media* is now used to describe companies that create little content of their own and are larger and more powerful than any of the media companies of the previous century. They also have little commitment to creating the public service and accountability reporting that journalism historically laid claim to.

By 2013, five companies controlled 64 percent of the ad revenue derived from the Internet—Google, Yahoo, Facebook, Microsoft, and AOL.[43]

Writer Dan Gillmor has suggested that Google's power has become so great the company is in effect the "Internet overlord."[44]

Writer Rebecca MacKinnon has argued that Google, Facebook, and a handful of others have such power over our lives that they operate as de facto sovereigns. "Our desire for security, entertainment and material comfort is manipulated to the point that we all voluntarily and eagerly submit to subjugation." She ends with a rallying cry: "We have a responsibility to hold the abusers of digital power to account, along with their facilitators and collaborators. If we do not, when we wake up one morning to discover that our freedoms have eroded beyond recognition, we will have only ourselves to blame."[45]

Those companies, which MacKinnon calls digital sovereigns, are also dissociated from geography, civic space, and even nation–the implications of which raise another level of uncertainty about the concept of corporate citizenship or social responsibility in the context of news.

Some, such as Harvard's Nicco Mele, author of *The End of Big*, have suggested that these large companies may be short-lived. To create new innovation, the conditions of the networked economy favor the nimbleness of individuals loosely connected. But even if Mele is right, these large companies seem likely to be replaced by other short-lived giants. The currency of the new media economy may lean more heavily on stock options, public offerings, getting in, getting out. And in this world, corporate responsibility and values seem antiquated, even irrelevant.

If the distribution companies begin to buy up news, or create it themselves, the managers of the news subsidiaries will fight and protest for their independence, but history suggests they will suffer from the position of minority status. "We look at the 1930s and we see steel and chemical industries starting to buy up the journalism of Europe," journalism scholar James Carey noted at the dawn of the Internet age. That altered how the press of Europe saw the rise of fascism. Militarism was good business. Today, he foresaw, American journalism is beginning to be "bought up by the entertainment business–and e-commerce. Entertainment and e-commerce are today what the steel and chemical industries were in the 1930s."[46]

The notion of freedom of the press is rooted in independence and diverse voices. Only a press free of government censors can tell the truth. In the modern context, that freedom was expanded to include independence from other institutions as well–parties, advertisers, business, and more. One by-product of the economic collapse of news is that the press as an independent institution is threatened. Not only can news not stand alone as a business, as it once did, but also its production is increasingly intermingled with other products (the rental of financial terminals at Bloomberg News) or with political causes (advocacy groups producing their own journalism). And while technology has created an unprecedented free flow of information and opinion, shrinking newsrooms have also meant a decline in accountability journalism. It is a fact and one about which all citizens should worry.

In the end, the question is this: Can journalism sustain in the twenty-first century the purpose that forged it in the three and a half centuries that came before?

Answering this question begins with identifying what journalism's purpose is. The next step is understanding the principles that allow those who gather the news to sustain that purpose on behalf of the rest of us.

Truth:
The First and
Most Confusing
Principle

A few days after John F. Kennedy was murdered, the man who succeeded Kennedy as president, Lyndon Johnson, sent for his secretary of defense. Johnson wanted to know what was really going on ten thousand miles across the globe, in a tiny country called Vietnam. Johnson didn't trust what he'd been told as vice president. He wanted his own information. Press reports at the time suggested the situation in South Vietnam had deteriorated in recent months following the takeover of a new government in a coup d'etat. How bad was it? Defense Secretary Robert McNamara flew to Saigon and spent three days talking to all the generals and touring the various battle zones.

On his way back, McNamara gave a press conference at Tan Son Nhat Airport. The enemy activity had eased, he announced, and he was "optimistic as to the progress that can be made in the coming year."[1] When he landed at Andrews Air Force Base the next day, McNamara took a helicopter to the White House to report to Johnson personally. Afterward, in brief remarks to White House reporters, he described his meeting with the president: "We reviewed in great detail the plans of the South Vietnamese and the plans of our own military advisors for operations during 1964. We have every reason to believe they will be successful. We are determined that they shall be." As Benjamin C. Bradlee, executive editor of the *Washington Post* at the time, would put it many years later, "And the world heard nothing more about the secretary's visit or his report to President Johnson."[2]

Eight years later, the *New York Times* and the *Washington Post* published a secret government-written history about what the leaders really knew and thought about the Vietnam War. Among the mountain of documents, which came to be called the Pentagon Papers, was the substance of what McNamara in fact had reported to the President that day. "The situation is very disturbing," McNamara's private memorandum to Johnson warned. "Current trends, unless reversed in the next 2–3 months, will lead to neutralization at best," he wrote, using the term at the time for a stalemate, "and more likely to a Communist-controlled state," in other words, utter U.S. defeat in Vietnam in early 1964. The new South Vietnamese government was "indecisive and drifting." The U.S. team helping them "lacks leadership, has been poorly informed, and is not working to a common plan." The situation with the enemy "has been deteriorating in the countryside since July to a far greater extent than we realized. . . ."

It was a startling appraisal, utterly at odds with everything McNamara had said publicly, starker and more alarming than anything that the American public would know.

The seriousness of the situation in Vietnam was hardly a mystery to reporters in Vietnam. Two days after McNamara's report to the President, David Halberstam of the *New York Times* authored a detailed assessment of the situation there. The struggle in Vietnam had reached "a critical point," wrote Halberstam, who had just returned from fifteen months in the country. Halberstam's thesis in some ways even mirrored McNamara's private memo.[3] Halberstam's sources, however, were anonymous, described in the couched language of "experienced Western observers" and unnamed "officials."

United Press International reporter Neil Sheehan had gone even further. His story about McNamara's visit to Vietnam suggested that the defense secretary had been blunt with Vietnamese leaders about how badly things were going. Yet Sheehan's sources were also unnamed, and he made no mention, or apparently had no idea, of how stark an assessment McNamara would give to Johnson.

"What might have happened," Bradlee would wonder two decades later, "had the truth emerged in 1963 instead of 1971," about what McNamara really thought and what he had really told the President?[4]

We use the words every day—*truth* and *lies, accurate* and *false*—and we think they convey something meaningful. McNamara *lied* during his press conferences. The Pentagon Papers revealed the *truth* of what he really thought and reported to Johnson. The press reported accurately what McNamara said in his press conferences. Some reporters even tried to convey, using unnamed sources, the sense that McNamara might have been more worried than he was letting on. But they did not get at the truth of what he had written and told the President. The Pentagon Papers would be a sensation eight years later, so much so that the Nixon White House would try—and fail—to use the Supreme Court to stop their publication. The war would go on another decade before the defeat McNamara predicted finally occurred.

Over the last three hundred years, news professionals have developed a loose set of principles and values to fulfill the function of providing news—the indirect knowledge by which people come to form their opinions about the world. Foremost among these principles is this:

Journalism's first obligation is to the truth.

On this there is absolute unanimity and also utter confusion: Everyone agrees journalists must tell the truth, yet people are befuddled about what "the truth" means.

When the Pew Research Center for the People & the Press and

the Committee of Concerned Journalists asked journalists in 1999 which news values they considered paramount, 100 percent answered "getting the facts right."[5]

In long interviews with our university research partners, journalists from both old and new media similarly volunteered "truth" overwhelmingly as a primary mission.[6] In forums, even ideological journalists gave the same answer. "What we're saying is you cannot be objective because you're going to go in with certain biases," said Patty Calhoun, the editor of the alternative weekly paper *Westword*. "But you can certainly pursue accuracy and fairness and the truth, and that pursuit continues."[7]

The desire that information be truthful is elemental. Since news is the material that people use to learn and think about the world beyond themselves, the most important quality it can possess is that it be usable and reliable. Will it rain tomorrow? Is there a traffic jam ahead? Did my team win? What did the President say? Truthfulness creates, in effect, the sense of security that grows from awareness and is at the essence of news.

This basic desire for truthfulness is so powerful, the evidence suggests it is innate. "In the beginning was the Word" is the opening line of the Gospel of John in the New Testament. The earliest journalists—messengers in preliterate societies—were expected to recall matters accurately and reliably, partly out of need. Often the news these messengers carried was a matter of survival. The chiefs needed accurate word about whether the tribe on the other side of the hill might attack.

It is interesting that oppressive societies tend to belittle literal definitions of truthfulness and accuracy, just as postmodernists do today (although for different reasons). In the Middle Ages, for instance, monks held that there was actually a hierarchy of truth. At the highest level were messages that told us about the fate of the universe, such as whether heaven existed. Next came moral truth, which taught us how to live. This was followed by allegorical truth, which exclaimed the moral of stories. Finally, at the bottom, the least important, was the literal truth, which the theorists said was usually empty of meaning and irrelevant. As one fourteenth-century manual explained, using logic similar to what we might hear today from a postmodern scholar or a Hollywood producer, "Whether it is truth of history or fiction doesn't matter, because the example is not supplied for its own sake but for its signification."[8]

Modern political operatives are enamored of similar notions and often preach the idea that in public life perception is reality. The operatives around Richard Nixon in 1968 extolled such notions to aggrandize their role in that election, for instance, as would operatives for politicians as diverse as Bill Clinton and Mitt Romney.[9]

Consider also what an anonymous advisor to George W. Bush told reporter Ron Suskind for a 2004 piece in the *New York Times Magazine* about how the government tries to control information in the new world: "[Journalists] are in what we call the reality-based community.... That's not the way the world really works anymore.... When we act, we create our own reality. While you are studying that reality ... we'll act again, creating other new realities, which you can study too."[10]

The tools for such information management arguably are even greater today. The technology that creates the idea of citizen journalism also empowers political powers to control the image of them that is presented to the public. A 2013 study of Twitter messages from reporters at fifty-one U.S. newspapers found that "politicians were quoted in tweets 12 times more often than citizens, and along with government employees, accounted for 75 percent of quotes," reflecting the extent to which new communications technology has opened the public mind to special interest messages.[11]

The goal of official message management, whether it was medieval church leaders or modern political operatives today, is not enlightenment so much as control. They don't want literal facts to get in the way of political or religious persuasion. An accurate understanding of the day offers contradiction and dissonance to orthodoxy.

As the modern press began to form with the birth of democratic theory, the promise of being truthful and accurate quickly became a powerful part of even the earliest marketing of journalism. The first identifiable regular newspaper in England proposed to rely "on the best and most certain intelligence." The editor of the first paper in France, though his enterprise was government-owned, promised in his maiden issue, "In one thing I will yield to nobody—I mean in my endeavor to get at the truth." Similar promises to accuracy are found in the earliest papers in America, Germany, Spain, and elsewhere.[12]

The earliest colonial journalism was a strange mix of essay and fact. The information about shipping and cargoes was accurate. The political vitriol was less so, yet it was also obviously more opinion or speech than strict information. Even James Callender, the notorious scandal monger who made his reputation with sex exposés of Alexander Hamilton and Thomas Jefferson, did not make his stories up, but trafficked in facts mixed with rumor.[13]

In the nineteenth century, as it disentangled itself from political control, journalism sought its first mass audience in part by relying on sensational crime, scandal, thrill seeking, and celebrity worship, but also by writing the news in plain language for regular people. The move away from party affiliation began with the *New York Sun* in the 1830s, and journalism gained new heights of popularity and sensation at the end of the century. These were the years of William Randolph Hearst, Joseph Pulitzer, and "yellow journalism." Yet even the Lords of the Yellow Press sought to assure readers that they could believe what they read, even if the pledge was not always honored. Hearst's *Journal*, which was guilty more of sensationalism than of invention, claimed it was the most truthful paper in town. Pulitzer's *World* operated under the motto "Accuracy, Accuracy, Accuracy" and was more reliable than is usually credited.[14]

To assure his readers they could believe what they read, Pulitzer created a Bureau of Accuracy and Fair Play in the *New York World* in 1913. In a 1984 article in the *Columbia Journalism Review*, Cassandra Tate described how the *World*'s first ombudsman noticed a pattern in the newspaper's reporting on shipwrecks: Each such story featured a cat that had survived. When the ombudsman asked the reporter about this curious coincidence, he was told:

> One of those wrecked ships had a cat, and the crew went back to save it. I made the cat a feature of my story, while the other reporters

failed to mention the cat, and were called down by their city editors for being beaten. The next time there was a shipwreck, there was no cat but the other ship news reporters did not wish to take a chance, and put the cat in. I wrote the report, leaving out the cat, and then I was severely chided for being beaten. Now when there is a shipwreck all of us always put in the cat.[15]

The irony, of course, is that the embellishments were all put there to create a sense of realism.

By the beginning of the twentieth century, journalists began to realize that realism and reality—or accuracy and truth—were not so easily equated. In 1920, Walter Lippmann used the terms *truth* and *news* interchangeably in his book *Liberty and the News*. But in 1922, in *Public Opinion*, he wrote: "News and truth are not the same thing.... The function of news is to signalize an event," or make people aware of it. "The function of truth is to bring to light the hidden facts, to set them into relation with each other, and make a picture of reality upon which men can act."[16] By 1938, journalism textbooks were beginning to question how truthful the news could really be.[17]

Over the next fifty years, after decades of debate and argument, sometimes by political ideologues and sometimes by postmodern deconstructionist academics, we came to the point where some denied that anyone could put facts into a meaningful context to report the truth about them. An epistemological skepticism began to pervade every aspect of our intellectual life, from art, literature, law, and physics to history. Columbia University historian Simon Schama suggested that "the certainty of an ultimately observable, empirically verifiable truth" was dead.[18]

With the digital age, some have suggested that what we considered truth was merely "consensus" arrived at by an oligarchical press system canvassing the opinions of a limited number of establishment sources, something changeable and far less solid than what we imagined. "Truth is a judgment about what persuades us to believe a particular assertion," NYU professor Clay Shirky has argued.[19]

The arguments doubting that there is anything such as truth, in other words, are long-standing. Truth, it seems, is too complicated for us to pursue–in our journalism or anything else. Or perhaps it doesn't even exist, since we are all subjective individuals. These are interesting arguments–maybe, on some philosophical level, even valid. But where does that leave what we call journalism? Is the word *truth* now something adequate for everyday conversation but something that doesn't hold up to real scrutiny?

Clearly, there are levels. "The journalist at the *New York Times* told us the other day that the New York Giants lost a football game by a score of 20-8," journalist and press critic Richard Harwood told us at one of the forums we organized to research this book. "Now that was a small piece of truth. But the story of why the Giants lost can be told in a hundred different ways–each story being written through a different lens that is fogged over by stereotypes and personal predilections."[20]

So what does journalism's obligation to the truth mean? The usual efforts to answer this question, at seminars or in philosophical tracts, end up in a muddle. One reason is that the conversation is usually not grounded in the real world. Philosophical discussions of whether "truth" really exists founder in semantics.

Another reason is that journalists themselves have never been very clear about what they mean by truthfulness. Journalism by nature is reactive and practical rather than philosophical and introspective. The serious literature by journalists thinking through such issues is not rich, and what little there is most journalists have not read. Theories of journalism are left to the academy, and many newspeople have historically devalued journalism education, arguing that the only place to learn is through osmosis on the job. As Ted Koppel, the highly respected network TV journalist, once declared: "Journalism schools are an absolute and total waste of time."[21]

The conventional explanations by journalists of how they get at the truth tend to be quick responses drawn from interviews or speeches or, worse, marketing slogans, and they often rely on crude metaphors. The press is "a mirror" on society, said David Bartlett, then president of the Radio and Television News Directors Association, echoing a common phrase of the time. Journalism is "a reflection of the passions of the day," leading television broadcaster Tom Brokaw told our academic research partners. News is whatever is "most newsworthy on a given day," said a CNN producer.[22] These explanations made journalists seem passive–mere recorders of events rather than investigators, selectors, or editors.[23] It's as if they thought truth was something that rises up by itself, like bread dough. Rather than defend their techniques and methods for finding truth, journalists tended to deny that they existed.

Whether it was secrecy, idealism, or ineptness, the failure by journalists to articulate what they were doing left citizens suspicious that the press was either deluding itself or hiding something. This is one reason the discussion of journalistic objectivity became such a trap. The term is so misunderstood and battered, the discussion mostly goes off track. It is also one of the reasons that a new era of digital pioneers, as they tried to contemplate the journalism they were disrupting, have tended to dismiss journalistic professionalism. They imagined journalists were largely stenographers, with random lists of sources, using fairly crude notions of balance to get at accuracy. Many if not most journalists were doing much more. But they had little vocabulary, let alone standard method, and even less journalistic literature, to explain themselves.

As we will discuss in more depth in chapter 4, on verification, originally it was not the journalist who was imagined to be objective. It was his or her method. Today, however, in part because journalists have failed to articulate what they are doing, our contemporary understanding of objectivity is mostly muddled and confused. Most people, as we noted earlier and will detail more later, mistake objectivity to mean neutrality.

Despite the public's confusion, there is little doubt that journalists believe themselves to be engaged in pursuing truth, not just free speech or commerce. They have to be–for this is what society requires of them.

And, as we will see, "journalistic truth" means more than mere accuracy. It is a sorting-out process that takes place between the initial story and the interaction among the public, newsmakers, and journalists. This first principle of journalism–its disinterested pursuit of truth—is ultimately what sets journalism apart from other forms of communication.

JOURNALISTIC TRUTH

To understand this sorting-out process, it is important to remember that journalism exists in a social context. Out of necessity, citizens and societies depend on accurate and reliable accounts of events. They develop procedures and processes to arrive at what might be called "functional truth." Police track down and arrest suspects based on facts. Judges hold trials. Juries render verdicts. Industries are regulated, taxes are collected, and laws are made. We teach our children rules, history, physics, and biology. All of these truths—even the laws of science—are subject to revision, but we operate by them in the meantime because they are necessary and they work.

This is what our journalism must be after—a practical or functional form of truth. It is not truth in the absolute or philosophical sense. It is not the truth of a chemical equation. Journalism can—and must—pursue the truths by which we can operate on a day-to-day basis. "We don't think it's unreasonable to expect jurors to render fair verdicts, or teachers to teach honest lessons, or historians to write impartial history, scientists to perform unbiased research. Why should we set any lower goals for poor journalists?" Bill Keller of the *New York Times* asked us. "Whether true objectivity is ever possible—I don't think that is what we're here for.... We strive for coverage that aims as much as possible to present the reader with enough information to make up his or her own mind. That's our fine ideal."[24]

Does this suggest that journalism should stick simply to accuracy, getting the names and dates right? Is that sufficient? The increasingly interpretative nature of most modern journalism tells us no. A journalism built merely on accuracy fails to serve contemporary civil society.

In the first place, mere accuracy can be a kind of distortion all its own. As long ago as 1947, the Hutchins Commission, a group of scholars who spent years producing a document that outlined the obligations of journalism, warned of the dangers of publishing accounts that were "factually correct but substantially untrue."[25] Even then, the commission cited stories about members of minority groups that, by failing to provide context or by emphasizing race or ethnicity pointlessly, reinforced false stereotypes. "It is no longer enough to report the fact truthfully. It is now necessary to report the truth about the fact," the commission concluded.

Mere accuracy is also not what people are looking for. In his book *News Values* journalist Jack Fuller described how philosophers imagine there are two tests of truth: one is correspondence, the other is coherence. For journalism, these tests roughly translate into getting the facts straight and making sense of the facts. Coherence must be the ultimate test of journalistic truth, Fuller decided. "Regardless of what the radical skeptics argue, people still passionately believe in meaning. They want the whole picture, not just part of it.... They are tired of polarized discussion...."[26]

Common sense tells us something similar. A report that the mayor praised the police at the Garden Club luncheon seem inadequate–even foolish–if the police are in fact entangled in a corruption scandal; the mayor's comments are clearly political rhetoric, and they come in response to some recent attack by his critics.

This is far from suggesting that accuracy doesn't matter, that facts are all relative–just another form of fodder for debate. On the contrary, accuracy is the foundation upon which everything else is built: context, interpretation, debate, and all of public communication. If the foundation is faulty, everything else is flawed. A debate between opponents arguing with false figures or purely on prejudice fails to inform. It only inflames. It takes the society nowhere. It is more helpful, and more realistic, to understand the truth we seek or can expect from journalism to be a process–or a continuing journey toward understanding–that begins with the first account of an event and builds over time. For instance, the first news accounts signal a new situation or trend. They may begin with reports of something simple–an accident, a meeting, an inflammatory statement. They may come in the form of a brief alert with few details. The time and place of the accident, the damage done, the types of vehicles, arrests, unusual weather or road conditions–in effect, the physical externalities of the case—are facts that can be recorded and checked. Once they have verified the facts, those engaged in reporting the news should strive to convey a fair and reliable account of their meaning, valid for now, subject to further investigation. Journalist Carl Bernstein has described this as reporters striving to provide "the best obtainable version of the truth."[27] Journalist Howie Schneider has called it "conditional truth," subject to revision with new information. The principles of the *Washington Post,* drafted by Eugene Meyer in 1933, describe telling "the truth as nearly as the truth may be ascertained."[28]

An individual reporter may not be able to move much beyond a surface level of accuracy in a first account, particularly if that account is written in real time as a blog post or an alert. But the first account builds to a second, in which the sources of news have responded to initial mistakes and missing elements, and the second account builds to a third, and so on. Context is added in each successive layer. In more important and complex stories, there are subsequent contributions on the editorial pages, in blogs, social media discourse, in official responses—the full range of public and private conversation. This practical truth is a protean thing that, like learning, grows like a stalactite in a cave, drop by drop, over time.

The truth is a complicated and sometimes contradictory phenomenon, but if it is seen as a process over time, journalism can get at it. First by stripping information of any attached misinformation, disinformation, or self-promoting bias and then by letting the community react, in the sorting-out process that ensues. As always, the search for truth becomes a conversation.

This definition helps reconcile the way we use the words *true* and *false* every day with the way we deconstruct those words in the petri dish of a philosophical debate. This definition comes closer to journalists' intuitive understanding of what they do than the crude metaphors of mirrors and reflections that are commonly handed out.

We understand truth as a goal—at best elusive—and still embrace it. We embrace it the same way as Albert Einstein did when he said of science that it was not about truth but about making what we know less false. For this is how life really is—we're often striving and never fully achieving. As historian Gordon Wood has said about writing history: "One can accept the view that the historical record is fragmentary and incomplete ... and that historians will never finally agree in their interpretations" and yet still believe "in an objective truth about the past that can be observed and empirically verified." This is more than a leap of faith. In real life, people can tell when someone has come closer to getting it right, when the sourcing is authoritative, when the research is exhaustive, when the method is transparent. Or as Wood put it, "Historians may never see and present that truth wholly and finally, but some of them will come closer than others, be more nearly complete, more objective, more honest, in their written history, and we will know it, and have known it, when we see it."[29]

Those who have worked in news or in public life say much the same thing: Getting news that comes closer to a complete version of the truth has real consequences. In the first hours of an event, when being accurate is most difficult, accuracy is perhaps most important. It is during this time that public attitudes are formed, sometimes stubbornly, by the context within which the information is presented. Is it a threat to me? Is it good for me? Is it something I should be concerned about? The answer to these questions determines how carefully I follow a new event, how much verification of the facts I will look for. Based on his experience, Hodding Carter, a longtime journalist who served as assistant secretary of state for public affairs in the Carter administration's State Department, has said that this is the time in which the government can exercise its greatest control over the public mind: "If given three days without serious challenge, the government will have set the context for an event and can control public perception of that event."[30]

The digital age adds pressures in both directions to this process of searching for functional or conditional truth. The first pressure is speed. In the context of gathering news, speed is almost always the enemy of accuracy. It offers those who seek to report less time to check facts. This is why cable news channels that report continuously (such as CNN and Fox News) tend to report more erroneous information than the broadcast channels (NBC, CBS, or ABC) that have hours to vet their reports for a single network evening newscast. Posting news in real time on Twitter or elsewhere online, thus, tends to make all news organizations as vulnerable as cable.

The second pressure is the growing orientation toward commentary and argument. As people compose polemics, they are focused on persuasion. They naturally tend to choose facts that help them make their case. But this pushes the emphasis away by degrees from fact checking, from getting to the bottom of what happened and arriving at the most complete understanding of the facts.

An open networked media environment also means that more rumors, more misinformation are passed along in public–creating more confusion for users and more pressure on news organizations.

Those pressures pulling against truth and accuracy are balanced against others brought by the digital age that move in the opposite direction. The opening of the media system to more voices, particularly through social media, has the potential to strengthen the process of verification magnificently. More sources are likely to spot falsehoods and point them out. And there are countless examples. During political speeches, such as Paul Ryan's vice presidential acceptance speech at the 2012 Republican Convention, people pointed out inaccuracies in almost real time. When some media outlets in 2011 mistakenly reported that Congresswoman Gabrielle Giffords had been shot to death by a gunman in Tucson while others reported she had been taken to a hospital, citizens pointed out the discrepancy on Twitter immediately, and news organizations had corrected the error within fifteen minutes.

As powerful and profound as the network is, however, it's an oversimplification–a hope that cannot be sustained–to think that in the networked culture the sorting out process always works efficiently–that the Internet, as some have put it, is a self-cleaning oven. In addition to the speed, a variety of other factors get in the way. In a fragmented media culture, more people may be operating in their own bubbles of self-selected interests and sources. We may, as we scatter to our own sources for information, lack a central gathering place or a common understanding of the basic facts. The initial account of an event is always the most important, and the more hastily it is put together, the more inaccurate it is likely to be. That problem is added to by the phenomenon of our simply moving on, deciding we have learned what we needed about something and are on to the next thing, like the student only paying half attention in class and getting a general sense of the topic but botching all the details. Only there is no test at the end of the unit to tell us we got it about half-wrong.

The more compelling sense is that truth requires commitment, a dedication to a process of verification, and that search is made more powerful when journalists and the public are knit together in a way that mixes the structure of traditional journalism techniques and authority with the power of the networked community.

Consider the case of Ian Tomlinson, a newspaper vendor who died after being caught in the middle of a protest over the G20 meeting in England in April 2009. The initial police account held that Tomlinson suffered a heart attack while walking home and that protesters were culpable for getting in the way of medics whose treatment might have saved his life. The next day's *Evening Standard* newspaper, the paper Tomlinson sold, bore the headline: "Police pelted with bricks as they help dying man."

The *Guardian* newspaper, skeptical of that version and of police secrecy surrounding the case, pursued two lines of inquiry to go deeper. One, traditional shoe-leather reporting, had journalists covering the protest go through their notebooks of interviewees to identify possible eyewitnesses; the paper also pored over its photos to see if anyone had inadvertently caught a glimpse of the incident. The effort found one eyewitness and photographic evidence that seemed to prove Tomlinson had fallen to the ground at the feet of police, one hundred yards from where he would later fall again and die.

The second line of inquiry reached out to readers on the Internet. After taking four days to conclusively establish that its photos indeed proved Tomlinson had fallen earlier, near police, the *Guardian* put its photographic evidence online and asked if anyone knew more. The paper thus became part of the online conversation questioning the circumstances of Tomlinson's death. Via Twitter, *Guardian* reporter Paul Lewis discovered photo albums on another social media platform, Flickr, that contained more images raising doubts about Tomlinson's death. But all of this was circumstantial evidence, feeding online speculation, Lewis thought, not yet proof of any wrongdoing. The crowd, like the *Guardian*, in other words, was uneasy, but it did not really know what had happened.

One member of that crowd was Chris La Jaunie, an investment fund manager in New York who had been in London during the protest. La Jaunie had shot video that he thought might be explosive; it showed a policeman pushing Tomlinson. He had considered releasing it on YouTube, but had had second thoughts. It might go unnoticed. It might be challenged. It would also lack any context, a lone video posted by an unfamiliar source. Believing the *Guardian* had been the most effective interrogator of the police version of events, he contacted Lewis. The paper verified his account, triangulated his footage with other evidence, and eight days later overturned what in effect was a police cover-up, establishing that Tomlinson had died as a result of actions by police.

The Tomlinson case, Lewis argues, illustrates the synergy of what the *Guardian* calls Open Journalism, which combines the professionalism of journalists and their access to the observations and knowledge of public witness and experience.[31]

One striking feature of the Tomlinson story is that there are parallels to it from earlier times, which reveal just how much the means of getting at the truth have changed, while the goal of pursuing it has not.

Fifty years earlier, in Orangeburg, South Carolina, three students were killed and more than twenty others injured in what police described as "an exchange of gunfire" with state troopers during a protest over civil rights. After hearing about the shootings, reporter Jack Nelson, the Atlanta bureau chief of the *Los Angeles Times*, flew to South Carolina to check out the story. While most reporters were gathered at press conferences, Nelson went to the Orangeburg Regional Hospital, where twenty-seven wounded students were being treated. He stuffed two reporter's notebooks in his inside jacket pocket, creating a bulge underneath that resembled a shoulder holster holding a handgun, and walked into the office of the hospital administrator, Phil Mabry. Nelson identified himself "as being from the Atlanta bureau" and said he wanted to examine the medical records of the wounded students. Mabry assumed Nelson was from the Atlanta office of the FBI. Nelson did not disabuse him.

The dutiful hospital administrator laid the medical records out on his desk. The records showed what had really happened. Most of the wounded students, and the ones who had died, had been shot in the back, caught in the cross fire as they were running away. Nelson corroborated the medical records with eyewitness interviews and other official records to prove the police account was false. He wanted his story to be airtight. His account proved the state police were lying and added momentum to the civil rights protests.[32]

Paul Lewis combined traditional shoe leather, documentary evidence, and the power of social media to get definitive proof of what happened to Ian Tomlinson. A half century earlier, Jack Nelson used toughness, bluff, the trained knowledge of where official documentary records could be located, and the formal and informal reporting techniques required to establish what really happened in Orangeburg. In both cases, truth was a process—but within reach.

Over time there have been people, even inside traditional journalism, who were unsure if truth was a practical goal for news. At different times, some journalists have suggested substitutes. Probably the two most common of these have been fairness and balance. If newspeople cannot know the truth, they can at least be fair and balanced. But both of these concepts, under scrutiny, are inadequate. Fairness is too abstract and, in the end, is more subjective than truth. Fair to whom? How do you test fairness? Truthfulness, for all its difficulties, at least can be tested.

Balance, too, is subjective. Balancing a story by being fair to both sides may not be fair to the truth if both sides do not, in fact, have equal weight. And in those many cases where there are more than two sides to a story, how does one determine which side to honor? Balance, if it amounts to false balance, becomes distortion.

Technology has added obstacles to the process before. By the late 1990s, as we detailed in our book *Warp Speed*, various forces were converging to weaken journalists' pursuit of truthfulness, despite the continuing allegiance most journalists professed to it. With the advent of the continuous 24-7 news cycle, which began with cable and grew with the Web, the news became more piecemeal; what were once the raw ingredients of journalism began to be passed on to the public directly. As the number of outlets for news proliferated, the sources who talked to the press, and wanted to influence the public, gained more relative power over the journalists who covered them; more outlets, in effect, made it more of a seller's market for information. As audiences fragmented, different news outlets began to adapt differing standards of journalism. In the continuous news culture, news channels trying to shovel out the latest information had less time to check things out. Amid growing competition and speed, there emerged what we called a new Journalism of Assertion that was overwhelming the more traditional Journalism of Verification, which had moved more slowly and put a higher premium on getting things right first.

That process was well under way before the arrival of the Internet as a force in our news culture. In the first years of the Web, as the audience further fragmented and a proliferating number of news outlets competed to get the attention of that audience, we saw the rapid rise of a third model of media—a Journalism of Affirmation, epitomized by talk show hosts like Rush Limbaugh and Rachel Maddow, who attracted audiences through reassurance, or the affirming of preconceptions. (We will talk more about these different models in later chapters.)

In short, what had been a fairly homogeneous notion of journalism that was grounded in reporting, even if it had somewhat differing styles in alternative weeklies versus daily newspapers or nightly local TV, was giving way to different models built on speed and convenience in one model and reassurance in another. The changes were subtle. Even some of the journalists who worked in these new media barely recognized the values shift occurring. Cable TV journalists did not readily acknowledge that they put less of a premium on verification. They just imagined they did it differently. The shift in the core appeal to the audience represented, however subtly, a shift in ethics. And that shift was predicated on more choice and more competition for the one thing that could not grow–the amount of time in the day. More outlets were competing for what was a finite level of audience attention.

With the Internet, there emerged a new and important fourth model–a Journalism of Aggregation–in which publishers such as Yahoo News, search engines such as Google, or Web communities such as Reddit–and with the rise of social media, in turn, individual citizens themselves–recommended and passed along content that they had no direct role in producing and, often, made no effort to verify. Google became one of the most powerful institutions on earth by aggregating for users the material produced by others, with the assurance that its computerized algorithm was ranking its searches based on the reputational record of the source. There is no doubting the incomparable richness of a curated news environment. The experience of sorting through numerous accounts of an event effortlessly in minutes offers a depth, context, and control that the reading of the single account in the past could not come close to. But it is also important to recognize that we now operate in a distributed media environment where most publishers are passing along work they cannot possibly vouch for–and may make no effort to–and that we accept this now without a second thought. The burden of verification has been passed incrementally from the news deliverer to the consumer.

Add to this pressure the shrinking resources in newsrooms dedicated to direct reporting, as the advertising dollars in legacy platforms were replaced by digital dimes. It is a world in which an initial error in reporting or editing or interpretation can turn into a kind of original sin that influences us forever.

The instinct for truth is no less important today–but it is more pressured. Peter Viereck, professor emeritus in history at Mount Holyoke College, has argued that in a networked and connected world, the value of a group dedicated to pursuing truth is now greater. "I can think of nothing more gallant," Viereck says, "even though again and again we fail, than attempting to get at the facts; attempting to tell things as they really are. For at least reality, though never fully attained, can be defined. Reality is that which, when you don't believe it, doesn't go away."[33]

In practical terms, more information makes truth more challenging, even though it means that at the end of the process the truth we arrive at will likely be more accurate. The process, however, becomes more demanding. Call it the paradox of learning in the Information Age. When information is a commodity in oversupply—when there is so much more input—knowledge becomes more difficult to acquire because one must sift and synthesize more information to set things in order. The knowledge acquired may be deeper and better, but it will likely also be more specialized.

This paradox may be the most daunting tension currently affecting our ability to know what's true. There is a gulf between the abundance of news and information available and our ability to sort through it all.

And when the media become background noise, our capacity to focus is diminished. It becomes more difficult to rise above the din. If Winston Churchill was correct that "a lie gets halfway around the world before the truth has a chance to get its pants on," greater technology has only speeded up the process, aiding truth and falsehood alike.[34]

These factors help to explain why the new partisan journalism of the twenty-first century, the Journalism of Affirmation, is even more appealing for some audiences. It makes things easier. It is a way of achieving order in a more confusing world, without so much sifting and heavy lifting. It offers comfort. They tidied up our mental rooms for us. The neo-partisans, be they Bill O'Reilly or Stephanie Miller or a growing array of ideological websites, create the impression for audiences that they are sense makers.

Rather than rush to add interpretation, we need to ensure that we also have a journalism that establishes what has truly happened before it rushes to tell us what it means—a journalism that first concentrates on context and verification. We should look for news that makes transparent how it was produced–the sourcing, evidence, and journalistic decision making that went into it. We should look for journalism that has explicitly tried to sift out rumor, innuendo, and spin and shows evidence of that effort. We need a journalism, in other words, that allows us to answer the question "Why should I believe this?" rather than "Do I agree with it?"

And the more journalism, through its transparency, encourages consumers to think about how the news was put together, the more it will increase their skills for making informed judgments about what constitutes reliable news.

What we need from our journalism in the twenty-first century, in short, is not so different from what we needed in the twentieth. What journalism looks like, however, how it is presented, and even the routines that journalists use to achieve those goals are very different. The new journalism cannot presume anymore to be the only content its audience sees. It cannot present itself as a singular omniscient account of events. It must assume that we have seen other, more partial information in real time, but it also must provide a coherent account on its own in case we have not. It must be conscious and try to correct false information that has previously been presented, particularly if there is a reason to think that misinformation has resonated in the marketplace of ideas. Put more simply, the best new journalism will compete in the marketplace of ideas by being more deeply reported and more transparent, by correcting the record for audiences that have been misinformed and by answering questions other accounts have left unclear.

The impact of this new journalism, in turn, will extend beyond its direct audience, for it will impact and change the work others produce about the same news events. And if it is produced by smart managers, they will spend more effort than they once did marketing this work to elevate its impact both on the public and other news producers and analysts.

We will explain the new ways in which this journalism must be created and presented in subsequent chapters. But it all begins with the recognition that the new journalism, even in a networked era, must be built on a foundation of truth–and that truth cannot be assumed to occur automatically based on the presence of more sources. The pursuit of truth is a process that requires an intellectual discipline and vigilance. It also requires memory—not forgetting about misinformation simply because the discussion has quickly moved on. And the need for this is greater, not lesser, in the new century, because the likelihood of untruth has become so much greater.

For truth to prevail, journalists must make clear to whom they owe their first loyalty. That is the next step.

3

Who
Journalists
Work For

In most businesses, accountability is tied to fairly straightforward metrics. Usually, success is measured in dollars. The bonuses of lawyers, doctors, businesspeople, and most of upper management are tied to how much money their operations bring in.

What is the best mark of value for someone producing journalism?

For years, journalists were evaluated mostly based on highly subjective judgments about the quality of their work. The number of stories reporters produced might be part of the mix, but that varied widely by beat and was not necessarily relevant to how their bosses, the editors themselves, were judged.

At the end of the twentieth century, a new trend emerged: As the industry began to worry more about efficiency and profit, under the assumption that it now was a mature industry whose audience could not grow, it began to tie the performance of top news managers to the profitability of the news enterprise rather than the quality of the content produced under their watch, just as it had previously done with its advertising and circulation executives. Quality factors started to make up half or less of the decision criteria about the performance of news executives and how much they should be paid.

The bonuses, at least for managers, began to be based in large part on how much profit their companies made.[1]

These corporate incentive programs formalized a new theory of newsroom management. In deed if not in name, by 2000 America's journalistic leaders had been transformed into businesspeople. Half of newspaper newsroom leaders reported that they spent at least a third of their time not on journalism but on business matters.[2]

At a minimum, the shift in focus did not have the desired effect. The effort to turn newsroom leaders into cost managers was part of the collective failure of the news industry to adapt to disruption. Ensuring that everyone was focused on maximizing profit and share price only broadened and reinforced the defensive fortress mentality in news companies, which became concentrated on protecting revenue rather than innovating the product. It made it more difficult for newsroom leaders to advocate for the public interest within their companies, and to push for risky, expensive experiments in coverage that might hurt short-term profitability. Publishers and executives talked openly about trying to blow up the culture of the newsroom because it resisted these business imperatives. These changes in the culture of news companies, not coincidentally, showed up in the data about why citizens began to lose their faith in and connection to the news. The public began to see the news as much more of a business and much less of a public service—precisely when the industry tied the compensation of newsroom leadership to those business demands.

Perhaps it made no difference. The fortress mind-set that blocked innovation, and even led more innovative people in news companies to flee, might have occurred anyway. But the move to make those who produced the news accountable not for the quality of their journalism but for the profit they helped generate came just at the moment that the industry needed to reimagine its product, not protect its revenue.

Today, in the networked news environment, evaluating success in journalism is even more complicated. Many emerging media outlets do not expect to generate revenue at the outset as much as build audience and trusted brand. That might suggest measuring success by the traffic the content generates. Yet it quickly becomes obvious that this is also problematic. The coverage of the local champion college football team will surely generate more page views than the work of the reporter whose enterprise has revealed critical problems with the city's water supply. The investigative reporter covering the CIA and the NSA, whose profile must be low to protect his often anonymous sources, is not likely to want to compete at promoting himself in social media with the film critic who appears on television, blogs avidly about movies and celebrities, and is highly visible on Twitter.

A number of people trying to contemplate the metrics of the Web have begun to think a more proper measure of journalism value should be "impact." In a morass of numbers, where page views, unique visitors, and time on site seem to create a muddle of conflicting opinions, with each rating company offering conflicting data, shouldn't the criteria of whether journalism has value—and will build your brand—be the good it does for democratic society? This new discussion is highly idealistic. And those pushing this argument are quick to admit that the task is complex and that any metrics are only proxies, just the beginning of the quest.

Wherever this comes out, the struggle over how to assess the value of a work of journalism goes to the heart of an underlying issue: We established in the previous chapter the idea that journalists must seek out the truth. But what conditions are necessary for those who practice journalism to be able to get at the truth, and also to communicate that truth to the public in a way that their citizens will believe it? The answer—the second principle of journalism—is loyalty.

No one questions that news organizations answer to many constituencies. Community institutions, local groups, parent companies, shareholders, advertisers, and many more interests must be considered and served by a successful news organization. Yet what newspaper publishers gradually came to understand in the nineteenth century—and what generations of news publishers across other technologies refined with significant hardship and later, under duress, began to forget in the twentieth—is that those who produce news in an organization (whether the ultimate motive is profit, prestige, community building, authority, audience reach, or some mix) must have one allegiance above all others. And this commitment forms the second element of journalism:

Journalism's first loyalty is to citizens.

A commitment to citizens is more than professional egoism. It is the implied covenant between someone producing a work of journalism and the public that consumes it that the work is honest. In some cases, this is a covenant among citizens themselves to be transparent about who they are and why they are sharing or creating content in the first place. Whoever produces the news, it is an understanding about purpose that tells the audience that the movie reviews are straight, that the restaurant reviews are not influenced by who buys an ad, that the coverage is not self-interested or slanted for friends or underwriters, that the work is not a veil whose real purpose is something different than it is presented to be.

The notion that those who report the news are not obstructed from digging up and telling the truth—even at the expense of the owners' other financial interests, the funders' political agenda, or the sponsors' products—is a prerequisite of telling the news not only accurately but also persuasively. It is the basis for why citizens believe what they are seeing or hearing or reading. They know they are not being misled or lied to. In short, loyalty to citizens is the most important asset of any publisher that claims to produce journalism. It is what makes the news content trustworthy. And that, in turn, is what makes the publication's advertising more credible. It makes the e-commerce transactions readers engage in on the site seem safer. It makes the events that generate revenue seem more worth attending. It also means that any new experiments to make advertising messages more compelling, whether they are called "native advertising" or "sponsored content" or something else, must also be designed in a way that does not undermine the credibility of the news enterprise. All of this begins with the idea of loyalty to the citizen, to the audience, to the concept that the public is being served rather than exploited or, worse, deceived.

Thus people who produce journalism have different loyalties from employees engaged in other types of work. They have a social obligation that at times overrides employers' or financial sponsors' immediate interests, and yet this obligation is the source of their employers' financial success.

Allegiance to citizens is the meaning of what we have come to call journalistic independence. As we will see, the phrase has often been used as a synonym for other ideas, including disengagement, disinterestedness, detachment, or neutrality. These other terms, ironically, have tended to create confusion and to reflect a fuzzy understanding of what the intellectual independence of journalism really means. Professional journalists contributed to their woes by passing that confusion on to the public, and citizens have understandably become skeptical, even cynical and angry, as a result.

That journalists' primary commitment is to the public is a deeply felt tradition among both journalists and citizens. In a survey on values by the Pew Research Center for the People & the Press and the Committee of Concerned Journalists, more than 80 percent listed "making the reader/listener/viewer your first obligation" as a "core principle of journalism."[3] In open-ended, in-depth interviews with developmental psychologists, more than 70 percent of journalists similarly placed "audience" as their first loyalty, well above their employers, themselves, their profession, or even their families.[4] "I always worked for the people who turned on the television set," said Nick Clooney, the father of the actor George and a former newscaster in Los Angeles, Cincinnati, and elsewhere. "Always. Whenever I was having a discussion with a general manager or a member of the board of directors, my bottom line was always, 'I don't work for you. You're paying my check, and I'm very pleased. But the truth of the matter is, I don't work for you, and if it comes down to a question of loyalty, my loyalty will be to the person who turns on the television set. . . . When I made that position clear, [it was] never questioned."[5]

This sense that the journalist has a loyalty beyond and above that to his or her employer is so deeply held that it manifests itself at the very best news organizations in dramatic, public rebellions of a sort inconceivable in other industries. In 2003, when reporters and editors at the *New York Times* felt that the two most powerful people in their newsroom—the executive editor and the managing editor—had violated this loyalty in condoning the conduct of and then trying to avoid responsibility for Jayson Blair, a reporter who plagiarized and fictionalized, the newsroom's anger effectively forced the publisher to remove these editors.[6] When the publisher's handling of controversial reporter Judith Miller's involvement in a leak investigation in 2005 evoked similar concerns, *New York Times* reporters Don Van Natta Jr., Adam Liptak, and Clifford J. Levy were not shy about revealing these shortcomings in the paper.[7] And then in a very public warning to her boss, columnist Maureen Dowd threatened in the opinion pages that if Miller were allowed back on her beat, the public shouldn't trust the newspaper. Eventually, Miller resigned.

The revolt was not unique. The *Los Angeles Times* had a similar response from its newsroom over a sweetheart deal with a local sports arena, which toppled the editor and publisher. The *Washington Post* backtracked on an ill-conceived plan for private dinners between lobbyists and lawmakers.

It is fair to ask whether this sense of mission has weakened as news organizations have lost revenue. Is the commitment to audiences first a luxury of high profit margins, something that we may look back on, as news organizations seek new kinds of revenue, as an artifact of a passing era?

There is too much evidence to suggest this impulse goes deeper—that the commitment of those trying to get to the bottom of things is to a strongly felt, almost spiritual sense of mission on the public's behalf. It is a sentiment that we have heard countless times from journalists we have met, from countless countries. "I see journalists all around the world as soldiers in an army of truth," Idriss Njutapvoul, a journalist from Cameroon who writes for the website Journal du Cameroun, told us in 2013.[8] There is something in the act of trying to find out the truth of events, and relate them in a way that connects to the public, that binds those who gather the news. The similarities among journalists working in different countries, in different traditions and media, are far more important than their differences.

And the public also expects this commitment from those who provide news, particularly professionals. For years, the Pew Research Center for the People & the Press has asked people whether they want news that reflected their point of view or news that reflected all sides. While trust, accuracy, and a host of other metrics fell, the numbers never significantly wavered. More than six in ten Americans, roughly two-thirds (64 percent) in 2012 preferred news that was not aligned with a particular point of view.[9]

This kind of understanding did not come easily. Though news produced on behalf of the public rather than the party first began to emerge in the 1830s, it was not until the latter part of the nineteenth century that a large number of leading daily newspaper publishers began to substitute editorial independence for political ideology. The most famous declaration of this intellectual and financial independence came in 1896, when a young publisher from Tennessee named Adolph Ochs bought the struggling *New York Times*. Ochs was convinced that a good many New Yorkers were tired of the tawdry sensationalism of William Randolph Hearst and Joseph Pulitzer, and that they would welcome a more tasteful–and accurate–style of journalism. Under the simple headline BUSINESS ANNOUNCEMENT, Ochs published on his first day as owner the words that would become his legacy. It was his "earnest aim," he wrote, "to give the news impartially, without fear or favor, regardless of party, sect or interests involved."

Other publishers had made similar claims to independence, but as authors Alex Jones and Susan Tifft put it in their history of the *Times*, Ochs "actually believed what he wrote."[10] Newspapers across the country reprinted the statement in full. As the *Times* went on to become the most influential paper in New York and then the world, others followed the Ochs model, staking their business plan on the idea that putting the audience ahead of political and immediate financial interests was the best long-term financial strategy. After buying the *Washington Post* in 1933, for instance, Eugene Meyer crafted a set of principles that stated, among other items, "In pursuit of the truth, the newspaper shall be prepared to make sacrifices of its material fortunes, if such a course be necessary for the public good."[11]

As owners began trumpeting editorial independence in their marketing, journalists seized on it to upgrade their professionalism. A generation of early press critics emerged, such as Will Irwin, a former newspaper reporter and editor of *McClure's Magazine,* who in 1911 published a bracing fifteen-part series in *Collier's* chronicling in bold detail the abuses of the press. Seizing on the new technology of the lightbulb, Irwin called on a new public service role for journalism, "an electric light in a dark alley."[12] Newspaper editors in turn reacted to the rhetoric of their bosses and the rebukes of the critics, and they tried to professionalize as a group. Malcolm Bingay, a columnist for the *Detroit Free Press,* has traced this development to the genesis of the American Society of Newspaper Editors, the primary trade association for those who run America's newspaper newsrooms. In 1912, a group of editors had gathered to preview Glacier National Park one summer night in the Rockies:

> As they sat around a campfire they heard [Casper] Yost [editorial page editor of the *St. Louis Globe-Democrat*] discuss an idea which possessed him. His dream was the creation of an ethical organization of American newspaper editors. . . . Little Casper, tagged Arsenic and Old Lace by his contemporaries, might more appropriately be remembered as creating the modern concept of responsibility of the press, a concept often lost today in the more dramatic scuffles about press freedom.[13]

The organization's code of ethics placed editorial independence above all: "Independence: Freedom from all obligations except that of fidelity to the public interest is vital," it stated. "Promotion of any private interest contrary to the general welfare, for whatever reasons, is not compatible with honest journalism. . . . Partisanship, in editorial comment which knowingly departs from the truth, does violence to the best spirit of American journalism; in the news columns it is subversive of a fundamental principle of the profession."

In the commercial era, at the height of its monopoly over audience attention, news organizations were periodically tested to see how seriously they took these statements of public commitment.

When one of its columnists, Foster Winans, was caught engaging in insider trading in the 1980s, the *Wall Street Journal* felt compelled to publicly reexamine and rewrite its code of conduct. "The central premise of this code is that Dow Jones' reputation for quality and for the independence and integrity of our publications is the heart and soul of our enterprise." This was a financial premise, not a purely journalistic one, just as it is for other news organizations as well. "Dow Jones cannot prosper if our customers cannot assume that . . . our analyses represent our best independent judgments rather than our preference, or those of our sources, advertisers or information providers."[14]

Newspapers became monopolies in the 1960s and generally toned down such declarations, except–like the *Journal*–in times of crisis. But television journalism, which is far more commercially competitive, continued to market itself in the public's name. Throughout the 1990s, for instance, at the very time of rising suspicions about the press, "On Your Side" and "Working 4 You" were two of the most popular slogans in local television news. Internal station research, as well as focus groups conducted by the Project for Excellence in Journalism, suggest they were also the most effective slogans.[15]

INDEPENDENCE TO ISOLATION

As with so many professional ideas, editorial independence began over time in some quarters to harden into isolation. As journalists tried to honor and protect their carefully won independence from party and commercial pressures, they sometimes came to pursue independence for its own sake. Detachment from outside pressures could bleed into disengagement from the community.

In part, ironically, this was a result of journalism's becoming professionalized. As journalists became better educated and the press organized itself into chains, companies began to use their newspapers and TV stations as farm systems to train journalists in small markets for assignments later in the bigger ones. By 1997, two-thirds of newspaper journalists, according to one survey, had not grown up in the community they were covering.[16] The majority of them felt "less involved" in their communities than other people who lived there, up markedly from only eight years earlier.[17] Journalists were becoming transients–residents only of the community of journalism, a class of "news Bedouins."

A second factor in the growing isolation was a change in journalism's tone. After Vietnam and Watergate, and later the advent of twenty-four-hour cable news, journalism became noticeably more subjective and judgmental.[18] Coverage was focused more on mediating what public people were saying than simply reporting it. One notable study found that on television, for instance, the length of time for each candidate quote, or sound bite, on network nightly news programs during election years began to shrink, from an average of forty-three seconds in 1968 to a mere nine seconds in 1988.[19] At the same time, the stand-up closes, in which the reporters summarized the story, became longer and more judgmental.[20] In newspapers, as various studies have found, stories began to focus less on what candidates said and more on the tactical motives for their statements.[21] A study of the front pages of the *New York Times* and the *Washington Post* found that the number of "straight news" accounts decreased, and the number of interpretative and analytical stories grew. Often, these analytical stories were not labeled or identified as analysis.[22] Phrases designed to pull back the curtain of public life, including terms like "spin doctors" and "photo op," began to emerge in the press. In time this engendered a new jargon about the objectionable behavior of journalists–terms like "feeding frenzy" and "gotcha journalism."

In some hands, this more interpretative style serves as much as anything else the desire of journalists to create a public persona. In the year leading into the 2000 presidential campaign, political columnist Michael Kelly satirized Democrat Al Gore for playing up his rural background. The piece "Farmer Al" ridiculed the fact that Gore had spent more of his youth living in a Washington hotel while his father served in the U.S. Senate than he had in Tennessee.

Al ran through the vast apartment. (The Gore farmhouse occupied six big rooms on the top floor of the Fairfax [Hotel] and Al was proud of that; there weren't many families in Washington whose penthouses boasted views of sunrise and sunset.) . . . He ate as he ran, just pausing to grab his trusty two-bladed ax from the umbrella stand.[23]

Kelly's thoroughly entertaining piece earned praise for exposing Gore's presumed hypocrisy. The problem was that twelve years earlier, before he had become a Washington columnist noted for his sharp edge, Kelly as a news reporter for the *Baltimore Sun* had presented the same facts as authentic rather than hypocritical:

> Down at the farm, at the insistence of his father and over the objections of his mother, life was different. "In the summer I would have to get up before dawn and help feed livestock," [Gore] says. "Then I would have to clean out the hog parlors. . . . Then I would work on the farm all day and feed the stock again at night before dinner." By all accounts, Mr. Gore was from early youth unusually serious and hardworking.[24]

Even some journalists had become concerned that too many of their colleagues had crossed a line from skepticism to cynicism, or even a kind of journalistic nihilism, the philosophy of believing in nothing. Phil Trounstein, then political editor of the *San Jose Mercury News*, was moved to write an essay on the subject for the Committee of Concerned Journalists. "It seems the worst thing a reporter or commentator can be accused of in certain circles is not inaccuracy or unfairness but credulousness."[25]

A key part of the problem, University of Pennsylvania professors Joseph N. Cappella and Kathleen Hall Jamieson argued in *The Spiral of Cynicism: The Press and the Public Good*, was the growing journalistic focus on the motives of public officials rather than their actions. By shifting from the "what" of public life to the "why," they argued, journalists "interiorized" public life, making it about the psyche and self of politicians and also making it less about the outcomes of public policy that actually affected citizens. This cynical focus tended to further disconnect journalists from citizens.

Finally, the creeping journalistic isolation coincided with a business strategy at many newspapers and later television stations to enhance profits by going after the most affluent or efficient audience rather than the largest. In television, that meant designing the news for women ages eighteen to forty-nine, who make most household buying decisions. In newspapers, that meant limiting circulation to the more affluent ZIP code areas, which cut the cost of production and distribution. Targeting the news meant a news company theoretically could get more out of less—higher advertising rates with a smaller audience. It also meant the paper or the TV station could ignore certain parts of the community in its coverage, which also saved money.

Isolation, in other words, became a business plan. After the *Minneapolis Star Tribune* dropped in circulation by 4 percent in three years in the mid-1990s, publisher Joel Kramer told the *New York Times*, "We are a healthier business because we are charging readers more and accepting a somewhat smaller circulation."[26] Perhaps nothing illustrated the thinking better than the story of a Bloomingdale's executive who told Rupert Murdoch that the store did not advertise in his *New York Post* because "your readers are our shoplifters." Though it was probably apocryphal, the story became an urban legend within the newspaper business because it so succinctly framed the industry's prevailing modus operandi.

A BACKLASH AGAINST DETACHMENT

Though few realized it at the time, there began in the 1990s what amounted to a reconsideration of the independence of the newsroom. The initial cause was that the business strategy of targeted demographics began to backfire. Making money without growing circulation had worked because the journalism business was such a monopoly that it had been able to take its advertising base for granted. By 1989, with transforming shifts in American retailing and communications technology, that situation began to unravel. Grocery and department stores—the financial backbone of newspapers—were being rocked by bankruptcy, mergers, and debt. The discount retailers that replaced them didn't buy newspaper advertising, since, as everything was discounted every day, they didn't need to announce their special sales. In the eleven years between 1980 and 1991, the amount of advertising space in big-city dailies dropped by 8 percent, according to Sanford C. Bernstein.[27] In 1991 alone, the industry suffered a 4.9 percent drop in retail advertising–the steepest one-year decline in history to that time. A similar dislocation was affecting television, where the audience began to slip away to pseudo news programs, cable reruns, and eventually the Internet.

To managers, all this meant the business of journalism was starting to suffer a structural decline, a decade before the Internet, and they began to refashion how they operated. For newspapers, that largely meant cutting costs and not investing more in the news to try to build more audiences. Between 1992 and 1997, smaller newspapers cut the percentage of their news budgets by 11 percent, and larger papers by 14 percent.[28]

As they cut costs, business managers also began to expect newspeople to begin justifying their journalism in short-term financial terms. The businesspeople had market research and all kinds of new technology–minute-by-minute ratings data in TV, focus group data, even infrared glasses that would track reader eye movements across a page. The hope was that if journalists somehow used the technology more, they could do more to build circulation and not be so unpopular with the public.

A gulf began to form between businesspeople and newspeople– and worse, between reporters and news managers. Journalists saw the business side as challenging their journalistic independence and feared that *accountability* was a code word for letting advertisers shape the news. The business side began to believe that if the newsroom was so intransigent about change, maybe the fabled detachment of the newsroom was the root of its stagnation. A culture war began to boil in the news business.

Journalists who made a case for the public-interest obligation inside their companies could be labeled as naïve, old-fashioned, and difficult. "If you mention 'public service' with corporate, you will be branded as an idealist, as an unrealistic person and you will not be listened to," said John Carroll, who won a record thirteen Pulitzer Prizes in five years at the helm of the *Los Angeles Times* from 2000 to

2005, and then resigned after fighting with his corporate bosses at the Tribune Company in Chicago.

The real fight was less over values than over the nature of change. The advocates of change saw themselves as fighting for the industry's survival. The resisters saw themselves defending a professional ethic that was the basis of the industry's success.

Nonetheless, some business practices were put into the newsroom that ran counter to everyone's best interests. One of the most basic techniques to create more newsroom accountability was the incentive program called Management By Objective, or MBO, that we noted at the beginning of this chapter. The concept, pioneered in the 1950s by management guru Peter F. Drucker, was simple: set goals and attach rewards for achieving them and a company can create a coherent system for both coordinating and monitoring what its executives are doing.

By the early part of the new century, the vast majority of news executives in TV and print worked under MBOs.[29] A good many of these programs were structured in a way that distorted and undermined the role of journalists or the needs of communities. In a survey by the State of the American Newspaper Project in 1998, 71 percent of editors said their companies employed such MBOs. Of those that did, half said they got 20 to 50 percent of their income from the programs. And the majority of these editors said that more than half of their bonus was tied to their paper's financial performance.

Tying a journalist's income to his or her organization's financial performance in effect changed the journalist's allegiance. Companies were explicitly saying that a good portion of the journalist's loyalty must be to the corporate parent and to shareholders—ahead of readers, listeners, or viewers. What if an advertiser made it clear that more income would come if the coverage of an issue began to ease off, or if a certain reporter was fired or moved off a beat? When has an advertiser ever urged more coverage of business corruption or price-fixing? How do you tell the news without fear or favor when you are explaining to the editor that one of his or her key goals is making money this quarter? MBOs tied to the bottom line divided that loyalty.

Sandra Rowe, while editor of Portland's *Oregonian*, captured the problem well. She said it was fine to teach your journalists about business. The question was, What religion are your journalists practicing? Are they journalists who understand business? Or are they businesspeople who understand journalism? The distinction is a matter of loyalty. Is the corporate culture based on the belief that devotion to serving the citizens will lead to solvency? Or is the corporate culture based on a dedication to maximizing profit, even at the expense of what the citizens require?

As we have noted, those efforts at creating accountability in the newsroom can be seen in retrospect to have been too simplistic, and too imitative of other industries. They failed to recognize how news was different. The incentives of newsroom managers should have been tied to innovation, to growing audience in new platforms, not to profit. But it is easier to see that now.

CITIZENS ARE NOT CUSTOMERS

Bringing business accountability to the newsroom brought the language of business as well. In some cases this meant applying the language of marketing to news, with readers and viewers becoming "customers," and to understand them became "marketing."[30]

Few would argue that journalists shouldn't market the services they offer the public, but precision in language matters, especially in times of change. News in a commercial setting is far more complex than simply delivering eyeballs to advertisers—a fact that is more obvious as the financing of news shifts toward consumers paying for the content online. The essential product of journalism is trust—the deeply felt sense that the content one receives is honest, that the editorial decisions, however flawed, were the decision of editors independent of revenue considerations, that what one is encountering is not unacknowledged product placement or commercial manipulation.

People who provide news build a relationship with their audience based on a mix of qualities that the audience senses–a combination of values, judgment, authority, intellect, experience, courage, and commitment to the community. Providing this service creates a bond with the public, which the news organization then rents to sellers of goods and services that want to reach those members of the public.

In short, the business relationship of journalism is different from traditional consumer marketing, and in some ways more complex. It is a triangle, with the news provider forming one line, the public another, and those trying to reach the public to sell them goods and services the third. In this triangle, the public is dominant–they form the longer line of the triangle–even though the revenue they provide is usually less than that provided by advertisers. Even entrepreneurial business magnates such as Henry Luce understood this relationship. "If we have to be subsidized by anybody, we think that the advertiser presents extremely interesting possibilities," he told top aides in 1938. His goal was not to compromise "more than a small fraction of our journalistic soul."[31] Luce's boast was that "there is not an advertiser in America who does not realize that Time Inc. is cussedly independent."

THE WALL

If journalists are committed to the citizen first, what about the rest of the people who work in news companies–the ad salespeople, the marketing department, the circulation department at newspapers, the publishers or division presidents, the CEO, the shareholders? What should citizens expect of them? What should their relationship be to the independence of the news products?

Traditionally, journalists in the twentieth century often talked about there being a firewall between the news and the business sides of news companies. Editors at Time Inc. often hailed the idea that Henry Luce talked about the separation in their company between church (news) and state (the business side). Robert McCormick, the famous and notorious publisher of the *Chicago Tribune,* early in the twentieth century created two separate banks of elevators inside his ornate Tribune Tower overlooking the Chicago River. He didn't want his advertising salesmen even to ride with his reporters.

Unfortunately, that notion of the journalist cloistered behind some wall in service to the audience while everyone else is committed freely to profit was a misguided metaphor. First, it encouraged the isolation we have described. Second, if the two sides of a news-providing organization are really working at cross-purposes, the journalism tends to be what gets corrupted.

The scandal involving the *Los Angeles Times* and the Staples Center sports arena in 2005 revealed how weak the wall metaphor really was. The paper arranged to share profits with arena owners in exchange for help selling ads. The arena owners sent stern letters to their subcontractors insisting that ads be bought. The stories assigned and written at the paper for the magazine about the arena were all positive. The newsroom was not told of the arrangement. The wall, in other words, was kept intact. When the arrangement was discovered, both reporters and readers were outraged.

More than two hundred letters, e-mails, faxes, and phone messages poured onto the desk of reader representative Narda Zacchino in less than a week. When Sharon Waxman of the *Washington Post* went to interview Zacchino, she saw a log of phone messages lying on the desk, the main ideas from each one highlighted with a yellow marker. "Basically, readers are saying that this shakes their faith, their trust in the paper," Zacchino told Waxman. "People are questioning a lot of things. They are asking whether advertisers have influence in our stories. Questioning our integrity. What concerns me are these questions over whether our reporting is honest: 'Does such and such corporation have a deal with you?'"

Eventually, media reporter David Shaw would discover a growing pattern by Times management of exploiting the readership on behalf of its advertisers, all without letting the newsroom know. All of this had occurred after a former cereal company executive named Mark Willes, with little background and a shallow understanding of the economics of journalism, took over the Times Mirror Company that owned the paper. The mythical wall, in other words, did little to protect anyone. The business side was selling the newsroom out and had enough power to circumscribe the newsroom without its knowing.

Tensions between the newsroom and the business side of news companies had been building for years. In retrospect, the simmering pre-digital war over whether good journalism was good business was grounded in a question about the future. Were legacy media operations such as print newspapers or broadcast television "mature industries" that could no longer grow their audiences? If so, then managing costs and paying more attention to advertisers made sense—but acknowledged inevitable decline. Or were legacy news organizations still businesses that, if they adapted, could continue to reach new audiences in new ways, with new content and products? Wall Street had largely decided these media could not grow. And it rewarded media companies that got tough with costs and reduced inefficiency.

Ironically, that supposedly future-oriented view—the decision that most traditional media were mature industries—became a self-fulfilling prophecy. Rather than invest in R&D to figure out new ways to deliver quality and reach audiences in new ways, the newspaper industry focused heavily on managing costs on the one hand and raising the price of its advertising on the other, making the argument that in a fragmented news environment, advertising had become a singular way to reach elite audiences. The industry did not change its business model, in other words, as much as it changed its argument about why it was a good business. So, as its foundation weakened, the industry raised prices. Newspaper revenues reached their peak in 2005, after all of the structural elements that would shrink the industry were well in place.[32]

As the business side began tightening its grip, a series of academic studies continued to find a strong correlation between financial investment in the newsroom and improving the bottom line. Supporting news gathering, the studies found, would create quality journalism, which in turn would drive up circulation. But it would also have another financial benefit. Econometric modeling by Esther Thorson at the University of Missouri established that more investment in news, which presumably translated into more quality, was also correlated with newspapers being able to charge more for advertising. The argument was never popular in boardrooms, however, where most of the debate occurred. For years this dispute was little but background noise for journalists and their public. Some scholars, such as Phil Meyer at the University of North Carolina, argued that the industry was committing suicide, placing itself on the path toward a death spiral of cuts to the product to maintain high profit margins. The cuts would only drive away more readers who had other choices for news, which in turn would lead to further cutbacks. It was, whether conscious or not, a strategy of liquidating the industry.

The news industry was barely aware of the research. At the dawn of the digital disruption, instead of investing in digital innovation, the newspaper industry focused on managing costs to protect profit margins. And the business began to quickly erode.

The issue wasn't so much loss of audience. Between 2006 and 2012, for instance, daily print newspaper circulation in the United States fell 17 percent, and Sunday circulation 16 percent, according to data from the Newspaper Association of America. Many of those lost print readers, however, had simply migrated to the Web version of the same papers, not abandoned the content. Total newspaper readership, which included online readers, held relatively steady. According to data from Scarborough Research, between 2007 and 2012, the percentage of American adults who read newspaper content in print or online dropped less than 10 percent, from 74 percent in 2007 to 67 percent in 2012.[33]

But the financial side of the industry suffered far more. Newspaper advertising revenue between 2005 and 2013 fell more than 55 percent, roughly triple the rate of print readers, and about five times the rate of total readership. The problem, to be precise, was that advertising dollars failed to migrate to the Web along with readers. There were a variety of reasons, among them the fact that people don't respond well to pop-up and banner ads, and that there is no scarcity of websites, so the cost of advertising fell.

The revenue losses, in turn, had a devastating effect on the news-gathering power at many news organizations. From 2000 to 2013, the reporting and editing ranks of newspapers fell by 30 percent, and by more at many major metropolitan newspapers, which were hit hardest financially. The news divisions of the three major broadcast networks were cut by more than half from the 1980s, prior to the advent of cable news. While some of the journalists who left legacy media moved to alternative news operations, most left the profession, or moved to public relations, think tanks, or other fields. An analysis of Census Bureau data by Robert McChesney and John Nichols, for instance, found that the ratio of public relations workers to journalists grew from 1.2 to 1 in 1980 to 3.6 to 1 in 2008—and the gap has almost certainly widened since.[34]

Broadcast television news, the dominant news platform of the late twentieth century, had its own version of loss of confidence even earlier. In the 1990s, as it began to feel the impact of cable news and syndicated infotainment programming, network evening newscasts became increasingly focused on tabloid crime and celebrity. The number one topic on network evening newscasts for the decade was crime, even though crime rates nationally were plummeting during the period. Making their newscasts more entertaining became the focus of broadcasters, rather than investing in new platforms such as cable and later online. The one exception was NBC, whose news division has thrived largely due to revenue from its cable news operations, particularly CNBC, and who amortizes its healthier news division across all its platforms.

In 2000, Peter C. Goldmark Jr., then chairman and chief executive of the *International Herald Tribune,* suggested in a meeting at the Aspen Institute that corporations needed to do something "to cement the value of the journalistic enterprise within these huge corporate empires.... Every CEO understands they have a fiduciary obligation to their shareholders. In terms of journalism, I put more faith in corporate leadership that understands that they have an equally solemn fiduciary responsibility arising from their ownership of a news organization—that they hold a public trust."[35]

Goldmark offered four suggestions: have the CEO meet annually with those of similar organizations to assess the journalistic health of their companies; designate a member of the board of directors to assume special responsibility for protecting the independence of the news organization; invite an annual review or audit of the independence and vigor of the company's news function; jointly, with similar companies, fund an independent council to track, promote, examine, and defend the independence of the press.

A decade later, when the economic impact of the Web was clear, the battle at the top of many legacy media companies between the idealists and the accountants was over. The idealists had lost. Shrinking revenue made notions of focusing on audience and quality seem an unaffordable vanity to many business managers.

An executive at one of the three broadcast networks told senior staff in a meeting in 2005, "The ethical anvil has been lifted," meaning the producers could dispense with traditional notions of journalistic propriety.[36] The most cogent explanation for why journalism in the public interest had lost leverage was probably offered by Polk Laffoon IV, the corporate spokesman of Knight Ridder, a company that had managed itself to the point that it was about to vanish altogether: "I wish there were an identifiable and strong correlation between quality journalism ... and newspaper sales," he said. "It isn't ... that simple."[37]

There were some notable exceptions to the loss of the faith in quality journalism as a business proposition. To a large degree, they were in organizations where there was no wall, where the business side embraced the values of the newsroom as the soul of the operation. In these companies, independent public-interest journalism was the product the company was selling, with profit as a predictable by-product that was strategically and necessarily required for long-term health.

In 2002, the Guardian Media Group in the United Kingdom responded to the challenge when it launched a major effort in transparency, creating an annual audit called "Living Our Values." The purpose of the independently produced audit was to make clear to readers the special nature of the relationship between a commercial news organization and the citizens. The annual audit would report to the public in documented detail on the social and ethical behavior of the company and its promise to produce a "liberal, progressive, internationalist newspaper," as well as its behavior as a commercial business in such areas as its relationships with its employees, its business partners, and other institutions in the community and the world. The *Guardian* audit would describe how the values shared by the business and the news sides combined to serve a public interest.

The *Guardian* has proven among the quickest to embrace the possibilities of new technology and the ability it offers to turn audience into staff. It has embraced data journalism, or the inclusion of large databases as a new form of reporting, more rapidly than most legacy media. It has done the same with employing social media tools such as Twitter and Facebook as a way of gathering information from its community of readers rather than as simply a way of marketing its traditional content. It has transformed its culture into a system in which the group formerly known as the audience is a part of the news-gathering process, in a way that complements rather than threatens traditional journalism.

Despite layoffs and a drop in stock prices, the *New York Times* also generally has maintained a commitment to quality journalism, best reflected by the flagship newspaper. Analysts even expressed a worry that the Times Company was too focused on newspapers and did not look to diversify its revenue by investing in other products. "We are a company committed to journalism," Arthur Sulzberger Jr., the company chairman and publisher of the *New York Times*, told Ken Auletta of the *New Yorker* in 2005. "That is our core strength. That is our hedgehog. We are not in the education or cooking business. You are going to see us make journalism investments."[38] In 2013, the *Times*' new CEO, Mark Thompson, echoed the same sentiment when he told the American Society of Newspaper Editors that in effect, as the chief business executive at the company, he worked for Jill Abramson, the paper's editor. For everything they did flowed from the journalism.

To a significant extent, the *Times* was scorned when it decided to charge for online content in April 2011. (Until then, only financial newspapers purchased for business reasons had succeeded in charging for content.) Yet the *Times* proved doubters wrong. By 2013, the paper had roughly seven hundred thousand digital-only subscribers (people who paid for the digital version of the paper but did not want it in print). By early that year the paper derived more than half its revenue from subscriptions rather than advertising. Some doubters continued to insist that the *Times* was unique, a national paper of such distinct quality that it could charge when others couldn't. The doubters were wrong about this, too. By 2013, more than 450 of the country's 1,385 newspapers were charging for digital content—and many more were about to follow, including many who had argued a year earlier that they would never charge. The newspaper industry saw the first gain in circulation revenue in a decade.

By 2013, the move to charging people for content online was also showing glimmers of another change. Some newspapers were beginning to reinvest some resources back into editorial quality. The Gannett Company, one of the pioneers, under former CEO Al Neuharth, of creating in the late twentieth century an expectation of quarterly profit growth, invested tens of millions in new news-gathering resources. The reasoning was one the fallen idealists had argued and lost with years earlier: If you are going to charge people a fair price for the content, the content has to improve. Quality was a business strategy after all. The move to charging for digital content, pioneered for general audiences at the *Times*, represents a significant shift back toward the concept that the core of the business of media is that journalism must deliver value to the audience—rather than the audience is something to be leveraged to advertisers. To grow, the journalism must change and the audience must grow. The advocates of that financial innovation were those who did not stop believing in the journalism.

The metaphor of the wall was always a myth—and in the end it failed journalists instead of protecting them. Top news managers and top business managers always conversed. The so-called wall was never anything more than an easy way to assure readers that journalists were independent, with the added benefit of avoiding contact at lower levels so that managers would not have to officiate the conflicts.

In reality, other characteristics historically have defined the culture of organizations where the news could be trusted, and those characteristics had more to do with journalistic commitment at the top than with insulation at the bottom. We identify five keys to a news company or organization maintaining its commitment to citizens:

1 • THE OWNER MUST BE COMMITTED TO CITIZENS FIRST

Rather than the newsroom being cloistered from the rest of the organization, journalism works best when both sides are committed to the values of honest independent news, not one side to business or ideology or some other cause and the other to public service. History suggests that this works only when the owner of the operation believes deeply in these core journalistic values.

Even some of the so-called defenders of the wall were, in reality, practitioners of this joint philosophy, with journalism being the predominant value. Contrary to legend, there is scant evidence that Henry Luce actually talked about church and state, according to historian Tom Leonard. Rather, Luce believed the whole company needed to be "cussedly independent."

As he looked back on his own career, Tom Johnson, former publisher of the *Los Angeles Times* and then president of CNN, came to the same conclusion as Luce had a generation earlier, and Ochs a generation before that:

> Media owners, or in the case of publicly traded companies, the board-elected CEO, ultimately decide the quality of the news produced by or televised by their news departments. It is they who most often select, hire, fire, and promote the editors, and publishers, top general managers, news directors, and managing editors—the journalists—who run their newsrooms. . . . Owners determine newsroom budgets, and the amount of time and space allotted to news versus advertising. They set the standards of quality by the quality of the people they choose and the news policies they embrace. Owners decide how much profit they should produce from their media properties. Owners decide what quality levels they are willing to support by how well or how poorly they pay their journalists.[39]

The historical protection for journalism, the benevolent patri-arch, has largely disappeared, although there are some exceptions. Now, in the wake of the disruption of the Web, the corporation culture has given up significant ground to private equity owners. It is too soon to generalize about the character of this group. Some, such as former Internet entrepreneur Aaron Kushner, show signs of imag-ining a new level of engagement with readers and a new concept of quality. Others appear to have moved toward publishing because the price was low enough that the risk seemed low. But there is little doubt that this shift matters—probably more than any other factor.

2 • HIRE BUSINESS MANAGERS WHO ALSO PUT CITIZENS FIRST

While the owner is the ultimate determiner of an institution's values, successful businesspeople also talk about hiring managers who share the mission, even if selling ads or building circulation is a different path from producing stories. Robert Dechard, the former chairman and chief executive of A. H. Belo, the newspaper and television com-pany, said that commitment and understanding should flow down the organization. "It comes down to selecting people who have good news judgment and experience in journalism and are sensitive to potential conflicts. I would prefer to have a person with that sound judgment."[40]

3 • JOURNALISTS HAVE FINAL SAY OVER NEWS

As news organizations experiment with new revenue models, those in charge of news have an even larger role to play. They must guard the editorial integrity of the operations, and protect the integrity of the commercial brand as well. That means they must raise their hand and speak out when they think an organization is crossing the line. Editors' failure to do this is why the *Washington Post*'s new publisher and editor both earned early black eyes when the paper tried to generate revenue by hosting private dinners that served no news-making value, to provide access to lawmakers (quite unlike the news-making events that Atlantic Media or Texas Tribune do to generate revenue). The leader of the newsroom, in the modern news operation, is, in effect, the protector of the brand.

4 • SET AND COMMUNICATE CLEAR STANDARDS INTERNALLY

Even if owners share the journalistic mission, and hire managers who agree, those standards must be clearly articulated down the ranks, to create an open atmosphere in which the businesspeople and newspeople, at least at certain levels, can talk to make sure they understand and appreciate one another's role.

Few editors are more experimental about trying new approaches, or new pay models, than Lewis Dvorkin, the "chief product officer" at Forbes Media. Dvorkin has been at the sometimes controversial forefront of exploring how to use social media, contributor content, sponsored content, and a host of other experiments in an effort to build audience and generate revenue at *Forbes*, the former print monthly financial magazine that is now "a multi-media financial news source." As he has moved, whether you hail or cringe at the experiments, Dvorkin has aggressively embraced one of the core concepts we advocate: the notion of trying to be transparent and honest about what you are doing. In a series of columns, Dvorkin has outlined his experiments. And early to embrace the concept of allowing "brands," or the group once called advertisers, to sponsor and create editorial content, he has always been careful to label that content. Regardless of whether one feels Dvorkin has strayed too far, he has accomplished three things at a time when others hesitated. He has revitalized the demand for *Forbes* content. He has experimented. And he has been open about his experiments by communicating with his audience.

5 • COMMUNICATE CLEAR STANDARDS TO THE PUBLIC AS WELL

The final key is to be clear with audiences—clearer than in the past—about how news organizations operate. Dvorkin's writings for *Forbes* are only one example. John Paton, the CEO of the newspaper company Digital First, also writes a blog where he muses about his experiments. These communications strengthen understanding internally as well. They serve another purpose, too. They commit the organization to live up to these promises, and raise the stakes if they do not.

The movement toward more explanation gained force not initially to explain radical changes with technology but in response to the growing credibility crisis about news that had begun a generation earlier. In his address to the American Society of Newspaper Editors in 1999, Edward Seaton, the president of that group and editor of the *Manhattan Mercury* in Manhattan, Kansas, advised that the best way for newspapers to rebuild trust and credibility was to "explain yourself. . . . As editors, we have to lead. We have to state our values. When we have standards, we have something that we can explain to the public and our staffs, something that everyone can hear and understand. We must do much more and better than we have. Our emphasis has to be on serving citizens, not our bottom line or technology."[41]

Some television stations have taken similar approaches. When he was news director at KGUN-TV in Tucson, Forrest Carr created and repeatedly broadcast a "Viewers Bill of Rights" that outlined precisely what citizens in Tucson should expect from his station and his people.

The list of seven rights included such items as supporting the public's right to know (the station "asks tough questions and conducts investigations"), the right to ethical news gathering (the station will live up to the ethics code of the Society of Professional Journalists), and the right to solution-oriented journalism (the station will attempt to find or spotlight solutions, not just focus on problems).

The language of a bill of rights may strike some as corny. But focus groups conducted by the Project for Excellence in Journalism in Tucson around the time of the station's introduction of the program suggested that they connected with people. "It might go back to the station having some guidelines, something called ethics in reporting," said one man.

The station's share of the Tucson television audience continued a steady climb. Carr also told us that the project had another benefit: making the values of the organization clear to those who worked there. Nothing he had ever done, Carr would say, helped him more in improving the culture of his own newsroom.

There is evidence that the "bill of rights" idea still has some resonance today. In June of 2013, the Louisville, Kentucky, FOX affiliate WDRB rolled out a "Contract with Our Viewers." The state-ment contained ten principles intended to convey its commitment to a set of core journalistic values, and to the audience. The contract contained promises not to "hype our product," to "strive to present reporting that is bias free," to use the term "breaking news" judi-ciously and not as a marketing gimmick. The contract promised not to take the viewer's time for granted.[42]

Whatever approach a news organization takes, the question of allegiance remains pivotal and is usually ignored or misunderstood. The reason it is so vital, however, is precisely that the press has be-come so unpopular. What is often missed in considering the decline in public trust of the press is that, at bottom, this credibility crisis is about motive. As citizens, we do not expect perfection of our jour-nalists—or even a journalism with every word spelled correctly. The problem is more fundamental.

Journalists like to think of themselves as the people's surrogate, covering society's waterfront in the public interest. Increasingly, however, the public doesn't believe them. People see sensationalism and exploitation, and they sense that journalists are in it for a buck, or personal fame, or perhaps worse, a kind of perverse joy in unhap-piness. When it was revealed that Bob Woodward had a practice of interviewing administration officials for his books and not letting much of the information obtained be part of the immediate record, readers challenged his allegiance. Was he an author working for himself or was he a *Washington Post* reporter working for the public? Some readers did not trust Woodward to decide whether something needed to be exposed immediately or could wait a year or two to make it into a book.

To reconnect people with the news, and through the news to the larger world, journalism must reestablish the allegiance to citizens that the news industry has mistakenly helped to subvert. Yet even this, ultimately, will not be enough. Truth and loyalty to citizens are only the first two steps in making journalism work. The next step is just as important: the method that journalists use to approach the truth and convey that method to citizens.

4

Journalism
of Verification

As he sat down to write, the Greek correspondent wanted to convince his audience that it could trust him. He was not writing an official version of the war, he wanted people to know, or a hasty one. He was striving for something more independent, more reliable, more lasting. As he had gone about his reporting, he had been mindful of the way memory, perspective, and politics blur recollection. He had double-checked his facts.

To convey all this, he decided to explain the methods of his reporting right at the beginning. This is the dedication to the methodology of truth that Thucydides drafted in the fifth century B.C., in the introduction to his account of the Peloponnesian War:

> With regard to my factual reporting of events . . . I have made it a principle not to write down the first story that came my way, and not even to be guided by my own general impressions; either I was present myself at the events which I have described or else heard of them from eyewitnesses whose reports I have checked with as much thoroughness as possible. Not that even so the truth was easy to discover: different eyewitnesses gave different accounts of the same events, speaking out of partiality for one side or the other, or else from imperfect memories.[1]

Why does this passage feel so contemporary more than two thousand years after it was written? Because it speaks to the heart of the task of nonfiction: How do you sift through the rumors, the gossip, the failed memories, the manipulative agendas, and try to capture something as accurately as possible, subject to revision in light of new information and perspective? How do you overcome your own limits of perception, your own experience, and come to an account that more people will recognize as reliable? Strip away all the debate about journalism, all the differences among media or between one age and another. These are the real questions faced daily by those who try to gather news, understand it, and convey it to others.

While not following any standardized code, everyone who produces what is viewed as news, or even the broader range of nonfiction, operates by relying on a method of testing and providing information–his or her own individual discipline of verification. Practices such as seeking multiple witnesses to an event, disclosing as much as possible about sources, and asking many sides for comment are, in effect, tools for the discipline of verification, which is the essential process of arriving as nearly as possible at the truth of the matter at hand. These methods may be intensely personal and idiosyncratic. Writer Rick Meyer at the *Los Angeles Times* would splice his facts and interviews into note card–like snippets and organize them on his office floor. Or the methods may be institutionalized, like the fact-checking department of the *New Yorker*. But by whatever name, in whatever medium, these habits and methods underlie the third principle of journalism:

The essence of journalism is a discipline of verification.

In the end, the discipline of verification is what separates journalism from entertainment, propaganda, fiction, or art. Entertainment–or its cousin "infotainment"–focuses on what is most diverting. Propaganda selects facts or invents them to serve the real purpose: persuasion and manipulation. Fiction invents scenarios to get at a more personal impression of what it calls truth.

Journalism alone is focused on the process employed to get what happened down right.

This is true be it the work of a network TV news division or a lone citizen posting eyewitness accounts on social media, and it is the first criterion by which any work claimed as journalism should be judged for competence.

Those who produce journalism often fail to connect their deeply held feelings about craft to the larger philosophical questions about journalism's role. They know how to check a story even if they can't always articulate the role that checking a story plays in society. But verifying facts resides in the central function of journalism. As Walter Lippmann put it in 1920, "There can be no liberty for a community which lacks the information by which to detect lies."[2]

This is why journalists often become so upset with people from other media, such as dramatists or filmmakers, when they tell stories of real-life events. In 2012, the public radio program *This American Life* "retracted" a program it had aired about manufacturing in China after it discovered that the author of the program, dramatist Mike Daisey, had blended names and incidents, both from his own visits to China and from accounts by others. "We're retracting the story," Ira Glass, the host and executive producer of *This American Life*, said in a statement, "because we can't vouch for its truth."[3]

Daisey, however, had no such doubts. "I stand by my work," he said in his own statement. "My show is a theatrical piece. . . . It uses a combination of fact, memoir, and dramatic license to tell its story, and I believe it does so with integrity. Certainly, the comprehensive investigations undertaken by the *New York Times* and a number of labor rights groups to document conditions in electronics manufacturing would seem to bear this out."

But, he added, "What I do is not journalism."[4]

The Daisey/*This American Life* example is only one in a long line of collisions over the meaning of truth between journalists and those in other forms of communication. *60 Minutes* correspondent Mike Wallace was livid in 1999 when the movie *The Insider* put invented words in his mouth and altered the time frame to suggest that he was worried about his "legacy" when he caved in to the tobacco industry on a story. "Have you ever heard me invoke the word *legacy*? That is utter bullshit ... and I'm offended."[5] The film's director, Michael Mann, countered that though things were changed to make the story more dramatic, the film was "basically accurate" to some larger definition of truthfulness, given that Wallace had indeed caved.

The antagonists in both cases were speaking different languages. To Mann and Daisey, truth was found in the larger contours of the story, not in the minutiae of every fact. To Glass and Wallace, truth could never be detached from an accurate account of the details. Both arguments may be defensible. But the journalistic process of verification must take both of them into account. It must get both the facts right and the truth.

From the moment news became a commodity that is instantly and continuously available in almost unlimited outlets, the process of verification–the beating heart of credible journalism in the public interest–came under new pressure. There are two principal sources of this pressure. The first is the temptation to publish immediately because something can always be corrected later. The second is the impulse to publish news simply because it's already "out there" in the new networked media system.

The problem was made more complex in the new reality created by the war against terrorism that was declared in the aftermath of September 11. This new reality conflicted with the popular notion of "we media" culture, which suggested that since citizens could communicate with one another at will, they could be closer to real truth and more accurate information.

No doubt they can communicate more easily. Whether or not the end result sustains a journalism of verification depends on the degree of commitment to that goal by those who produce the information in competition with other powerful mediating institutions that produce information for persuasion or manipulation.

THE LOST MEANING OF OBJECTIVITY

Perhaps because the discipline of verification is so personal and so haphazardly communicated, it is also part of one of the great confusions of journalism—the concept of objectivity. The original meaning of this idea is now thoroughly misunderstood and close to being lost. Yet getting at its intention, and finding new language that does so, can help point a way for a better journalism in the future.

When critics, including many in journalism, reject the notion of objectivity, they usually do so on the grounds that no person can ever be objective. As Dan Gillmor, author of *We the Media,* wrote in a much-circulated 2005 essay called "The End of Objectivity," "We are human. We have biases and backgrounds and a variety of conflicts that we bring to our jobs every day."[6] Gillmor was advocating that journalists drop the word *objectivity* and replace it with *thoroughness, accuracy, fairness,* and *transparency.*

His is not the only voice to be so raised in nearly eight decades of skepticism about the notion of objectivity. What dominates the argument, however, is a general confusion. When the concept of objectivity originally migrated from social science to journalism, it was not meant to imply that journalists were free of bias. Quite the contrary.

The term began to appear as part of journalism early in the last century, particularly in the 1920s, out of a growing recognition that journalists were full of bias, often without knowing it. The call for objectivity was an appeal for journalists to develop a consistent method of testing information—a transparent approach to evidence—precisely so that personal and cultural biases would not undermine the accuracy of their work.

In the nineteenth century, journalists talked about realism rather than objectivity.[7] This was the idea that if reporters simply dug out the facts and ordered them together, the truth would reveal itself naturally. Realism emerged at a time when journalism was separating from political parties and becoming more accurate. It coincided with the invention of what journalists call the "inverted pyramid" structure, in which a journalist orders a story's facts from most important to least important, thinking it helps audiences better understand the events.

At the beginning of the twentieth century, however, some journalists began to worry about the naïveté of realism. In part, reporters and editors were becoming more aware of the rise of propaganda and the role of press agents. At a time when Freud was developing his theories of the subconscious and painters such as Picasso were experimenting with Cubism, journalists were developing a greater recognition of human subjectivity. In 1919, Walter Lippmann and Charles Merz, an associate editor for the *New York World*, wrote an influential and scathing account of how cultural blinders had distorted the *New York Times* coverage of the Russian Revolution.[8] "In the large, the news about Russia is a case of seeing not what was, but what men wished to see," they wrote. Lippmann and others began to look for ways for the individual journalist "to remain clear and free of his irrational, his unexamined, his unacknowledged prejudgments in observing, understanding and presenting the news."[9]

Journalism, Lippmann declared, was being practiced by "untrained accidental witnesses." Good intentions, or what some might call "honest efforts," by journalists were not enough. Faith in the rugged individualism of the tough reporter–what Lippmann called the "cynicism of the trade"–was also not enough. Nor were some of the trends of the times, such as bylines and columnists.[10]

The solution, Lippmann argued, was for journalists to acquire more of "the scientific spirit.... There is but one kind of unity possible in a world as diverse as ours. It is unity of method, rather than aim; the unity of disciplined experiment." Lippmann meant by this that journalism should aspire to "a common intellectual method and a common area of valid fact." To begin, Lippmann thought, the fledgling field of journalism education should be transformed from "trade schools designed to fit men for higher salaries in the existing structure." Instead, the field should make its cornerstone the study of evidence and verification.[11]

Although this was an era of faith in science, Lippmann had few illusions. "It does not matter that the news is not susceptible of mathematical statement. In fact, just because news is complex and slippery, good reporting requires the exercise of the highest scientific virtues."[12] In the original concept, in other words, the journalist was not objective, but the journalist's method could be.

This original understanding of objectivity also has some important implications that are crucial to a twenty-first-century understanding of media. First, it means that objectivity is not the absence of a point of view, or "the view from nowhere," as New York University professor Jay Rosen has called it. Instead the aim of objectivity as a disciplined unity of method transparently conveyed comes close to what Gillmor and others have advocated as an alternative. Another implication is that the impartial voice employed by many news organizations–that familiar, supposedly neutral style of news writing–is not a fundamental principle of journalism. Rather, it is a device news organizations use to highlight the fact that they are trying to produce something obtained by objective methods. The third implication is that this neutral voice, without a discipline of verification, often is a veneer atop something hollow. Journalists who select sources to express what is really their own point of view, and then use the neutral voice to make it seem objective, are engaged in deception. This damages the credibility of all journalistic enterprise by making it seem unprincipled, dishonest, and biased. This is an important caution in an age when the standards of the press are in doubt.

This idea is worth repeating for emphasis. In this original understanding of objectivity, neutrality is not a fundamental principle of journalism. It is merely a voice, or device, to persuade the audience of one's accuracy or fairness.

It is interesting, too, that those in the commercial press, Left and Right, who produce opinionated journalism often deny it and claim fairness instead. Fox News marketed itself as "fair and balanced." From the Right, commentator Ann Coulter offered to expose the "lies" of the Left. Al Franken, when he was a liberal commentator, marketed his book as "truth." They echoed Hearst and Pulitzer and the yellow press of the nineteenth century, who claimed that their sensationalized reporting was more accurate than their competitors'. Rarely do people in journalism–even on the opinion end of the craft–market themselves as better arguers, but instead as more accurate or closer to the truth.

Another implication of the original meaning of objectivity as method is that it reconciles how various other forms of American journalism fall inside the broad principles of a single discipline, one that well accommodates the citizen contributions of today, or the alternative press that typically came from the Left in the 1960s and 1970s, or the magazine journalism of opinion from all sides of the political spectrum. If producing news starts with accuracy, a careful method or discipline of verification made transparent, and some unity of method to this process of verifying facts, then it can encompass a range of presentations. (We will discuss this in greater detail in the next chapter, on the meaning of the concept of independence in journalism.)

Unity of method rather than aim, as Lippmann put it more than ninety years ago, is the one unity that can be assessed in a diverse culture. And that method relates to the gathering of information, not the style of presentation. Lippmann was not alone in calling for a greater sense of professionalization, though his arguments are the most sophisticated. Joseph Pulitzer, the great populist journalistic innovator a generation earlier, had just created the Graduate School of Journalism at Columbia University for many of the same, though less clearly articulated, reasons. The Newspaper Guild was founded in large part to help professionalize journalism.

Over the years, however, this original and more sophisticated understanding of objectivity was utterly confused and its meaning largely lost. Writers such as Leo Rosten, who authored an influential sociological study of journalists, used the term to suggest that the journalist was objective. Not surprisingly, he found that idea wanting. So did various legal opinions, which declared objectivity impossible. Many journalists never really understood what Lippmann meant.[13] Over time, journalists began to reject the term *objectivity* as an illusion. They remained largely "accidental witnesses."

People in the alternative press often felt antagonistic toward so-called mainstream journalists for their faith in objectivity, when really what divided them was their positions about neutral voice, not how they went about gathering and verifying information. Newspaper people often move effortlessly to magazine work such as the *New Yorker*, where they produce journalism in a voice not dissimilar to what the alternative press might be employing or even the more subjective forms of TV news.

In the meantime, reporters have gone on to refine the concept Lippmann had in mind, but usually only privately, and in the name of technique or reporting routines rather than journalism's larger purpose. The notion of an objective method of reporting exists in pieces, handed down by word of mouth from reporter to reporter. Developmental psychologist William Damon at Stanford University, for instance, identified various "strategies" that journalists have developed to verify their reporting. Damon asked his interviewees where they learned these concepts. Overwhelmingly the answer was that they had learned them by trial and error, on their own, or from a friend. Rarely did journalists report learning them in journalism school or from their editors.[14] Many useful books have been written on the subject. One group, calling itself Investigative Reporters and Editors, for instance, tried to develop a methodology for how to use public records, read documents, and produce Freedom of Information Act requests.

But by and large, the differing approaches and strategies for verification were never pulled together into a unified method, let alone a curriculum or intellectual discipline. Nor have the older conventions of verification been expanded to match the new forms of journalism. Although journalism may have developed various techniques and conventions for determining facts, it has done less to develop a system for testing the reliability of journalistic interpretation.

Most important, in the twenty-first century, the notion that journalists or anyone else can arrive at a truthful account of things or follow an objective method of verification seems even more eroded in the public mind. This amounts to a threat not only to the notion of journalism but also to the possibility of civil society's confronting and solving its problems. The public sphere becomes an arena solely for polarized debate, not for compromise, consensus, and solution.

If journalists are to make a case for the values that have guided their work for nearly three hundred years, or even for the instincts of early chroniclers like Thucydides, they must understand the principles and methods of first getting the facts right, and they must reveal that method to the public.

More recently, a whole new field of data visualization and data journalism is evolving that has brought a new rich potential to journalism. This data realm offers the possibility of getting closer to the promise of the "scientific spirit" that Lippmann had in mind. At the same time, it contains the inherent danger that audiences will attach a false sense of authority to the numbers simply because they are quantitative, when in fact their analysis, or even the algorithms that produced them, are human creations. The growing field of data journalism, in other words, creates the potential for a greater discipline of method. But it also may lull audiences into inferring its presence where it doesn't exist. Data do nothing to lessen the requirement for transparency. They may even raise it.

JOURNALISM OF ASSERTION VS. JOURNALISM OF VERIFICATION

Well before the arrival of the Web, changes in the modern press culture were weakening the methodology of verification journalists had developed, even if that method was not adequately named or codified. In the age of the twenty-four-hour news cycle, journalists spent more time looking for something to add to the existing news, usually interpretation, than trying to independently discover and verify new facts. Facts had become a commodity, easily acquired, repackaged, and repurposed. "Once a story is hatched, it's as if all the herd behavior is true," Geneva Overholser, a journalist who has watched changes in media as an editor, ombudsman, and then educator, observed. "The story is determined by one medium—one newspaper or TV account. . . . Partly because news organizations are being consolidated and partly because of electronic reporting, we all feed at the same trough."[15] And this was before the full impact of the Web was felt, which only accelerated those influences.

Simply put, the Web makes redistributing content so convenient, and accelerates the pace of news flow so much, that the combination increases the potential that erroneous information will be passed on.

Each new breaking news story today seems to bring new examples. CNN and Fox mistakenly reported that the Supreme Court had struck down health care reform because their reporters were so eager to get on the air a moment before their rivals that they did not read further into the court's decision. The suspects in the Boston marathon bombings were reported to have been killed or captured when in fact they had not. Perhaps the most regretful case involved mistakes made in reporting the killing of twenty schoolchildren in December 2012 in Newtown, Connecticut.

At approximately 9:30 A.M. on the morning of December 14, Adam Lanza entered Sandy Hook Elementary School and began shooting. At 11:17 A.M., on its Twitter feed @CNN reported "CNN's@SusanCandiotti reports the suspect is Ryan Lanza and is in his 20s." Candiotti would repeat the mistake on the air shortly after 2 P.M., although she acknowledged it had not been confirmed by state police. At 3 P.M. the AP said it had confirmed Ryan Lanza's identity. Some news organizations, following CNN's lead, showed Ryan Lanza's Facebook photo and published some of his posts.

This was not the only mistake. A number of news organizations, including the *New York Times*, would report that Lanza's mother was a teacher at the school and that she had been killed there by her son.

The problem was that Ryan Lanza was not the shooter. His brother Adam was. And their mother was not a teacher at the school, nor was she even present there at the time of the shooting. Adam Lanza had already killed her in her home.

Not all of the mistakes could be attributed to haste. The mistake about Lanza's mother may also reflect a felt need by some reporters for the story to have a logic or motive. "It's hard for us to accept the idea that something so horrible was completely random," said W. Joseph Campbell, the author of *Getting It Wrong: Ten of the Greatest Misreported Stories in American Journalism*, a study of media-driven myths. "The idea that she had little or no connection to the school makes it harder to wrap your mind around such a horrific and senseless act."[16]

At times, the breakdown in verification can be the result not simply of erroneous information being passed along but of journalists expecting certain facts because they fit a larger popular master narrative.

One of the more enduring cases was the popular narrative that Vice President Al Gore, then the Democratic Party nominee for president, continually exaggerated his past accomplishments to impress people. One account referred to Gore's "Pinocchio problem," another called him a "liar," and a third "delusional."[17] A key bit of evidence was Gore's supposed assertion that he had discovered the Love Canal toxic waste site in upstate New York, which helped change federal policy. The problem is, Gore had never made any such assertion. He had told a group of New Hampshire high school students that he first learned about hazardous waste dangers when a constituent told him about a polluted town in Tennessee called Toone, and Gore wanted to hold hearings. "I looked around the country for other sites like that," he told the students. "I found a little place in upstate New York called Love Canal. Had the first hearing on the issue, and Toone, Tennessee—that was the one that you didn't hear of. But that was the one that started it all."[18]

The next day, however, the *Washington Post* misquoted Gore completely as saying, "I was the one that started it all." In a press release, the Republican Party changed the quote to "I was the one who started it all." The *New York Times* printed the same misquote as the *Post*. Soon the press was off and running, relying on the faulty accounts ingrained in the databases of the two papers. It didn't catch anyone's attention that the AP had the quote correct. The matter was not cleared up until the high school students themselves complained.

As journalists spend more time trying to synthesize the ever-growing stream of data pouring in through the new portals of information, the risk is that they can become more passive, more receivers than gatherers. To combat this, a better understanding of the original meaning of objectivity as a discipline or method could help put the news on firmer footing. We are not the only ones to advocate for this. "Journalism and science come from the same intellectual roots," said Phil Meyer, University of North Carolina journalism professor, "from the seventeenth- and eighteenth-century enlightenment. The same thinking that led to the First Amendment led to the scientific method. . . . I think this connection between journalism and science ought to be restored to the extent that we can. . . . I think we ought to emphasize objectivity of method. That's what scientific method is–our humanity, our subjective impulses . . . directed toward deciding what to investigate by objective means."[19]

Seen in this light, ideas such as fairness and balance, or the notion of gathering multiple points of view in stories, take on new meaning. Rather than high principles, they are as we have said before really techniques–devices–that can help guide anyone trying to gather and verify an account of an event. Fairness and balancing multiple points of view should never be pursued for their own sake or invoked as journalism's goal. Their value is in helping get us closer to more thorough verification and a reliable version of events. But they need to be used carefully, as any technique does, not overvalued.

Balance, for instance, can lead to distortion. If an overwhelming percentage of scientists, as an example, believe that global warming is a scientific fact, or that some medical treatment is clearly the safest, it is a disservice to citizens and truthfulness to create the impression that the scientific debate is equally split. Unfortunately, all too often journalistic balance is misconstrued to have this kind of almost mathematical meaning, as if a good story is one that has an equal number of quotes from two sides. As journalists know, often there are more than two sides to a story. And sometimes balancing them equally is not a true reflection of reality.

Fairness, in turn, can also be misunderstood if it is seen to be a goal unto itself. Fairness should mean that the journalist is being fair to the facts and to a citizen's understanding of the facts. It should not mean "being fair to my sources, so that none of them will be unhappy." Nor should it mean asking, "Does my story seem fair?" These are subjective judgments that may steer the journalist away from the need to do more to verify his or her work. Fairness, in other words, is also an aim, not a method, and ultimately it is subjective.

Trying to create the appearance of fairness can also lead to presenting false equivalencies, the idea that different perspectives have equal moral weight. Consider CNN's coverage in March 2013 of the conviction of two high school football players, Trent Mays and Ma'lik Richmond, for raping a sixteen-year-old girl at a party. The two young men were sentenced to one-to-five years in juvenile detention.

The two teenagers were anguished at the verdict.

CNN anchor Candy Crowley and legal analyst Paul Callan seemed to lose sight of who was the victim in the case as they tried to convey the emotional scene to viewers.

"A sixteen-year-old just sobbing in court. Regardless of what big football players they are, they still sound like sixteen-year-olds," Crowley said. "When you listen to it and you realize, that they could stay [incarcerated] until they are twenty-one. They are going to get credit for time served. What's the lasting effect though on two young men . . . ?"

Trying to be sympathetic to the emotion of the scene is one thing. Losing a grip on the context of the story is another.

In a networked world where consumers have more control, and content may be distributed in ways in which it is disassociated from its institutional source (a chart or graphic, for example, might be shared on Twitter without the accompanying article), employing a more rigorous method of gathering the news, and then being more transparent in communicating that method in each piece of content, not only comes closer to the original meaning of objectivity, it also empowers the news consumer with the tools necessary to make good decisions about what to trust.

In the old order, people relied on responsible gatekeepers to identify what stories they should know about and what facts they should hear. The journalists at these trusted brands—which in the case of many newspapers by the end of the twentieth century were monopolies—were not trained to make their presentation all that transparent. A lot of explanation about how the news was gathered might make the narrative unwieldy. It was enough that the brand was trusted. And that is how we encountered the content. We read the story in the newspaper or watched it inside the newscast. This was, as we have described elsewhere, the "trust me" era of news.

Now, as power has shifted to the consumer of news in our information system, we have entered the "show me" era of news. In a world where we rely on recommendations from friends, search results, references from social media, e-mailed stories, curated and aggregated distribution, it now becomes far more important for each piece of content, each work of news, to have its own internal integrity, for the evidence and the choices that went into producing that content to be clear.

We have entered an era in which the consumer does not say, "I believe this because I trust everything from this source." The citizen should demand to be shown why he or she should believe any particular piece of content. The news has been atomized, broken into stories away from institutions. Each atom of news must prove itself.

In this sense, clarifying such common misunderstandings about concepts like fairness and balance, along with improving the discipline of verification employed in the production of news, may be the most important step in improving the quality of news we receive and public discussion we build from that news. In the end, a discipline of verification is what separates journalism from other fields of communication and creates an economic reason for it to continue.

What would this journalism of objective *method*—rather than merely good intention—look like? What should citizens expect from the press as a reasonable discipline of reporting? What should we expect to see from news that comes from unfamiliar sources, from fellow citizens, or even partisan producers, for us to be able to consider it reliable and useful? As we listened to and studied the thoughts of journalists, citizens, and others concerning the news, we began to see a core set of concepts that form the foundation of the discipline of verification. They are the intellectual principles of a science of reporting:

1. Never add anything that was not there originally.
2. Never deceive the audience.
3. Be as transparent as possible about your methods and motives.

4. Rely on your own original reporting.
5. Exercise humility.

Let's examine them one at a time.

An important parallel to the new journalism of assertion is the rise of fiction posing as nonfiction. It has had different names in different areas. On television, producers have called it docudrama. In the publishing world, some—such as author James Frey—have hijacked the memoir genre to pass fiction off as biographical truth. In 2006 Frey was exposed to have fictionalized much of his memoir *A Million Little Pieces*. But all of it is making stuff up. In some cases it is just lying. Some writers who practice narrative nonfiction, such as John Berendt, the author of *Midnight in the Garden of Good and Evil*, argue that, in order to hold a reader's attention, some details—such as subjects' thoughts, or pieces of dialogue—can be invented in order to add color to the story.

Perhaps John McPhee, a *New Yorker* writer noted for the strength of his narrative style, best summarized the key imperative: "The nonfiction writer is communicating with the reader about real people in real places. So if those people talk, you say what those people said. You don't say what the writer decides they said.... You don't make up dialogue. You don't make a composite character.... And you don't get inside their [the characters'] heads and think for them. You can't interview the dead. Where writers abridge that, they hitchhike on the credibility of writers who don't."[20]

In 1980, John Hersey, the Pulitzer Prize–winning author of *Hiroshima*, the story of the effects of the first use of the atomic bomb in World War II, attempted to articulate a principle to help make journalism compelling without crossing the line between fact and fiction. In "The Legend on the License," Hersey advocated a strict standard: never invent. Journalism's implicit credo is "nothing here is made up."

Today, we think Hersey's standard of "never invent" needs to be refined.

Along with Roy Peter Clark, the senior scholar at the Poynter Institute in St. Petersburg, Florida, we developed an updated pair of ideas for navigating the shoals lying between fact and fiction.

DO NOT ADD

Do not add things that did not happen. This goes further than "never invent" or make things up, for it also encompasses rearranging events in time or place or conflating characters or events. If a siren rang out during the taping of a TV story, and for dramatic effect it is moved from one scene to another, it has been added to that second place. What was once a fact becomes a fiction.

Usually, when people do add or embellish, they hide it—a tip-off in itself that invention is not acceptable. And when authors of nonfiction have invented and admitted it, critics and readers have generally reacted poorly. This was the point of Hersey's original essay, which challenged author Tom Wolfe, among others. Biographer Edmund Morris discovered this when he wrote *Dutch*, his authorized biography of Ronald Reagan, in which he made himself a character in the book witnessing Reagan in his early life, before the author was actually born. Morris said he was trying to make a point about how Reagan himself created fictional reality. Yet this intermingling of fantasy and reality did little to illuminate Reagan and much to damage the credibility of the book. "Why would I want to read that?" former *Washington Post* editor Benjamin C. Bradlee exclaimed in reaction.[21]

DO NOT DECEIVE

Never mislead the audience. Fooling people is a form of lying and it mocks the idea that journalism is committed to truthfulness. This principle is closely related to the first one. If you move the sound of the siren and do not tell the audience, you are deceiving them. If acknowledging what you've done would make it unpalatable to the audience, then it is self-evidently improper. This is a useful check. How would the audience feel if they knew you moved that sound to another point in the story to make it more dramatic?

"Do not deceive" means that if one is going to engage in any narrative or storytelling techniques that deviate from the most literal form of eyewitness reporting, the audience should know. On the question of quoting people, a survey that we conducted of journalists found broad agreement: Except for word changes to correct grammar, some signal should be sent to audiences—such as ellipses or brackets—if words inside quotation marks are changed or phrases deleted for clarity.[22]

If someone reporting events reconstructs quotes or events that person did not witness, the audience should know these specific quotes were reconstructed and be told they were verified. A vague author's note at the beginning or end of a book or story that tells audiences merely "some interviews involved reconstruction" is not adequate. Which interviews? Reconstructed how? These kinds of vague disclosures are not disclosures at all.

We believe these two notions—Do Not Add and Do Not Deceive—serve as guideposts for navigating the line between fact and fiction. But how, as citizens, are we to identify which journalism to trust? Here, some other concepts are necessary.

TRANSPARENCY

If those doing journalism are truth seekers, it must follow that they be honest and truthful with their audiences, too—that they be truth presenters. If nothing else, this responsibility requires that those engaged in journalism be as open and honest with audiences as they can about what they know and what they don't. How can you claim to be seeking to convey the truth if you're not truthful with the audience in the first place?

In practice, the only way to level with people about what you know is to reveal as much as possible about your sources and methods. How do you know what you know? Who are your sources? How direct is their knowledge? What biases might they have? Are there conflicting accounts? What don't we know?

Call it the Spirit of Transparency. We consider this idea the most important single element in creating a better discipline of verification.

Most of the limitations journalists face in trying to move from accuracy to truth are addressed, if not overcome, by being honest about the nature of their knowledge, why they trust it, and what efforts they make to learn more.

Transparency has a second important virtue: It signals one's respect for the audience. It allows the audience to judge the validity of the information, the process by which it was secured, and the motives and biases of the persons providing it. This also makes transparency the best protection against errors and deception by sources. If the best information one has comes from a potentially biased source, naming the source and acknowledging the source's perspective will reveal to the audience the possible bias of the information–and may inhibit the source from deceiving as well. It will also compel the reporter to find the most authoritative sources possible.

Transparency also helps establish that the journalist has a public-interest motive, which is the key to credibility. The willingness to be transparent is at the heart of establishing that the reporter is concerned with truth. The lie, or the mistake, is in pretending omniscience, or claiming greater knowledge than one has.

How does the Spirit of Transparency work? It starts at the top, where it may mean public meetings, speeches, or editors' columns, especially during controversy. It flows down to individual stories, where it may demand specificity. If a piece reports "experts say," how many experts did the reporter actually talk to? Perhaps the most valuable thing about transparency is that its natural ally is the open architecture of the Internet. In a digital landscape, the consumer is also a critic, who may comment on stories, ask questions of the news producer, research additional sources, or offer his or her own commentary on a piece of content in social media. This dialogue of news has empowered the consumers of news to ask the most important question one can pose about the credibility of the information one is offered: "How do you know that?" Asking that question of a news provider can encourage a clear accounting of the original sources of assertions, conclusions, labels, and facts.

This clear and detailed identification of sources is the most effective form of transparency news publishers have at their disposal, and it forms the basis of a more open relationship with the public. While journalists were in many ways slow to embrace the Web, they did recognize this new relationship with audiences, and how the higher level of transparency and proof made possible by digital distribution was an empowering tool in the production of news. In 2002, for instance, the *Los Angeles Times* employed extensive footnotes detailing the sources of quotes, facts, scenes, and other information in "Enrique's Journey," a six-part Pulitzer Prize–winning series about a Honduran teenager journeying to the United States to find his mother. More than seven thousand words of footnotes kept the narrative clean of overattribution but also provided detailed information about sourcing to the reader.

Since the first edition of this book appeared in 2001, the concept of transparency, considered controversial at the time, has gained substantial momentum. Much of this is due to the arrival of digital technology, the interactive tools that it created, and the dialogue that generated about news. While newsrooms generally have suffered enormous financial disruption, the shift toward disclosure and evidence has been overwhelmingly positive. The Web and its dedicated outlets for journalism debates, criticism, and gossip—such as Jim Romenesko's blog, Nieman Journalism Lab, Poynter.org, Gigaom, and many, many more—helped push organizations to be more candid in explaining their work. News operations started blogs in which editors and producers explained newsroom decisions. The use of hyperlinks transformed digital stories from the flat narratives that they would have been in print into dynamic pathways from which consumers could delve deeply into topics, catch up on the story so far, and use stories as reference portals to which they could keep coming back.

The Web also created scores of new ways of presenting news and information that made the legacy forms of television or print seem paltry, from data visualization and interactive graphics, to archives, multimedia, curation, and much more. In our book *Blur*, we noted that in covering a news event in print, there were roughly seven elements a news provider could offer to convey the story—a headline, a narrative story, a chart or graphic, a photo, a map, a sidebar (second story), and perhaps a pull-quote (taking an interesting quote from a story, blowing it up, and using it as a graphic element to pull people into reading the story). In a digital form, a news publisher had perhaps ten times as many elements to choose from, from databases, to original documents, to audio and video interviews with sources or reporters, and much more.[23] All of these tools empower transparency, encourage engagement, and can make news more credible. Strategies for using these tools to make news transparent are still evolving. Yet to see these tools as a threat, or more work to be burdened by, is a mistake. The key is to see them as opportunities.

The tools must be used with conviction. One area where news publishers were already moving toward greater transparency, even before the Web, was in the explanation of anonymous sourcing. One impetus for this was growing survey data in the late 1990s that showed that excessive use of anonymous sourcing irritated the public and was a culprit in the decline in their trust of newspeople.

A *New York Times* story on self-prescribed drugs attempted transparency when attributing a quote to a character who had done such self-medicating. The paper described her simply as Katherine K. "'I acquire quite a few medications and then dispense them to my friends as needed. I usually know what I'm talking about,' said Katherine, who lives in Manhattan and who, like many other people interviewed for this article, did not want her last name used because of concerns that her behavior could get her in trouble with her employer, law enforcement authorities or at least her parents."[24]

Why Katherine wanted anonymity is obvious, but the *Times'* explanation for why it agreed to provide it, while a lengthy one, left unclear what standards it was applying. Was it because the paper did not want to put her in legal jeopardy or was it afraid she would get in trouble with her parents?

The Spirit of Transparency first involves the journalist asking for each event, "What does my audience need to know to evaluate this information for itself?" The answer includes explaining as much as is practical about how the news organization got its information.

A second element of transparency involves answering the question, "Is there anything in our treatment of this that requires explanation? Were any controversial decisions made to leave something in or take something out?" In an age of incredulity toward journalists, it is critical to explain editorial decisions that might be misconstrued.

A third element of the Spirit of Transparency involves something that may seem counterintuitive for most journalists: Those who produce news should acknowledge the questions they cannot answer. Traditionally, journalists were trained never to raise a question the story could not answer. Write around the holes in the story. Make stories seem airtight, even omniscient. In the twenty-first century, when journalists cannot control everything the public knows about public events, when they are no longer gatekeepers, that view is no longer sensible—if it ever was.

These ideas about transparency can solve myriad problems. Consider the case of Richard Jewell. The *Atlanta Journal-Constitution* broke the story that police briefly thought Jewell might be the bomber at the 1996 Olympics. The story came from law enforcement sources who wished to remain anonymous and said that Jewell, who was initially hailed as a hero for alerting police to the pipe bomb, had become a suspect in the investigation. The story also said Jewell fit the profile of a "lone bomber."

To make matters more complicated, the paper had to deal with its own rules, which prohibited the use of anonymous sources. So how did the *Journal-Constitution* handle the story? It used what the paper called a "Voice of God" approach, in which the journalists did not attribute this information but simply stated it as their own understanding of the facts.

The piece never mentioned all the things police did not know. This included the fact that they had no physical evidence linking Jewell to the crime. The police had also not interviewed Jewell as a suspect. Nor had they yet worked out a timeline to see if Jewell could have called in the tip to the police and still gotten to the place where he found the knapsack in the time allotted.

The paper insists it didn't get anything wrong. It simply reported what police were thinking. However, had the news organization noted all the things that police had not yet done to establish their unfounded suspicions of Jewell, the story might have been less explosive, but far more complete—and accurate. It also would have avoided sparking the years of litigation that followed its publication.[25]

The Spirit of Transparency is the same principle that governs the scientific method: explain how you learned something and why you believe it, so the audience can do the same. In science, the reliability of an experiment, or its objectivity, is defined by whether someone else can replicate the experiment. In journalism, only by explaining how we know what we know can we approximate this idea of people being able, if they are of a mind to, to replicate the reporting. This is what is meant by objectivity of method in science, or in journalism.

Even as he began to develop doubts about whether journalists could really sort out the truth, Walter Lippmann recognized this:

> There is no defense, no extenuation, no excuse whatsoever, for stating six times that Lenin is dead when the only information the paper possesses is a report that he is dead from a source repeatedly shown to be unreliable. The news, in that instance, is not that "Lenin is Dead" but "Helsingfors Says Lenin is Dead." And a newspaper can be asked to take responsibility of not making Lenin more dead than the source of the news is reliable. If there is one subject on which editors are most responsible it is in their judgment of the reliability of the source.[26]

Unfortunately, too much journalism fails to reveal anything about methods, motives, and sources. Television newscasts, as a matter of course, will say simply "sources said," a way of saving valuable time on the air, yet most of these sources are hardly confidential. Similarly it has been a standing rule in most offices on Capitol Hill that staffers be quoted anonymously at all times, that only the representative be on the record.

Withholding information from the public in ways like this is a mistake. As citizens become more skeptical of both journalists and the political establishment, such disservices to the public bring journalism under greater suspicion.

MISLEADING SOURCES: A COROLLARY TO TRANSPARENCY

The Spirit of Transparency also suggests something about the way those engaged in journalism deal with their sources. Obviously journalists should not lie to or mislead their sources in the process of trying to tell the truth to their audiences.

Unfortunately, journalists, without having thought the principle through, all too often have failed to see this. Bluffing sources, failing to level with them about the real point of the story, even flat out lying to sources about where one is heading with a story, are all techniques many journalists have applied in the name of truth seeking. While at first glance candor may seem a handcuff on reporters, it won't be in most cases. Many reporters have come to find that it can win them enormous influence. "I've found it is always better to level with sources, tell them what I'm doing and where I'm going," concluded Jill Zuckman, who worked as a political correspondent for the *Boston Globe* and the *Chicago Tribune* and later went into government. *Washington Post* reporter Jay Mathews long made a habit of showing sources drafts of stories. He believed it increased the accuracy and nuance of his pieces.[27]

At the same time, those engaged in journalism should expect similar veracity from their sources. Indeed, we would go one step further. If a source who has been granted anonymity is found to have deliberately misled the reporter, the source's identity should be revealed. Part of the bargain of granting a source anonymity is that in exchange the source tells the truth. If the source has lied, and used the shield of anonymity to do so, the source should be exposed. That source has broken the covenant. Journalists should not only employ this technique on behalf of the public. The practice should be common enough that sources know it—and fear it.

There is a special category of misleading that journalists practice with sources. It is called masquerading. This occurs when journalists pose as someone else to get a story. The "undercover" reporting technique is nothing new. At the beginning of the twentieth century, muckrakers like Nellie Bly, who among other remarkable achievements posed as an inmate in an insane asylum to expose mistreatment of the mentally ill, used masquerade. Television is particularly inclined to use masquerade and tiny hidden cameras to expose wrongdoing.

What does avoiding deception and being transparent with audiences and sources suggest about masquerade? These ideas do not preclude journalists' use of masquerade. Rather, they suggest that journalists should use a test similar to the concepts justifying civil disobedience in deciding whether to engage in the technique. Citizens should also apply this test in evaluating what they think of it. There are three steps to this test:

1. The information must be sufficiently vital to the public interest to justify deception.
2. Journalists should engage in masquerade only if there is no other way to get the story.
3. Journalists should reveal to their audience whenever they mislead sources to get information, and should explain their reasons for doing so, including why the story justifies the deception and why this was the only way to get the facts.

With this approach, citizens can decide for themselves whether journalistic dishonesty was justified or not. And journalists, in turn, have been clear with the citizens to whom they owe their first loyalty.

We have dealt at length with this notion of a more transparent journalism because it will help over the long run to develop a more discerning public. This is a public that can readily see the difference between journalism of principle and careless or self-interested imitation. In this way, journalists can enlist the new power of the marketplace to become a force for quality journalism. This transparency means embedding in the news reports a sense of how the story came to be and why it was presented as it was.

During the reporting on the Clinton-Lewinsky scandal, the *New York Times* did just this in explaining to readers why a story about the allegations of a woman named Juanita Broaddrick was held for a time and then placed on page 16. Broaddrick was alleging that President Clinton had forced himself sexually on her twenty-one years earlier in Arkansas, although she had not made the allegations at the time or even earlier in the Lewinsky scandal. Nor was she pressing the case legally.

Reporters Felicity Barringer and David Firestone interviewed their own managing editor, Bill Keller, and included his explanation in the story: The merits of Broaddrick's allegations were ultimately "probably unknowable ... legally it doesn't seem to go anywhere. ...

Congress isn't going to impeach him again ... and 'frankly we've all got a bit of scandal fatigue,'" Keller reasoned in the story. Some citizens might have disagreed with Keller's decision, but at least they now had some explanation for the news they were receiving, not some false sense that news was an objective reality rather than the product of human judgment.[28]

Two elements are important here. First, the reporters felt it was important to let readers know how news decisions were made and just what standards were applied to those decisions. Second, the atmosphere inside the newsroom of the *New York Times* was such that the reporters felt comfortable questioning the managing editor's decision, pen in hand, with the intention of quoting his comments in the story.

ORIGINALITY

Beyond demanding more transparency from journalism, we also should look for another quality from the news we produce and consume. Journalist Michael Oreskes, when he was Washington bureau chief of the *New York Times*, offered this deceptively simple but powerful idea in the discipline for pursuing truth: do your own work. This idea has become even more important as technology has made the distribution of others' work easier and more common—and turned facts into a seeming commodity of diminished value.

One of the first major stories to break at the dawn of the digital age was the sex and legal scandal involving President Bill Clinton and White House intern Monica Lewinsky. The story is instructive precisely because news organizations were then less familiar with the concept that stories were already, in the phrase that became popular at the time, "out there." Throughout the scandal, news organizations found themselves in the uncomfortable position of trying to decide what to do with often explosive exposés from other news organizations that they could not verify themselves. To make matters more complicated, these stories usually were based on anonymous sources, meaning that the news organization had to take even greater responsibility for the veracity of the story than if they were quoting someone. Based on such sourcing, three different news organizations reported that a third-party witness had seen the President and Lewinsky in an intimate encounter–stories that were later found to be inaccurate. Should a news organization have reported these exposés because they knew others might, and that in the newly proliferating world of media, the story would be public anyway somewhere else?

Oreskes concluded that the answer was an adamant no. "The people who got it right were those who did their own work, who were careful about it, who followed the basic standards of sourcing and got their information from multiple sources. The people who worried about what was 'out there,' to use that horrible phrase that justifies so many journalistic sins, the people who worried about getting beaten, rather than just trying to do it as well as they could as quickly as they could, they messed up."[29]

Originality is a bulwark of better journalism, deeper understanding, and more accurate reporting. Some ancient axioms of the press say much the same thing: "When in doubt leave it out." In the era before curation and aggregation, the tradition of "matching" stories was rooted in the same idea. Rather than publishing another news outlet's scoop, journalists tended to require one of their reporters to call a source to confirm it first. This tradition of matching was a way for news organizations to avoid having to credit their rivals, which in this earlier era was considered an embarrassing admission of being scooped. Yet the tradition of matching had another more important and salutary effect. Stories that couldn't be independently confirmed would not be repeated.

This concept of originality dovetails with the notion of transparency. There are levels of knowledge in reporting, and those who produce news should be aware of them and consider acknowledging them to their audience. Journalism is first concerned with the physical externality of events. A dump truck ran a stoplight and crashed into a bus. The President said these words. This many people died. The document said this. The closer you are to this physical and external level of information, the easier it is to verify the information.

Even here, of course, there are levels. Documents or facts that a reporter can see and verify for him- or herself are at the highest level of solidity. If one is relying on others to convey these facts, it then becomes important to know how those intermediary sources know what they are relaying. Were the sources eyewitnesses? Or are they secondhand sources (such as a press secretary who was briefed on a meeting but not present) or someone even further removed (a police public relations officer who did not interview witnesses but who was in turn briefed on what was said).

But as reporting moves toward the interior world, trying to report on what someone believes or what motivates the person, journalism necessarily becomes more speculative. What was the truck driver thinking when he ran that light? Why did the President say these words? What motivated the shooter in Newtown, Connecticut?

Interior thoughts may be something the journalist feels the audience should know, but it's more difficult to obtain solid proof for these kinds of details. There may be multiple interpretations and different levels of knowledge. This softer level of proof should be indicated to the audience. If the newsroom decided the best way to address motive and answer the "why" was through an expert, it should signal to the public why the expert was chosen and describe his or her expertise in or involvement with the topic. Newsrooms should not hide behind experts to abdicate their responsibility for getting as close to the truth as possible.

Why do we suggest this? Because the more honest the journalist is with the audience about what he or she knows and doesn't know, the more the audience will be inclined to trust the story. Level with people. Make no claims to an omniscience you cannot justify. Acknowledging what you don't know gives you more authority, not less.

HUMILITY

A fifth and final concept is that those engaged in reporting should be humble about their own skills. In other words, not only should they be skeptical of what they see and hear from others, but just as important, they should be skeptical about their ability to know what it really means. Jack Fuller, the former editor-publisher of the *Chicago*

Tribune, suggested in his book *News Values* that journalists needed to show "modesty in their judgments" about what they know and how they know it.[30] A key way to avoid misrepresenting events is a disciplined honesty about the limits of one's knowledge and of the power of one's perceptions.

An incident described to us by the veteran religion writer Laurie Goodstein illustrates the point. The event was a Pentecostal prayer revival on the steps of the U.S. Capitol. The gathering featured faith healings, calls for school prayer, condemnations of abortion and homosexuality—a fairly typical revival meeting. A reporter for a newspaper covering the event related all this, but added this sentence: "At times, the mood turned hostile toward the lawmakers in the stately white building behind the stage." Then the reporter quoted a Christian radio broadcaster speaking from the stage: "Let's pray that God will slay everyone in the Capitol."[31]

The reporter assumed the broadcaster meant slay as in "kill." But Goodstein explained, "Any Pentecostal knows that asking God to slay someone means to slay in spirit, slay in the sense of holy spirit, praying that they are overcome with love for God, for Jesus."

The problem was the reporter didn't know, didn't have any Pentecostals in the newsroom to ask, and was perhaps too anxious for a juicy story to double-check with someone afterward whether the broadcaster was really advocating murder of the entire Congress. "It made for a very embarrassing correction," said Goodstein. It also makes a strong case for the need for humility.

Humility also means that you are open-minded enough to accept that the next person you talk to could change the entire meaning of your story or even convince you that you have no story.

Together, these five ideas amount to a core philosophy that frames the discipline of verification. They also establish a closer relationship between the journalist, by which we mean anyone producing news, and the citizen, and that closer relationship is mutually beneficial. By employing the powerful tools of transparent, narrative storytelling, those gathering and reporting news engage citizens with important information. At the same time, by being more open about their work, those engaged in journalism are encouraged to be more thoughtful in acquiring, organizing, and presenting the news.

THE CHALLENGE OF VERIFICATION IN THE DIGITAL AGE

In the twelve years since the first edition of this book, we have been asked one question more often than any other: Is a discipline of verification still possible in an age when the rumors, gossip, innuendo, and panic that may flow through a crowd are all public in real time? How does one play the role of steward over facts after the fact—when false information has already spread?

At a symposium at the Newhouse School of Journalism at Syracuse University, the question came to us in real time. The subject of the event was how the press should deal with child molestation accusations. Back in 2011, Bernie Fine, a basketball coach at the school, had been the subject of those accusations. The local paper had investigated and decided it couldn't prove them, but years later, the press decided the charges needed to surface. The case was explosive and ongoing. During one of the symposium's afternoon sessions, a therapist who treated molestation victims in Syracuse declared suddenly that though he could provide no details, there was another coach at the school who was still actively molesting children and the school was protecting him. Other panelists were aghast.

A reporter for the local paper came up to us as soon as the session ended. What was he supposed to do with this utterly unsubstantiated allegation? The panel was being live tweeted. And live streamed. The accusation was already out there—with the press having no part of it.

The best way forward in a case such as this, we believe, is transparency and humility. There was no way the reporter could simply ignore the allegation. It was already "published" by tweet and webcast. So the first step, in whatever reporting time existed before publication, was to seek corroboration. Track down the man who had made the statement and demand what evidence there was to substantiate or justify making this allegation public. (He refused further comment.) Ask the police if any complaints had been filed. Find out if the university had heard the allegation before (though note that the university and police had been implicated in not acting quickly in the case that was the subject of the symposium).

The next step was to contextualize the now public allegation as much as possible for the audience. Explain that the accuser had offered no evidence to substantiate his claim. Report that other therapists on the panel were appalled that such an unsubstantiated accusation be made public. Put the public allegation in context. Don't just repeat it.

The third step was to share with the public what would need to be established to prove the accusation. Doing so would show how careful the public would need to be. In effect, in a networked media environment, the journalistic responsibility involves arming the public with as much information as possible so that people can determine for themselves whether to believe them. The audience, in other words, must be treated as adults, informed rather than protected. (Some who have worked through this problem with us have suggested monitoring social media to see how large an impression the accusation had made before publishing anything more and whether the nature of the reaction should let that also guide what you published next.)

Finally, the last step of verifying allegations after they are public involves the added responsibility the open system of the Web puts on those who aspire to verification. The news organization now had a community obligation to check the allegation out. Rather than ignore unsubstantiated accusations like a public ostrich, in other words, someone operating as a journalist now has more responsibility to track them down because they are already public. That meant the accusing therapist wasn't off the hook. The news organization should be thorough in making sure he took responsibility for what he had said.

This amounts to a new formula for verification of unsubstantiated material that is already public. The modern news provider has to inform the public about what needs to be substantiated for a citizen to believe an uncertain accusation, and then lead the community in the search to find the answer. The process of verification thus has become more public, and more collaborative. But it has not vanished.

BIAS

The discipline of verification, and particularly the notion of transparency, is one of the most powerful steps journalists can take to address the problem of bias. By bias we don't mean simply political or ideological bias. Bias encompasses all kinds of predilections, both appropriate and troubling. We mean bias in a broader sense that covers all the judgments, decisions, and beliefs of those who gather and report news. This could include a bias for truth or facts or giving voice to the voiceless, as well as a bias toward one's own personal social, economic, or political leanings. The critics are right that we're all shaped by personal history and the biases of the culture in which we live. Looked at this way, it becomes impossible to communicate without engaging some of these biases, including those that make a story compelling.

Understood in this broader and frankly more realistic sense, bias is not something that can or even should necessarily be eliminated. Rather, the job of those engaged in journalism is to become more conscious of the biases at play in a given story and decide when they are appropriate and useful, and when they are inappropriate. The journalist needs to become a manager of his or her own bias and the biases, if the setting is an institutional one, of the operation that is publishing the work.

There is some validity to the axiom that bias is in the eye of the beholder—or that a biased story is just one you disagree with. The problem with this interpretation is that it too easily becomes an excuse to let everyone off the hook. You can't please everyone, so why worry about it? Problem solved. Dismissing the issue this way, however, doesn't address the frustrations of the audience, and it doesn't improve the reporting.

Managing bias involves several components that relate to the discipline of verification. The first task is to become more systematic and conscious about getting the facts right, using any number of the techniques described below. Adopting a method of verification, rather than simply having faith in one's own and others' good intentions, is the most effective way for those engaged in gathering and reporting news to overcome their preconceptions.

The second way to manage or curb bias is to move toward the Spirit of Transparency. This changes the relationship with the audience from one of talking down to one of sharing as equals. Explaining their decision making forces those engaged in news to evaluate and sometimes reconsider what they are doing. Journalists have also told us that more transparency has a remarkable impact in defusing assumptions that audiences would otherwise make about the motives of journalists.

TECHNIQUES OF VERIFICATION

Obviously, these concepts are not specific enough to constitute "a scientific method" of reporting–that is for individual journalists to refine. The key is that they are clear about it. But by way of illustration, we would like to offer some concrete methods from journalists around the country. While they are not encyclopedic, any journalist could fashion a superb method of gathering and presenting news from adapting the following few techniques.

EDIT WITH SKEPTICISM

When Sandra Rowe was editor of the *Oregonian* in Portland, Oregon, she employed a system at her paper that she and her successor, Peter Bhatia, call "prosecutorial editing." The term may be an unfortunately aggressive one. Reid MacCluggage, a former editor and publisher of *The Day* in New London, Connecticut, has suggested a better one, "skeptical editing."[32]

The approach involves adjudicating a story–in effect, line by line, statement by statement–editing the assertions in the stories as well as the facts. How do we know this? Why should the reader believe this? What is the assumption behind this sentence? If the story says that a certain event may raise questions in people's minds, who suggested that? The reporter? A source? A citizen?

Amanda Bennett, when working as an *Oregonian* managing editor, said the notion–which she learned at the *Wall Street Journal*–was designed for "rooting out not so much errors of fact but unconscious errors of assertion and narrative–to root out the things that people put in because 'they just know it's true.' "[33]

If a story says that most Americans now have a personal computer, the editor would ask for verification. If a story said "according to sources," the editor would ask, "Who are the sources? Is there more than one?" If there was only one, the story would have to say so. If a story said that candidate Smith's flip-flop on some tax bill proposal raises questions about his ideological consistency, the editor would ask, "What questions?" and "In whose mind?" If the answer was merely the reporter and the reporter's friends, the story would either have to say so or that line would come out.

Whenever practical, said Rowe, this kind of editing involves the editor and the reporter sitting side by side, and the reporter producing original material. "The more of it we did, the more we were sending true fear" through the newsroom, said Rowe.[34] Bennett began teaching it in the newsroom in front of groups of reporters and editors. "People didn't know it was okay to ask these questions," Bennett said. The purpose, in large part, is to "make that role of asking questions okay, and to make it conscious." Rather than including more in stories, more was taken out, unless it could be absolutely verified.[35]

The technique, Bennett and Rowe believe, makes editors and reporters better and more thorough. The objective of the *Oregonian*'s skeptical editing is to create an atmosphere in which people can question a story without questioning the integrity of the reporter. It becomes part of an atmosphere of open dialogue in a newsroom, which goes bottom-up as well as top-down.

KEEP AN ACCURACY CHECKLIST

Several news organizations began to use accuracy checklists to remind their journalists of the importance of verification. Some of the
checklists we collected are more conceptual and ask questions like:

- Is the lead of the story sufficiently supported?
- Is the background material required to understand the
  story complete?
- Are all the stakeholders in the story identified, and have
  representatives from that side been contacted and given a
  chance to talk?
- Does the story pick sides or make subtle value judgments?
  Will some people like this story more than they should?
- Have you attributed and/or documented all the
  information in your story to make sure it is correct?
- Do those facts back up the premise of your story? Do you
  have multiple sources for controversial facts?
- Did you double-check the quotes to make sure they are
  accurate and in context?

Others we have seen are more factual and concrete:

- Did you double-check the quotes to make sure they are
  accurate and in context?
- Have you checked websites, phone numbers, and unusual
  names?
- Did you check that all first references in your story have a
  first and last name?
- Have you checked ages, addresses, and titles to make sure
  they are correct? If so, have you written "everything else
  cq" above your byline to signal those things are correct?
- Do time references in your story include day and date?

Some editors consider such checklists too mechanistic, and if
they are handled badly, we agree they can erode the confidence of
reporters by seeming to quash the creative element of storytelling.

But properly handled, such questions can bring reporters and editors together to make their work more accurate and credible.

ASSUME NOTHING

When he was president of the Chicago Innocence Project, a nonprofit investigative reporting group that exposes wrongful convictions, journalist David Protess used the cases of death-row inmates to teach journalism students at Northwestern University's Medill School of Journalism the importance of verifying presumed facts. Among the lessons were: Don't rely on officials or news accounts. Get as close as you can to primary sources. Be systematic. Corroborate.

Each year Protess received thousands of letters from people on death row who claimed wrongful conviction. Each year he chose a handful that he assigned his students to examine. In 1999, the appeal of Anthony Porter, who was facing execution after a murder conviction, was one of the cases Protess used to introduce his aspiring journalists to the value of skepticism.

"Maybe the best way to understand my method is what I do for the students when they come into my class," Protess explained in an interview with us while still at Medill. "I draw a set of concentric circles on the blackboard. In the outermost circle are secondary source documents, things like press accounts. . . . The next circle in is primary source documents—trial documents like testimony and statements. The third circle in is real people—witnesses. We interview them to see if everything matches what's in the documents. We ask them questions that may have come up looking at the documents. And at the inner circle are what I call the targets—the police, the lawyers, other suspects, and the prisoner. . . . You'd be surprised how much is in the early documents. There is a lot there, especially early suspects the police passed by."

At the inner circle of the Porter case, Protess and his students found Alstory Simon, a suspect the police quickly overlooked. Using Protess's systematic approach to cross-checking the documents and sources, Protess and his students found a nephew who had overheard Simon confess to the murder on the night of the killings. Simon was ultimately convicted of the crime for which Porter was about to die. On March 19, 1999, Anthony Porter became the fifth prisoner wrongfully convicted of murder in Illinois to be freed by the work of Protess and his students. Protess's work is an extraordinary demonstration of the power of methodical journalistic verification.

TOM FRENCH'S RED PENCIL

If Protess's method is exhaustive, Tom French's is wonderfully simple. French specialized in writing long, deep narrative nonfiction for the *St. Petersburg Times* in Florida. He won the 1998 Pulitzer Prize for feature writing. He also wrote on deadline.

French developed a test to verify any facts in his stories. Before he handed a piece in, he took a printed copy and went over the story line by line with a red pencil, putting a check mark by each fact and assertion to tell himself that he had double-checked that it was true.

BE CAREFUL WITH ANONYMOUS SOURCES

As citizens, we all rely on other sources of information for most of what we know. Those who produce journalism also most often depend on others for the details of their reporting. One of the earliest techniques journalists developed to assure audiences of their reliability was the practice of providing the sources of their information. Mr. Jones said so and so, in such and such a speech at the Elks Lodge, in the annual report, etc. Such dependence on others for information has always required a skeptical turn of mind. One axiom was: "If your mother says she loves you, check it out." If the source of the information is fully described, the audience can decide for itself whether the information is credible.

That isn't possible when a source is anonymous. At that point, audiences must invest more trust in the news provider that the source is believable. As we argued above, one way to mitigate this is to share more information with the audience about the anonymous source, while still protecting the source. Yet over time this has become more complex.

As news sources have become more sophisticated in the art of press manipulation, confidentiality has shifted from a tool journalists used to coax reluctant whistleblowers into confiding vital information to something quite different—a condition press-savvy sources imposed on journalists before they would even agree to an interview.

As dependence on anonymous sources for important public information has grown, journalists have begun trying to develop rules to assure themselves and their audience that they are maintaining independence from the anonymous sources of their news. Joe Lelyveld, when he was executive editor of the *New York Times*, required that reporters and editors ask themselves two questions before using an anonymous source:

1. How much direct knowledge does the anonymous source have of the event?
2. What, if any, motive might the source have for misleading us, gilding the lily, or hiding important facts that might alter our impression of the information?

Only after they were satisfied by the answers to these questions could they use the source. And then, to the maximum degree possible, they had to share with the audience information to suggest how the source was in a position to know ("a source who has seen the document," for example) and what special interest that source might have ("a source inside the Independent Prosecutor's office," for example). This effort at more transparency was a crucial factor in enlarging the audience's ability to judge for itself how much credence to give a report, but more important, it signaled the standards of the organization serving up their news.

The late Deborah Howell, who was ombudsman of the *Washington Post*, Washington editor of the Newhouse newspapers, and editor of the *St. Paul Pioneer Press*, developed two other rules for anonymous sources that reinforced Lelyveld's:

1. Never use an anonymous source to offer an opinion of another person.
2. Never use an anonymous source as the first quote in a story.

Glenn Guzzo, the former editor of the *Denver Post*, had another set of questions he wanted reporters and editors to be able to answer when they requested approval for keeping a source anonymous to their audience.

1. Is the information essential to the story?
2. Is the information fact, not opinion or judgment? (He would not allow anonymity for judgmental statements.)
3. Is the source in a position to truly know—is this an eyewitness?
4. What other indicators of reliability are there (multiple sources, independent corroboration, experience with the source)?
5. What descriptors can you use so the audience can decide what weight to assign this source?

The three versions of these questions or tests also offer practical instructions for how to convey news, even after one has decided to use what an anonymous source is offering.

The point is not that anyone adhere rigidly to any one of these tests, but that those engaged in practicing journalism apply conscious judgment when deciding to allow a source to remain confidential, and that they share some of that reasoning with the audience. Public opinion surveys reveal that the public does not like anonymous sourcing, though they do appreciate that the practice may have value.[36]

How would such a disclosure read? An example might be as follows: "... according to an attorney with access to the details of the case. The publication granted anonymity to the attorney because of the importance to the public of having this information and our belief that identifying him would put him in legal jeopardy."

TRUTH'S MULTIPLE ROOTS

In the end, everyone in the journalistic process has a role to play in the journey toward truth. Publishers and owners must be willing to consistently air the work of public-interest journalism without fear or favor.

Editors must serve as the protectors against debasement of the currency of free expression—words—resisting effort by governments, corporations, litigants, lawyers, or any other newsmakers to mislead or manipulate by labeling lies as truth, war as peace.

Reporters must be dogged in their pursuit and disciplined in trying to overcome their own perspectives. Longtime Chicago TV newscaster Carol Marin explained it this way to us: "When you sit down this Thanksgiving with your family and you have one of the classic family arguments—whether it's about politics or race or religion or sex—you remember that what you are seeing of that family dispute is seen from the position of your chair and your side of the table. And it will warp your view, because in those instances you are arguing your position. . . . A journalist is someone who steps away from the table and tries to see it all."[37]

And, if journalism is conversation, in the end that conversation includes discourse among citizens as well as with those who provide the news. The citizens, too, have a role. They must, of course, be attentive. They also must be assertive. If they have a question or a problem, they should ask it of those who have provided the reporting: How do you know this? Why did you write this? What are your journalistic principles? These are fair questions to ask, and citizens deserve answers.

Thus those engaged in journalism must be committed to truth as a first principle and must be loyal to citizens above all so that citizens are free to pursue it. And in order to engage citizens in that search, they must apply transparent and systematic methods of verification. The next step is to clarify their relationship to those they report on.

5

Independence from Faction

I n 1971, a few months after the historic confrontation between the *New York Times* and the federal government that the publication of the Pentagon Papers touched off, William Safire, a speechwriter for President Nixon, was seated next to *Times* publisher Arthur "Punch" Sulzberger at a fund-raising dinner. During their conversation Safire mentioned that he was planning to leave government service.

Safire's comment fell on receptive ears. Since the election of Nixon in 1968, Sulzberger had been under pressure to find a conservative voice to balance the *Times* op-ed pages. The pressure was coming from Scotty Reston, the paper's Washington correspondent, former bureau chief, and executive editor, who worried about how the political world viewed the paper, as well as from members of the *Times* board of directors, who believed a greater balance of voices would ensure the success of a plan to launch a national edition. At the time, the op-ed page was dominated by liberals, including Tom Wicker, Anthony Lewis, Flora Lewis, and more moderately, Reston himself. Sulzberger had come to the conclusion that he agreed: A strong conservative voice was a genuine need.

Safire was an appealing choice. He was raised in New York and still had many friends in the city. His clear and sometimes stinging prose included memorable criticisms of the press. The fact that Katharine Graham, the publisher of the *Washington Post*, had tried to hire Safire but couldn't agree on a salary made the idea even more attractive.

Yet if the addition of Safire eased the pressure on Sulzberger from one side, it lighted a firestorm of criticism from longtime readers on the other, as well as from some in the *Times* newsroom. From both quarters came expressions of dismay that a presidential speechwriter could pass himself off as a journalist.

By what criteria could a partisan political activist suddenly call himself a journalist? Certainly something more than merely having a column was required to be a journalist at the *Times*. When Safire finally arrived three weeks before the Watergate scandal broke wide open, he recalled years later, he was thoroughly "ostracized by my Washington bureau colleagues as an unreconstructed Nixon flack. The only reporter who would even have lunch with me was Martin Tolchin, a long-before classmate at the Bronx High School of Science."[1]

Two unrelated events changed Safire's status. The first was personal. "At the annual bureau picnic, the three-year-old child of a reporter fell in a pool and started to drown," Safire said; "as the only adult standing nearby, I jumped in fully clothed to fish him out. The general opinion changed to 'he can't be all bad.'" The second was journalistic. *Times* reporter John Crewdson had broken a story on secret wiretaps placed on sixteen reporters and one Nixon aide. The aide was Safire. "That was a seemingly unprecedented assault on press freedom and was later made illegal; however, since I was the aide wiretapped, that made me 'one of them,' in Nixonian terminology, and when I blew my stack about secret taps in a *Times* column, that was reported in *Time* magazine as 'Safire Afire' and helped establish my independence. It was like getting a shower; I was no longer a pariah."

Thirty-two years later, Safire would retire from the *Times* with a Pulitzer Prize and the esteem not only of his colleagues in journalism but also of millions of readers. What earned him that acclaim?

It certainly wasn't neutrality, or a tepid tone, or the desire to be evenhanded. Safire remained a dyed-in-the-wool conservative who could skewer adversaries, end careers, and be strident when moved to be. What was it, then, that separated Safire from a partisan, activist, or propagandist?

The question is increasingly pertinent to the delivery of news and information in the twenty-first century. Technology has opened media to millions of new voices; everyone on Facebook and Twitter is a publisher. And as commercial newsrooms have shrunk, think tanks, corporations, political activist groups, and nonprofits, all with clear social agendas, have become newsrooms and moved to generate coverage for issues that affect them—sometimes with an eye to correcting the slant, shallowness, or other limitations they perceived in commercial media. And as digital thinkers have noted, all the rest of us can publish, too. Amid all this, what is it that makes something journalism?

Two of the values outlined in previous chapters, truthfulness and a commitment to citizens, are a part of the answer. So, as we will describe later, are playing a watchdog role and providing a forum for public debate. But for now let's deal with where the role of opinion fits in journalism.

News with a point of view cannot be discounted from being journalism. If it were, columnists and editorial writers would be excluded from the profession. Reporters such as Paul Gigot of the *Wall Street Journal* and Thomas Friedman of the *New York Times* would somehow have shed their standing as journalists when they became columnists. Magazine writers such as Nick Lemann (who also served as dean of Columbia Journalism School) would be denounced for crossing a line when they drew conclusions in their reporting. Authors such as Robert Caro and the late David Halberstam, whose thoroughness elevated their work from journalism to history, would not have been honored for the depth, courage, and compassion of their reportorial judgment, but cast out for having them. Columnists such as Ruth Marcus, David Brooks, Paul Krugman, and Michael Gerson would be castigated rather than honored. Some of the most celebrated work, known as Knowledge Journalism because its authors are experts who also report, would be denounced because it was too informed, too useful.

Every year the Pulitzer Board awards a prize for commentary under the heading "Journalism." And many have argued that the American alternative press is closer to the historical roots of journalism than large corporate-owned papers that profess that they provide a neutral news account.

All of these precedents are worth remembering when people complain that the new media made possible by the Web is not journalism because it is commentary. The element of judgment and opinion cannot, by any tradition or distinction, disqualify it from being journalism, nor does it make all commentary journalism.

The point is worth restating to make it clear. Being impartial or neutral is not a core principle of journalism. As we've explained in the previous chapter on verification, impartiality was never what was meant by objectivity. But if neutrality is not a cornerstone of journalism, what then makes something journalism, as opposed to propaganda? Propagandists publish. Political activists publish. Al Sharpton has a cable talk show from the Left. Rush Limbaugh has a talk show from the Right. Scores from both sides of the political aisle write partisan blogs. Are they journalists? Is anyone who publishes or broadcasts a journalist?

After he retired from the *Times*, we asked Safire (who died in 2009) to ruminate on the qualities that guided his thinking and propelled that transformation from politician to journalist. A central issue has to do with allegiance.

> Where does loyalty lie—with your old personal friends and colleagues, with your political ideology or party, with your news medium, with the cold facts—or with The Truth?
>
> In real life, it's a fluctuating combination of all these. You don't burn a good long-term source to get a pretty-good story. You don't let your ideology turn you away from a good story. (You don't let a copy editor change "story" to "article" without a fight.) You don't let a series of hard facts lead you to a softly untruthful or misleading conclusion.

You don't become a hero by joining a pack savaging your ideological soulmates. You don't quote from this paragraph selectively, reporting accurately but corrupting its whole meaning.

In other words, Safire held the same fidelity to accuracy and facts as does any other journalist, and that allegiance to hard facts and truthful conclusions separated him from his old partisan team. He was his own man, still conservative, but now working for his readers.

Safire also believed his experience in politics helped inform his second career as journalist. He believed just as clearly that this was a transformation one could not repeat. "Going back and forth every few years confuses the reader/viewer and must trouble the inveterate switcher as well," he said. Journalism is more than just having a perch at a TV station or on an op-ed page, although Safire believed political experience was good training for becoming a reporter.

Having learned to skirt an issue or fuzz up a statement on the inside helps a journalist detect such manipulation of words when on the outside. When on the inside, you develop lifelong relationships with people you trust (and you remember those less trustworthy). After you have crossed the street, these friendships can lead to confidential sourcemanship: the art of getting information from insiders, or predecessors of insiders, that you as a journalist are not supposed to get. Nothing beats a confidential source with whom you have shared a political foxhole. You know what to expect from that person, who knows how far you will go to protect a confidence.

Safire believed that opinion journalists had more liberty than other journalists to call things as they see them without the qualifiers of a straight reporter. They may even have more obligation. "I like to think I helped launch a field called 'opinionated reporting,'" Safire said. "This was not the sneaky business of slanting a purported news story; it was the digging for a fresh fact that illuminated, or at least called attention to, a candidly labeled op-ed opinion column."

There was one other matter that bothered his new colleagues

at the *Times* that Safire chose not to clear up. "[There] was still the 'nattering nabobs of negativism' problem," Safire would recall, referring to a speech he had helped write that would become one of the most famous denunciations of the American media ever delivered by a major political figure. "I wrote that phrase in a 1970 speech given by Vice President Agnew in San Diego denouncing defeatists in general, not the press in particular; but because it followed a televised speech he made, written by Pat Buchanan, excoriating the media for 'instant analysis' and other sins, my alliterative phrase, generously credited to me by Agnew, was associated with his caustic attack on the press. (I never tried to straighten that out, because having a reputation of media critic didn't hurt me a bit with readers.)" This, too, is revealing. Safire was less concerned with how his new colleagues perceived him than with how the audience reacted.

These qualities thus emerge as the fourth key principle of journalism:

Journalists must maintain an independence from those they cover.

This even applies to those who work in the realm of opinion, criticism, and commentary. It is this independence of spirit and mind, intellectual independence rather than neutrality, that journalists must keep in focus.

Editorialists and opinion journalists are not neutral. Their credibility is rooted instead in the same dedication to accuracy, verification, the larger public interest, and a desire to inform that all other journalists subscribe to. "Do you need to present both sides to be impartial?" Safire wondered. "Clearly no. Don't be afraid to call somebody a 'terrorist' who strikes terror into a populace by deliberately killing civilians. That killer is not a 'militant' or 'activist,' which are suitable terms for political demonstrators or firebrands, nor is he or she a 'gunman,' which is not only evasive but sexist. To be excessively evenhanded is to be, as the Brits say, kak-handed—clumsy."

Safire also felt phony evenhandedness was a disservice to his readers. "Playing it straight does not mean striking a balance of space or time. When one side of a controversy makes news—issues a survey or holds an event—it's not the reporter's job to dig up the people who will shoot it down and give them equal attention. Comment, yes; 'balance' by column inch or stopwatch, no."

That does not mean seeking out straw man arguments to knock down. For political activists and propagandists, facts are often stretchable and more selectable, and ideas tend to be tactics rather than the point of the exercise. The goal is not just to win an argument. It is to get to a particular political outcome. That is not true of opinion journalists, for whom the goal is about exploring ideas. Some of the best opinion journalists indeed like to engage the strongest arguments of their opponents, not knock down the weakest. Michael Gerson, who was a speechwriter for George W. Bush before becoming a columnist for the *Washington Post* writers group, has said that taking account of the arguments on the other side is a way of making his own ideas stronger and more interesting. And E. J. Dionne, whose column also appears in the *Post*, on the art of argument cites writer Christopher Lasch, who contended that when writers seriously engage in opposing ideas, they are also prone to learn from them and change their own.

In some ways, this fourth principle—that journalists must be intellectually independent—is rooted more in pragmatism than in theory. One might imagine that one could both report on events and be a participant in them, but the reality is that being a participant clouds all the other tasks a journalist must perform. It becomes difficult to see things from other perspectives. It becomes more difficult to win the trust of the sources and combatants on different sides. It becomes difficult if not impossible to then persuade your audience that you put their interests ahead of those of the team that you are also working for.

INDEPENDENCE OF MIND

As we talked to journalists around the country from different fields, probed their motives and their professional goals, it became clear that Safire, Gerson, and Dionne had articulated key but subtle notions that are widely shared. The late Anthony Lewis, a liberal opinion columnist for the *New York Times*, said that the difference is grounded not only in a commitment to truthfulness but also in a kind of faith that this commitment implies. "Journalists who end up writing columns of opinion have a point of view.... But they still prize facts above all. C. P. Scott, the great editor of *The Manchester* (Great Britain) *Guardian*, put it, 'Comment is free but facts are sacred.' I think we tend to go from the particular to the general; we find facts and from them draw a conclusion," Lewis continued. Media "provocateurs like Ann Coulter or veteran conservative talk show host John McLaughlin are the other way around. All they care about are opinions, preferably shouted. Facts, if any, are incidental. They follow the advice of the Queen of Hearts, 'Sentence first—verdict afterward.'"[2]

Independence of spirit even reaches into opinion writing that is non-ideological—the work of art critics and reviewers. John Martin, former dance critic of the *New York Times*, said that as he moved to judgment and opinion he believed he retained a kind of journalistic independence. "I feel that my first responsibility is to tell what happened, and secondarily, to express my opinion, let's say, or an interpretation, or, as briefly as possible, to put this particular performance in its place in the scene. And I think that, in a way, is reporting, too."[3]

It has become fashionable in recent years to wonder who is and isn't a journalist. We think this is the wrong question. The question people should ask is whether or not the person in question is doing journalism. Does the work proceed from an adherence to the principles of truthfulness, an allegiance to citizens, and to informing rather than manipulating—concepts that set journalism apart from other forms of communication? In this connection Twitter should not be confused with being a "source" or falling into any one category of content. Twitter is a platform, a delivery system, and the work that one finds there can range from teenage gossip to journalists seeking sources. The content from a professional journalist on Twitter or on Facebook may be a picture of the family vacation or a joke the reporter tells in a bar, something that falls well outside his or her professional content. Emily Bell, who runs the Tow Center for Digital Journalism at Columbia University's Graduate School of Journalism, is fond of commenting on the television show *Girls* on Sunday night, although these tweets are clearly personal. Much the same could be said of blogs, a form of writing that encompasses everything from highly personal accounts aimed at a few friends, to more public diaries about hobbies, and some of the most important journalistic coverage (as in the case of the popular Scotusblog) of the Supreme Court. In many ways social media platforms such as Twitter, Facebook, Instagram, and others are making social interaction a more public form of communication. But this does not define the nature of the communication. That is determined by the content. The new delivery systems and formats may be journalism or they may be political activism. They may be lie-mongering or they may be incisive academic debate. The issue is not where the information appears. The issue is the nature of the work itself.

The important implication is this: Freedom of speech and freedom of the press belong to everyone. But communication and journalism are not interchangeable terms. Anyone *can* be a journalist. Not everyone *is*.

The decisive factor is not whether someone has a press pass or an audience. Phil Donahue, who had one of the first popular daytime talk shows on television, years before Oprah Winfrey, suggested to us long ago that the man who walked into the bar at Chernobyl and said, "The thing blew," at that moment had committed an act of journalism. If he was reporting an event he had witnessed or had checked out, not passing along a rumor, he was doing journalism. Donahue's hypothetical example would come to be borne out—again and again—when technology made public spaces something more than physical places such as bars. Consider IT consultant Sohaib Athar, who happened to be living in Abbottabad, Pakistan, at the time of the U.S. raid on the compound where Osama bin Laden was hiding. Athar's tweets on that day in May of 2011—observing an unusual helicopter, noting the sound of an explosion, and surmising that the activity seemed to go beyond routine Taliban operations–go down as the first known reporting on the raid that killed Osama bin Laden.

It is one thing to understand the intellectual difference between an opinion journalist and a partisan propagandist. Living up to that distinction can be harder. Friendships, opportunities, and flattery all will conspire to seduce the opinion writer to cross the line.

The case of Maggie Gallagher is instructive. At one of our forums in 1997, Gallagher, then a columnist with the Universal Press Syndicate and the *New York Post*, was among the most articulate thinkers we encountered on the line between opinion journalism and activism and propaganda. "I think there are three criteria that I use and remind myself of in my ambition to remain a journalist–one with a point of view," Gallagher said at the time. "One is an ultimate commitment to the truth. . . . I don't relate anything to my readers that I don't believe is true."[4]

That requires being "open with the readers, to make it clear to the audience what your views are and what your biases are. . . . That's the difference between a journalist and a propagandist. I don't seek to manipulate my audience. I seek to reveal, to convey to them the world as I see it," she said.

And to accomplish all this finally, Gallagher said, it becomes essential to maintain distance from faction:

I think it's possible to be an honest journalist and be loyal to a cause. It's not really possible to be an honest journalist and be loyal to a person, a political party or a faction. Why do I say that? I think it relates to my basic belief that there is some relationship between journalism and one's perception of the truth. One can believe that certain things, ideas, proposals, would be good for America and can openly state that. But to be loyal to a political party, a person or faction means that you do not see your primary goal as commitment to speaking the truth to people who are your audience. There's a fundamental conflict of loyalty there.

In the first edition of this book, we were so struck by Gallagher's articulation of these distinctions that we spotlighted them in the opening of this chapter. In 2005, however, it came to light that Gallagher had violated the principles she herself had outlined.

Howard Kurtz, then a media writer at the *Washington Post*, revealed that Gallagher had a $21,500 contract to write for the Department of Health and Human Services. Gallagher's work, Kurtz wrote, was to promote President Bush's marriage initiative as a way of strengthening families. Her contract, which ran for ten months in 2002, included drafting a magazine article for a department official, writing brochures, and conducting a briefing. The story followed the disclosure that the Bush administration's Education Department was paying conservative commentator Armstrong Williams more than $240,000 to promote Bush's No Child Left Behind program. The revelations cost Gallagher her newspaper column, which she later resumed, though by then she was president of a lobbying group against same sex marriage and was clearly identified and speaking as an activist.

Gallagher said she saw her own case as different from Williams's. "I'm a marriage expert. I get paid to write, edit, research and educate on marriage," she wrote. "If a scholar or expert gets paid to do some work for the government, should he or she disclose that if he writes a paper, essay or op-ed on the same or similar subject? If this is the ethical standard, it is an entirely new standard."[5]

Actually it is not a new standard. It is an old one, fundamental to both the academy and to journalism: If there is a potential conflict of interest, it should be revealed, and if the revelation casts one in a clearly compromised position, don't take the work. Indeed, Gallagher's failure to disclose suggests that she knew what she was doing compromised the independence essential to her claim as a journalist.

THE EVOLUTION OF INDEPENDENCE

Ancient Greek philosophers understood that humans are political by nature and that an organized community requires some sort of political activity. It was into this crucible of political affairs that the first periodicals were born, inviting the broad public to become involved in the political decisions that affected their lives.

As we outlined in chapter 3 when discussing journalists' loyalty to citizens, the history of journalism over the last three hundred years, particularly in the American tradition, was distinguished by a move away from fealty to political party toward public interest. "Journalistically, the twentieth century can be defined as the struggle for democracy against propaganda, a struggle inevitably waged by an 'objective' and 'independent' press,'" journalism scholar James Carey of Columbia University wrote.[6]

In essence, the press swapped partisan loyalty for a new compact—that journalism would harbor no hidden agenda. Editorials and political opinion, which before had mixed with and sometimes even constituted the news on the front page, were now set apart by space or label. From these simple decisions—things that seem obvious today—much of today's standard journalistic ethic was formed, especially those principles concerning political positioning by reporters.

Those ethics strengthened generally through the twentieth century as journalists aspired to greater professionalism and also as the number of competing newspapers in cities shrank, leaving the survivors to appeal to a more mass audience, something to which television news organizations also aspired.

In the twenty-first century, one of the biggest questions is whether this notion of journalistic independence will endure. New technology, and the audience fragmentation it spawned, has led to the creation of niche media outlets built around ideology and the appeal of affirming the audience's preconceptions (Journalism of Affirmation), although many of these are owned by corporations and their purpose is commercial, not strictly partisan. (Fox News, MSNBC, websites such as the Daily Caller, and the Internet operations of conservative pugilist Glenn Beck are a few examples.) For now, there is no analogous market for ideology at the local level, though there are some statewide online news sites funded by nonprofits, such as Watchdog.org, a network of conservative websites that contend they are doing investigative reporting of state government. At the same time, advocacy groups, think tanks, and commercial businesses have moved into producing as traditional newsrooms have shrunk, to ensure and shape coverage on their core topics. These trends will continue, and will throw into doubt the future of the American press tradition of independence from faction, and will also weaken the economic possibilities of the mass markets that encouraged nonpartisan journalism in the first place. As the sorting out process of the new media system goes on, the question is whether audiences in the twenty-first century will continue as they did in the twentieth to respond more to news that is produced with genuine intellectual independence.

INDEPENDENCE IN PRACTICE

The rules have been modified and strengthened over time, to the point that reporters and editors at many traditional news organizations were forbidden from participating in such political action as public rallies on politicized issues. In 1989, *New York Times* Supreme Court reporter Linda Greenhouse was criticized for participating in a "Freedom of Choice" demonstration in support of abortion rights. She called her participation anonymous activism and made note of the fact that she did not call attention to herself. "I was just another woman in blue jeans and a down jacket," she said afterward. But the *Times* said her marching jeopardized the appearance of her reporting and reprimanded her.[7]

The Greenhouse incident came at a time when journalism was becoming more sensitive to the charge of liberal bias. The nature of the political debate had been changing since the 1960s, stimulated in part by the creation of an active network of conservative think tanks injecting new ideas into the public debate. And Republican lawmakers were more vocal in asserting press bias.

The advent of new digital publishing platforms refueled the debate about what journalists can and cannot do or say in their private lives. In April 2004, Rachel Mosteller was fired from the *Durham Herald-Sun* for keeping a blog, "Sarcastic Journalist," in which she talked about newsroom life. Her blog did not identify the company or her coworkers. In January 2006, the weekly *Dover Post* fired a reporter because his personal blog contained, among other things, disparaging references to people who sought coverage from the newspaper. In 2010, CNN parted company with Octavia Nasr, a senior editor for Middle Eastern affairs, after she posted a tweet in response to the death of a Shiite cleric: "Sad to hear of the passing of Sayyed Mohammed Hussein Fadlallah ... one of Hezbolla's giants I respect a lot."

INDEPENDENCE REEVALUATED

Even as the rules of independence became stricter in the past decades, there were always those who challenged–or evaded–them.

In the March 2003 lead-up to the Iraq War, conservative columnist George Will wrote a column dismissing the idea that America should wait for approval from its allies before invading the Middle Eastern country. To support his view that waiting for permission was foolish, Will quoted at length from a speech by British House of Lords member and newspaper owner Conrad Black. In his speech, Black said that America had the most successful foreign policy because when its objective was threatened, America removed the threat.

What Will did not disclose in his column was that for years he had been paid to sit on the international advisory board of Black's newspaper company, Hollinger International. The *New York Times* said that for every meeting Will attended, he received $25,000; Will said he did not remember how many meetings he was present at. The *Washington Post* Writers Group, which syndicates Will, was also not aware of the conflict. Asked by the *Times* if he should have told readers about receiving money from Black, Will replied: "My business is my business. Got it?"[8]

The Conrad Black episode was not the first of its kind for Will. In 1980, then a strong backer of Republican presidential candidate Ronald Reagan, he coached Reagan in preparation for the candidate's debate with President Jimmy Carter. Will then took to the airwaves after the debate as an ABC commentator and hailed Reagan's performance, saying Reagan was a "thoroughbred" under pressure.

Such secret counsel to politicians had plenty of precedent. Among others, Walter Lippmann wrote speeches for various presidents, including Lyndon Johnson, and the belated discovery of the secret work tarnished Lippman's reputation.

What was new in the Will case was that the columnist continued to say he didn't care. When news of the coaching of Reagan eventually surfaced, Will basically called criticisms of his coaching nitpicking. "Journalism (like public service, with its 'conflict of interest' phonetics) is now infested with persons who are 'little moral thermometers' dashing about taking other persons' temperatures, spreading, as confused moralists will, a silly scrupulosity and other confusions."[9]

Will was not making an ideological argument. He was implying something else, something that others, regardless of ideology, would echo: that the morality or ethics of journalism was subjective and invalid.

There was only one problem with Will's argument, the same one that reveals why the concept of independence is grounded in pragmatism rather than theory. Will had kept his coaching of Reagan secret. He did not want to tell his readers that he had helped produce the performance by President Reagan that he then glowingly reviewed. If he had, his praise of Reagan would have been discounted. Not by ethicists. By the audience.

Will's pattern is an old one, but it continually undermines the credibility of the journalist as activist. In 2008, various cable commentators, such as Chris Matthews, Paul Begala, and Donna Brazile, presented themselves as unaligned commentators when in private they were supporting or advising either Barack Obama or Hillary Clinton in the race for the Democratic nomination. CNN would later institute a policy barring its "political contributors" from being paid by candidates, though less than direct paid relationships with political groups seemed to allow the news channel to honor the rule in the breach rather than the spirit. The distribution of talking points to friendly political commentators, which turns people presented as media personalities into functional party mouthpieces, using precisely the same words and concepts that parties want to project on a given subject in a uniform way, has also become common practice.

Another device is political candidates wooing commentators by "consulting" with them for their ideas. In 2005, as an example, the Bush administration consulted with various journalists on drafts of the President's second inaugural speech, among them William Kristol of the *Weekly Standard* and syndicated columnist Charles Krauthammer. Both commentators said these were general consultations about policy, not speech preparations, and contended unapologetically that as such they had done nothing wrong.[10] Both also praised the speech after it was delivered.

There is a different problem, besides failure to disclose, with such consultations. While those who allow themselves to act as insiders see little problem, they are usually deluding themselves as to what is really going on here. As a rule, politicians are far less interested in what any journalist might actually contribute to a speech, which probably already has more authors than it needs, and far more interested in making the journalist imagine that his or her rhetorical and intellectual powers are so magical that the journalist just had to be consulted. Often these negotiations are far more likely attempts to ensure good press than to elicit whatever a journalist has to contribute.

Others have made several stronger challenges to the concept of independence of spirit and mind in journalism. They are worth examining one at a time.

One concern is the worry that journalistic independence has wandered into a kind of self-imposed solitary confinement from society at large. As Elliot Diringer, a former reporter with the *San Francisco Chronicle* who later joined the Clinton White House, told our academic research partners, "There is this notion that you should be disinterested to the point ... that you should withdraw from civic affairs if you are a journalist. And I find that somewhat troubling. I don't know why being a concerned citizen should be antagonistic with being a journalist."[11]

There have been two major responses to correct this sense that those operating by traditional news conventions were distant and alienated. One was the movement called Public or Civic Journalism, which gathered steam in the 1990s before being overrun by the interactive relationship with community made possible by the new technology. These movements argued that journalism should not just point out problems but also examine possible answers. Proponents of the movement did not see this approach as a rejection of the journalistic principle of independence. Critics argued it put journalists in a position of advocate because they identified with outcomes. But that divide, in the end, was more an argument over careful execution than philosophy.

Much of the tension over how close those who report the news should become to helping create solutions continues to have some resonance in the recognition that the purpose of journalism is not just to report but to create community. This involves creating channels, forums, and alliances, and helping connect people who are working on problems. As the history of news outlined in our chapter on purpose should make clear, community creation has always been at the heart of news—from the earliest days of newspapers growing out of the conversation that occurred in coffeehouses to the communities of citizens and journalists that form and re-form around breaking news stories or communities of interest on social platforms such as Twitter. The difference between a path forward or a path into the ditch is in the execution, and in the intent of the people operating in the role of journalist. Are they posing as journalists, pretending to provide news and information, when in fact their real motive is to manipulate others toward a predetermined outcome? Or are they really information providers and forum communicators who do not presume to have the answers but want to present information and then help convene the community to address problems together?

The other reaction to the sense that the independent news provider is somehow not to be trusted has been to abandon the principle of independence altogether, reaching out to the audience by arguing from one side or the other. In this new incarnation, partisans function as "media people"—talk show hosts, commentators, or guests on TV or radio. Usually they purport to be independent experts—they are identified as former federal prosecutors, legal scholars, or other disinterested professionals–when in fact they are party surrogates. They might better be described as "media activists." As we will explain more in chapter 7, on the forum function of journalism, these people increasingly are far less expert than they pretend, and often they have little regard for accuracy. Rather than addressing the public anger toward the press, this partisan approach takes advantage of it. Psychologist Philip Tetlock surveyed more than 250 people who make a living from sharing their expertise and comments. His twenty-year study tried to assess the probability that various outcomes the experts predicted would or would not happen. The results showed these experts to be poor forecasters. They fared worse than they would have if they had given all possible outcomes equal weight.[12]

Perhaps the best example of this phenomenon comes from the political Right, where conservative media mogul Rupert Murdoch has created an entire news network that focuses heavily on argument and ideology: Fox News. Privately, journalists inside Fox argue that they are creating balance by giving airtime to conservatives. Here there is a case to be made.

But publicly Fox tends to make a more subtle and less intellectually honest argument, wrapping its programming in the mantle of independence. The network's first marketing campaign featured the slogan, for instance, "We report, you decide," which it later dropped in favor of "Fair and Balanced." This had echoes of the way Hearst and Pulitzer claimed to advertise themselves not as they were but as they wanted people to imagine them: as accurate and fair, not as simply a source one was likely to agree with. It is an appeal to each audience member's sense of him- or herself as reasonable. If you like us, that is because we are more accurate, more complete, not because you agree with us.

The appeal of this new partisan press rests on reinforcing the preconceptions of the audience, instead of on being a watchdog of the powerful. Yet this new Journalism of Affirmation is different from the old American partisan press of the colonial age, which was controlled by a party and existed to advance a political agenda, to persuade and even educate. The Journalism of Affirmation, as it formed in places such as Fox and MSNBC, exists as a corporate strategy: Politics is a means to an end, a financial one.

It is also important to make a distinction between this Journalism of Affirmation, which denies its partisanship, and real alliances and the traditional forms of opinion journalism, which is both more transparent and more independent, the kind of work found in journals such as the *Weekly Standard* and the *Nation*, in many blogs written today by scholars, and in the commentary of opinion writers such as David Brooks or Paul Krugman. One is clear in its intent and remains committed to all the principles of intellectual independence. The other purports to be one thing—neutral—while using the language and form of balance to create something else, a kind of propaganda to amass an audience.

This distinction has an important implication. Open in its intent, journalism of opinion is also open in its allegiance to a set of intellectual principles, which it holds above faction or party. David Brooks describes himself a Libertarian, in the same manner that George Will in the *Washington Post* called himself an American Tory and Victor Navasky at the *Nation* refers to himself as a progressive. The Journalism of Affirmation, claiming fairness, balance, and neutrality, lacks that agility or that candor. Watch these commentators carefully—Rachel Maddow, Al Sharpton, Rush Limbaugh, Sean Hannity, Bill O'Reilly—or, online, consider Michelle Malkin, Glenn Beck, and writers at sites such as Breitbart.com. Their currency is emotional mobilization more than ideas. Much of their conversation focuses on the wrongness of the other side, or the anticipation that there lies trouble ahead for the obviously misguided opponent. This is the essence of the Affirmation: be afraid, or be angry, or be assured they will get their comeuppance. As one talk radio host told us after we finished a segment on his program one evening: "My show isn't really about ideology. It's about outrage."

There is another difference as well. Journalism of opinion, be it in the column of a conservative or a liberal, is not fundamentally about reporting the news but about making sense of it. It assumes that the reporting occurs elsewhere. While the journalism of opinion may involve reporting, there is no claim that this is occurring outside the realm of the opinion and that interpretation is its primary concern.

The Journalism of Affirmation stakes more of its claim on reporting (we report, you decide). Fox, MSNBC, and places such as Huffington Post have opened the door to political operatives and celebrities because these people are popular and have an audience. They are no longer newsmakers to be interviewed. They are part of the team, paid for their affiliation. So former White House press secretary Dana Perino and political aide and PAC activist Karl Rove are commentators on Fox, and civil rights activist Al Sharpton has a show on MSNBC. They ask or are asked questions as if they are observers of the scene, not actors in it. On CNN, democratic activist Donna Brazile and Republican consultant Alex Castellanos comment on races while advising the candidates.

The outright bias of these hosts does not damage their notion of accuracy, precisely because the Rashomon bias (that there is no such thing as accuracy or truth) is so easy it becomes an excuse. The notion that the only authentic approach to information is through opinion is appealing to some people because it requires no professional discipline or technique or even idealism. There is a simplicity to it, like a faith in pure markets or the idea that any emotion is valid if it is strongly felt.

This blurring of journalistic identities has taken on another dimension. It has changed attitudes about personal relationships between journalists and those they cover. The *New York Times*, for instance, allowed Todd Purdum to cover the Clinton administration even after he had a relationship with former White House press secretary Dee Dee Myers, whom he eventually married. The situation, which probably would not have been allowed a few years earlier at the *Times*, did not even engender much comment. A generation earlier *Times* reporter Laura Foreman was found to have been romantically involved with a corrupt politician on whom she was reporting when she was working at another paper. When the affair was discovered, *Times* executive editor Abe Rosenthal famously declared,

"I don't care if you sleep with elephants, as long as you don't cover the circus." The Myers-Purdum relationship was so open, by contrast, that it was replayed as a charming and apparently acceptable subplot on *The West Wing*, a TV drama about the White House. And why not, when CNN's premier foreign correspondent, Christiane Amanpour, while covering the war in Kosovo in the late nineties, was engaged to (and later married) James Rubin, then spokesman for the U.S. State Department.

Unlike the Foreman case, situations like Myers and Purdum, Amanpour and Rubin are arguably considered more acceptable in a contemporary media culture because they are open. But is openness good enough? Can anyone reasonably be expected to cover those to whom they have personal, even intimate, loyalties? How can this be squared with the obligation that the first professional loyalty of a journalist is to the citizen?

Disclosure is important. As citizens, we deserve to know if a reporter is actively involved with the issues or people he or she is covering. But having listened to journalists and worried citizens, we conclude that disclosure is not sufficient. As Gerson, Dionne, and others who write with a point of view understand, it is vital to maintain some personal distance in order to see things clearly and make independent judgments.

Nor is the remedy nearly as onerous as some contend. Purdum could have a different beat, Rubin or Amanpour a different post. Indeed, at a time when so many citizens doubt the professionalism of journalists, such support for this principle of independence would demonstrate to a skeptical public how seriously news organizations take their responsibilities and how they are willing to live up to them to their own inconvenience, embarrassment, and, occasionally, sacrifice and unpleasantness.

INDEPENDENCE FROM CLASS OR ECONOMIC STATUS

The question of independence is not limited to ideology. It may, indeed, be easier to deal with here than in other areas. The solution to bias, as we outlined in chapter 4, on verification, is to develop a clearer method of reporting. Yet to fully understand the role intellectual independence can play in gathering and reporting news, it is important to look at other kinds of conflicts and interdependencies.

As journalists in the twentieth century became better trained and educated (and in certain quarters better paid), another complication to the concept of independence set in. New York journalist Juan Gonzalez, who worked as a columnist for the *New York Daily News* and was president of the Hispanic journalist group, was also a thought leader about the impact of class on journalistic perspective. "The biggest problem ... is that the American people feel there is a class divide between those who produce the news and information and those who receive it. That the class divide manifests a class bias toward most Americans whether they are conservative or center or liberal: if they're working class and they're poor, they're considered less important in the society. I think that's the principal bias."[13]

Richard Harwood, who held many top jobs at the *Washington Post,* including being its ombudsman, agreed. "Journalists, as members of [the] cognitive elite, derive their worldviews, mind-sets, and biases from their peers. Their work is shaped to suit the tastes and needs of this new upper class. I must say there's a lot of evidence that the mainstream press is staking its future on this class because it's increasingly going upscale ... and rejecting or losing working people, lower-income people."[14]

Tom Minnery, a former journalist who later became vice president of Focus on the Family, an evangelical Christian organization based in Colorado Springs, Colorado, has argued that this class bias helped accelerate commercialization of the news. "The direction of coverage ... is a distortion of the way life is lived in the United States by a vast, broad middle of the country's population," Minnery argued. "In the United States, 1 percent of the population owns 35 percent of all the commonly traded stock. You would think from watching the evening news or reading newspapers that we are all at home watching the streaming ticker across the bottom of CNBC." Or, he continued, watch the morning network shows "and see extensive, lovingly detailed coverage of the latest gizmos and googaws....

The confluence of commerce and news coverage is now so deep and profound that we can't even see the edges of it anymore."[15]

In short, Harwood and Minnery were arguing, the commercialized media had begun to serve consumer society rather than civil society.

Some argue that the Web has largely fixed this, democratizing information, auto-correcting falsehood, creating a wiki culture of accuracy, fairness, and contextualization. But it isn't that simple. There remain digital divides, class divides, digital competence divides, as well as divides in how active and influential different people are in different spaces. For all that we imagine the world has changed, as of 2012, just 18 percent of Internet-connected American adults were on Twitter, yet a majority of journalists were active there.[16] The reality, however, often not acknowledged in the discussion of technology's benefits (the tech discussion is usually looking forward rather than taking current stock) is that most of the reporting in American media, and elsewhere in the world, continues to come from commercial media outlets.

This potential class isolation is reinforced by strategic targeting of elite demographics, and it will only intensify as online media increasingly tries to use targeting based on online behavior to identify audiences. As the Web matures, digital publishers will increasingly be expected to make a profit–not simply attract a crowd–which also will influence what Web ventures are launched and financed. People increasingly see the press as part of an "other world" from which they feel alienated, rather than as a public surrogate acting on their behalf. The result will continue to be a threat to the public service dimension of the news.

The biggest exception to media isolation is localism. People tend to distrust the media. Yet what they have in mind when they imagine media is national media, and particularly cable news. For instance, Pew Research Center data we were involved in developing found that by 2011, 66 percent of Americans thought the media often got the facts wrong, and 63 percent thought the media were biased. When we asked what media they thought of when they heard that question, 63 percent mentioned a cable news outlet, especially CNN and Fox News Channel.[17]

When the survey asked people the same questions about the media they used most often, the perception changed drastically. Just 30 percent said the media usually got the facts wrong, and 49 percent said they were biased. Which media did they have in mind now? Most said their local newspaper or television station.

There is some basis, looking forward, to worry about the future of localism. The Web, various data suggest, will inevitably pull our news consumption away from local issues tied to civic geography for the simple reason that it makes so many national and international sources more readily available. More national digital operations will also be launched for the simple reason that they are more likely to amass a large audience, and thus will get financial backing and attract commerce. While not an inherently good or bad phenomenon, the Web will nonetheless pull us toward subjects about which we are more Balkanized and ideologically polarized, and niche interests where our common ground is smaller. The Web traffic and survey data we have seen suggest this trend is already under way.

The solution is not to repudiate the concept of journalistic independence–and to move in its place toward ideological content to make news more engaging and trustworthy. This approach makes little sense as a way to revive the financial health of a community news site or newspaper media publishing operation. The way to start would not be to lop off a local outlet's appeal to a substantial share of its market.

Instead, the way to create a journalism that serves the public interest, and the interests of a more robust democracy, is to recruit more people from a diversity of classes and backgrounds to combat insularity. The journalism that people with different perspectives produce together is better than that which any of them could produce alone.

Before the Web disrupted the revenue base of many larger institutional newsrooms, this was precisely where those interested in making news better were heading. "If you're going to change the composition of the journalistic workforce there has to be some kind of a program that takes people that are already in other careers ... [and] offers them an opportunity to help diversify in a class way," Gonzalez suggested.[18] More recently, this notion, of recruiting people with more diverse life experiences into journalism, has animated some of the more innovative efforts in journalism education. It was a key idea of Steve Shepard, the founding dean of the City University of New York's new journalism school, created in 2006. It is at the core of the Fellowships in Global Journalism, an idea developed by Rob Steiner, a former *Wall Street Journal* reporter, at the University of Toronto's Munk School of Global Affairs. Steiner's idea was to attract professionals with deep expertise in other fields and train them as journalists, to elevate the substance and expertise of the journalism being created.

INDEPENDENCE FROM RACE, ETHNICITY, RELIGION, AND GENDER

The last thirty years of the twentieth century saw a growing awareness of the need for reflecting the diversity of American society in newsrooms. Trade groups such as the American Society of Newspaper Editors created industry-wide diversity goals for newspapers. Various news organizations revamped their style books to root out racist language. Almost all of that promised was only partly fulfilled. The newspaper industry failed to meet the goals. As we will outline in discussing the principle of personal conscience, there are problems with the concept of diversity if it is narrowed simply to mean ethnic, gender, or other numerical targets. Those are a necessary means, but they should not be the end of diversity.

Yet there is another issue within the question of diversity that must be wrestled with first. It is the question of the degree to which ethnicity and gender and other markers can be equated with identity or expertise. Do we think that only African-Americans can capably cover African-Americans, and Asian-Americans alone capably cover Asian-Americans, and so on? Shouldn't a good journalist be able to cover anything?

"The argument for diversity based on representation ... at its core, presupposes that persons of the same race and gender think alike because of their shared experiences of racism and sexism," African-American business executive Peter Bell has argued. "The argument, I believe, ignores and/or minimizes the influence of class, education, region, family, personal psychology and religion in shaping our personal ideas and beliefs. . . . Observable traits such as race and gender . . . serve as a proxy, and I would argue a crude proxy, for ideas. . . . What is the black position on any given issue? The answer, of course, is there isn't one."[19]

Many journalists, even those in minority groups, have had similar doubts. "To simply say . . . that you're going to have an Asian and a black and a person in a wheelchair in your newsroom, and that this is somehow going to give you some license to say that you're diverse, is to fall into the same category of determining your content on the basis of demographics," award-winning TV and radio correspondent John Hockenberry, who is disabled, has argued. "You can determine revenue on the basis of demographics, but you can never determine content. . . . Far from hiring in the newsroom being an indicator of where diversity comes from, it's knowing your audience, and to be truly interested in your audience from the top to the bottom, from the left to the right, and from all economic levels."[20]

The criticisms touch a serious point: To what extent does background influence a journalist's work? If those who cover events are chosen simply by ethnic heritage or skin color, isn't that just another kind of racial and ethnic stereotyping? It implies that there is such a thing as a single black perspective or a single Asian perspective.

Somewhere between rigid newsroom quotas and the fears of a new "politically correct" orthodoxy lies a richer area. There was already ample evidence that newsrooms lacking diversity were unable to do their jobs properly. They missed news. Their coverage had holes. Journalist Clarence Page recalled: "One editor in northern Illinois tried to beg off [of minority coverage] saying that he really didn't have much of a minority population in his town, even though I knew for a fact that his town has a 17 percent Latino population–17 percent. . . . A rural Wisconsin editor told me that he really didn't have any minorities in his area, even though his newspaper was just down the road from a major Indian reservation."[21]

The myopia of traditional definitions of news is proof enough that personal perspective colors journalism. Media companies, recognizing this problem, enlisted the help of organizations like the Maynard Institute, which developed a workshop that helped media outlets better understand the concerns of the full range of their audiences and helped expand the news organizations' sources of information.

But if one accepts that factors such as race do matter, how do we reconcile the undeniable influence of personal perspective with the goal of maintaining something called journalistic independence?

Independence from faction suggests there is a way to produce journalism without either denying the influence of personal experience or being hostage to it. The key is whether one maintains allegiance to the core journalistic principles that build toward truthfulness and informing the public. Just as it should be with political ideology, the question is not neutrality, but purpose. This journalistic calling for independence from faction should sit atop all the culture and personal history a reporter brings to an event he or she is covering and trying to understand. Whatever adjective attaches itself to someone who is described as a journalist–Buddhist, African-American, disabled, gay, Hispanic, Jewish, WASP, or even liberal or conservative–it becomes descriptive but not limiting. He or she is a journalist who is also Buddhist, African-American, conservative–not Buddhist first and journalist second. When that happens, racial, ethnic, religious, class, and ideological backgrounds inform the journalist's work, but do not dictate it.

John Hockenberry's skepticism about the influence of his own disability proves how this can work. Hockenberry once avoided doing "stories on disability" but later came to understand what he could bring to such pieces. "When I arrived at [the NBC News program] *Dateline*, a producer came to me and said, 'We want to do a story, a hidden-camera story, about the disabled in employment and in hiring.' . . . Even though my motives had something to do with this issue of not being pigeonholed as the disability reporter, what I said was [that] in my experience in encountering discrimination, it's inconclusive. I see people who sort of look at me wrong or maybe they make some sort of decision and I never really quite understand ... how it affected me.

"This young man [the producer], a Korean-American named Joe Rhee, said, 'John, discrimination doesn't happen while you're there. It happens the moment you leave. That's why we have the hidden cameras.'"[22] The result was a story that showed how companies in every case passed over a paraplegic man to hire a nondisabled applicant. "It was the combination of our collaboration in that newsroom that brought together a story that actually did something that mattered," Hockenberry said.

Hockenberry's experience shows that the goal of a newsroom is not simply to create numerical diversity—in this case, the disability story would not have been done if the disabled reporter were working alone. The ultimate goal of newsroom diversity is to create an intellectually mixed environment where everyone holds firm to the idea of journalistic independence. Together the journalists' various experiences blend to create a reporting richer than what each would create alone. And in the end that leads to a richer, fuller view of the world for the public.

The journalist is committed to society. The model is not disinterested. It is not cynical. It is not disengaged. The journalist's role is predicated on a special kind of engagement—being dedicated to informing the public, but not to playing a direct role as an activist. It might be called "engaged independence."

Few people have thought as probingly about the role of the journalist in the community as Gil Thelen, who has worked as a newspaper editor and educator. Thelen was an early experimenter with the concept of Civic Journalism, which developed ideas designed to reconnect journalists with community. But he also fought the publishers to protect the principle of journalistic independence. He ultimately left a newspaper in the Knight Ridder organization over the separation of news and business interests.

Thelen has described the journalist's role in community as that of a "committed observer." Journalists' needs, he explained, are "interdependent" with those of their fellow citizens. If there is a key issue in town that needs resolution and is being explored by local institutions, "we have a commitment to reporting on this process over the long term, as an observer." It would be irresponsible to cover the issue haphazardly or ignore it because it seems dull. The journalist should be committed to helping resolve the issue, Thelen argues, and the way he or she does that is by playing the role of the responsible reporter.

In this sense, the term *observer* is not passive. It also implies connector, translator, contexualizer, interpreter. But it distinguishes the journalist from other community actors, activists, and combatants. The focus of those engaged in journalism is on accurately understanding and conveying what others are saying and doing—rather than being simply another actor working for a particular solution or outcome. This difference makes the journalist a more reliable observer.

Thelen's ideas are echoed in the words of other journalists, who talk about the press creating a common language, a common understanding, or being part of the glue that defines and holds a community together. This is the proper understanding that many journalists have about the role of engaged independence.

The notion that journalists should be engaged in community as observers, translators, and connectors is also echoed in the writings of people exploring the potential of social media. Among the most dynamic of these voices is Monica Guzman, who writes a column for the *Seattle Times*. "In a world where everyone can participate in newsgathering, cultivating self-informing communities is itself an act of journalism," she has written. "To accomplish it, we need to not only learn the language of these spaces, but also smart ways to join, respect and inspire the voices within."[23] In this way, Guzman has argued, community is not a means to an end for journalism. It is the end.

No one has earned more recognition for using the community of voices to create a new connected journalism than Andy Carvin. When the Arab Spring began in 2011, Carvin was NPR's social media strategist. He quickly began to monitor the information being shared on Twitter by people on the ground in Cairo's Tahrir Square and elsewhere—then he began to triangulate, highlight, and redistribute it, tapping those same people to help verify the reports of others. Some sources he knew. Others he checked out. Carvin curated the collection in a way that was thoughtful and transparent, and his Twitter feed, @acarvin, became a kind of news service of a growing number of authentic, credible voices few others could find.

Carvin calls the skills he used "situational awareness," seeing the big picture by following his collection of on-the-ground voices speaking in real time. As Guzman has put it, "Carvin turned the random chatter into collected wisdom and gave that wisdom right back to the people who needed it most. All without writing a single traditional news story."

Every day, there are new examples of journalists who connect with their communities in order to better serve them, while maintaining the independence that allows journalism an authenticator's perspective. The *Guardian*'s belief in Open Journalism, in which the community participates in the process of news gathering, is one. Open Journalism may come as close as we've seen to the notion of journalism as organized intelligence that combines the experience and diversity of the community, the power of machines, and the skills, access, and discipline of open-minded inquiry that journalists are trained to perform. The *Guardian*'s editor, Alan Rusbridger, says the approach has ten core ideas behind it:

- It encourages public participation.
- It is not inert (the journalist to the public), in short not a static product.
- It involves the public in the pre-production process.
- It forms communities of interest.
- It is open to the Web, links to it, collaborates with it.
- It aggregates and curates.
- It recognizes that journalists are not the only voices of authority.
- It aspires to achieve and reflect diversity.
- Publishing is the start, not the end, of the process.
- It is open to challenge, correction, and clarification.

The principles of Open Journalism and the techniques of Andy Carvin represent a powerful shift in the way journalists do their work. But they also support, not repudiate, the elements of journalism. They are, in other words, a strong reflection of the idea that the principles that the public requires of journalism haven't changed, but the ways those principles are fulfilled in the network age have.

These new ideas of connection and observation as the qualities of the reliable journalist also put in clear relief the way in which journalism is a form of participation—but one that demands commitment to accuracy and is distinct from other types of activism, even for those producing journalism in settings that are not otherwise journalistic. Those functioning as translator, observer, and communicator at a think tank, an activist special interest group, or a corporate setting are not relieved of these obligations because of the funding source. Their work will lose its credibility and authority if they are not willing to engage in the same level of transparency and faithfulness to accuracy and verification. In the twenty-first century, journalistic independence, as it has always been for the opinion journalist, is intellectual. In this sense, we consider independence a core principle of producing journalism no matter where that journalism is produced.

Some journalists developed highly personal techniques for testing whether they are maintaining the kind of intellectual independence this participation demands. Paul Taylor, former chief political correspondent at the *Philadelphia Inquirer* and the *Washington Post*, who went on to create the Social and Demographics Project at the Pew Research Center, used a before-and-after method to check himself when he was a journalist. When he was assigned to a story that involved substantial reporting and research, Taylor used to write a lead before he had started his information gathering. Then he would test that lead against one he crafted at the end of the reporting process. If the two leads were too similar, he would know he hadn't learned very much, that he might not have done enough reporting, and that he might have been simply rewriting his own preconceptions.

In the end, no rigid prohibition against any kind of personal or intellectual engagement will guarantee that a journalist remains independent from factions, political or otherwise. In the end it is good judgment, and an abiding commitment to the principle of first allegiance to citizens, that separates the journalist from the partisan. Having an opinion is not only allowable and natural, but it is also valuable to the natural skepticism with which any good reporter approaches a story. But a journalist must be smart enough and honest enough to recognize that opinion must be based on something more substantial than personal beliefs if it is to be of journalistic use. It is not about believing in people or groups of people. It is a craft based on reporting, learning, understanding, and educating. Creating barriers to this process of discovery is, in the end, being disloyal to the public.

The importance of this independence becomes even more obvious when we consider the next special obligation of journalism, its role as watchdog.

6

Monitor Power and Offer Voice to the Voiceless

I n 1964, the Pulitzer Prize went to the *Philadelphia Bulletin* in a new reporting category. The award honored the *Bulletin* for exposing police officers in that city who were involved in running a numbers racket, a kind of illegal lotto game, out of their station house. The story presaged what would become a new wave of scrutiny about police corruption in American cities. The award had one other significance as well. It marked formal recognition by the print establishment of a new era in American journalism.

The new Pulitzer category was called "Investigative Reporting." The newspaper executives from around the country who run the Pulitzer under the auspices of Columbia University had added it in place of an older designation that they decided no longer required special recognition, "Local Reporting." They were putting new emphasis on the role of the press as activist, reformer, and exposer.

In doing so, the journalism establishment was acknowledging a kind of work they saw increasingly being done in recent years by a new generation of journalists. Reporters like Wallace Turner and William Lambert in Portland and George Bliss in Chicago were reviving a tradition of pursuing and exposing corruption that had largely been absent from reporting during World War II and the years immediately following. The war years featured storytellers like Ernie Pyle of the Scripps Howard wire service, who evoked the heroic spirit of the Allies at war, the sturdy British people, and the simple but gutsy American GI. After 1964, that began to change. Eight years after the introduction of the investigative reporting category to the Pulitzers, when Bob Woodward and Carl Bernstein of the *Washington Post* helped uncover the Watergate scandal inside the Nixon White House, investigative reporting would suddenly gain celebrity and sex appeal and would redefine the image of the profession.

All of journalism was changed, especially Washington journalism. A. M. Rosenthal, then executive editor of the *New York Times,* was so disturbed by the way the *Washington Post* dominated the Watergate story that he ordered a reorganization of his newspaper's Washington bureau to create a formal team of investigative reporters. So long as Rosenthal was executive editor, the job of Washington bureau chief would be only as secure as the strength of the bureau's investigative reportage. CBS News launched its own investigative news show, *60 Minutes,* which became the most successful news program network TV ever produced. Local television news, not to be left out, was soon awash in investigative teams–or "I-Teams"–of its own.

Some old-timers began to grumble. Investigative reporting, they harrumphed, was little more than a two-dollar word for good reporting. In the end, all reporting is investigative. While that is an oversimplification–investigative reporting is qualitatively different from other kinds of work in various ways–the critics were correct in one sense. What the Pulitzer Prize board formally recognized in 1964 had been, in fact, more than two hundred years in development.

Investigative reporting's roots were firmly established in the very first periodicals, in the earliest notions of the meaning of a free press and the First Amendment, and in the motivation of journalists throughout the profession's history. These roots are so strong, they form a fundamental principle:

Journalists must serve as an independent monitor of power.

This principle is often misunderstood, even by journalists, to mean "afflict the comfortable." Moreover, the watchdog principle is being threatened in contemporary journalism by overuse and by a faux watchdogism aimed more at pandering to audiences than doing public service. Perhaps even more serious, the watchdog role is threatened by a new kind of corporate conglomeration, as well as the grim search for new revenue models by news operations that have found digital advertising dollars wanting.

When print periodicals first emerged in Europe in the early seventeenth century, they saw their role as investigatory. During the English civil war, when press freedom in England seemed to flicker to life, periodicals immediately began to promise that they would investigate what was going on and tell their readers. The *Parliament Scout*, which began publication in 1643, "suggested something new in journalism—the necessity of making an effort to search out and discover the news."[1] The next year a publication calling itself *The Spie* promised readers that it planned on "discovering the usual cheats in the great game of the Kingdome. For that we would have to go undercover."

These early efforts at investigative work became part of the reason the press was granted its constitutional freedom. Periodicals like *Scout* and *Spie* were, for the first time, making the affairs of government more transparent. They marked the ambition of the press to be what would later be called the Fourth Estate, and stated publicly that the affairs of government should be known to all, not just to the privileged. Until the journals appeared, the internal workings of government were primarily the knowledge of limited elites—those with business before the state or those directly involved in the administration of government. The general public's information on its rulers largely came from uninformed gossip or official government messages. Suddenly, in contrast to the proclamations and town criers who provided the information those in power wanted distributed, these new periodicals aspired to tell people what the government actually did. Though government often clamped down on these early printers, as it would so often throughout the world, they established investigative reporting as one of the earliest principles that would set journalism apart from other means of communication with the public. It was the watchdog role that made journalism, in James Madison's phrase, "a bulwark of liberty," just as truth, in the case of John Peter Zenger's challenge to English libel law, became the ultimate defense of the press.

These early efforts were often frustrated. The British government forbade note-taking during parliamentary debates. People had to remember what was said and then run outside to recall or paraphrase the event before the paper went to press. These early journalists were dismissed as "newsmongers," and historians look back on that early parliamentary press as often dishonest and corrupt. Yet the instinct toward transparency and serving as watchdog that they represented, however crudely, proved enduring and ultimately would triumph.[2]

In the years to come, as conflict between a protected press and government institutions increased, it was this watchdog role that the Supreme Court fell back on time and again to reaffirm the press's central role in American society. Beginning with the case of *Near v. Minnesota,* which forbade the government from restraining publication of any journal except when the story threatened "grave and immediate danger to the security of the United States," the Court has methodically built a secure place within the law where journalists are protected so that they may aggressively serve the public's need for information concerning matters of public welfare.[3] A full two hundred years after the American Revolution, Supreme Court Justice Hugo Black continued to focus on the press's watchdog responsibilities when he wrote, "The press was protected so that it could bare the secrets of government and inform the people. Only a free and unrestrained press can effectively expose deception in government."[4] With support from state and federal legislatures during the 1960s and 1970s, the press gained greater access through the Freedom of Information Act and the so-called sunshine laws, which provided public access to many documents and activities of the government. Beginning in the twenty-first century—especially during the administration of George W. Bush and intensified under the administration of Barack Obama—unprecedented efforts were launched to withhold government information from the public and even to criminalize the efforts by the press to publish it. It is unresolved how the courts will react to these efforts.

The watchdog principle means more than simply monitoring government; it extends to all the powerful institutions in society. And that was true early on. Just as the *Spie* went "undercover" in order to discover the "cheats in the great game of the Kingdome," nineteenth-century journalist Henry Mayhew stayed out in the open to document the plights of that same kingdom's unknowns. Mayhew roamed the streets of Victorian London reporting on the lives of street people for the London *Morning Chronicle*.[5] By so doing, he gave the watercress girl and the chimney sweep individual faces, voices, and aspirations. He revealed their humanity to a population that regularly passed them unnoticed.

Combining the search for voices that went unheeded and cheats that went undiscovered, the earliest journalists firmly established as a core principle their responsibility to examine the unseen corners of society. The world they chronicled captured the imagination of a largely uninformed society, creating an immediate and enthusiastic popular following.

At the end of the twentieth century, nearly nine out of ten journalists believed the press "keeps political leaders from doing things they shouldn't do." The watchdog role was second, after informing the public, among the answers journalists volunteered as to what distinguished their profession from other types of communication.[6]

Even at the height of digital disruption, news organizations considered their watchdog responsibility one that, while expensive, could not be abandoned. A 2010 Pew Research Center survey of news executives found that strong majorities had serious reservations about the idea of taking funds from interest groups or from the government.[7] James Hamilton, an economist who specialized in studying media at Duke and now at Stanford, did an analysis of the cost of investigative reporting at the *Raleigh News and Observer*. He determined that an investigative series would cost $200,000. Yet among the intangible benefits of such a series—in the case of a News & Observer series exposing problems in the North Carolina probation system—were not only a better functioning probation system, but saved lives as well.[8] Even a skeptical public agrees. A Pew Research Center survey from 2011 found that a majority (58 percent) support the watchdog role of the press, and that support is almost equally present among Democrats, Republicans, and independents.[9]

As firmly as journalists believe in it, however, the watchdog principle is often misunderstood. At the turn of the century, Chicago journalist and humorist Finley Peter Dunne translated the watchdog principle to mean "comfort the afflicted and afflict the comfortable."[10] Dunne was half kidding, but the maxim stuck. On the day the *St. Paul Pioneer Press* won the Pulitzer Prize in 2000 for uncovering a cheating scandal on the University of Minnesota basketball team, the paper's sports editor in a speech cited his boss's fondness for repeating the phrase.[11]

Unfortunately, the notion that the press is there to afflict the comfortable and comfort the afflicted misconstrues the meaning of the watchdog role and gives it a liberal or progressive cast. The concept is deeper and more nuanced than the literal sense of *afflicting* or *comforting* would suggest. As history showed us, it more properly means watching over the powerful few in society to guard, on behalf of the many, against tyranny.

The purpose of the watchdog role also extends beyond simply making the management and execution of power transparent, to making known and understood the effects of that power. This logically implies that the press should recognize where powerful institutions are working effectively as well as where they are not. How can the press purport to monitor the powerful if it does not illustrate successes as well as failures? Endless criticisms lose meaning, and the public has no basis for judging good from bad.

Like a theme in a Bach fugue, investigative reporting has swelled and subsided through the history of journalism but never disappeared. It has defined some of the most memorable and important eras in U.S. history:

- The press in colonial America found its purpose as tribune of a people chaffing under a distant government that interfered with the energy of its development. James Franklin's *New England Courant* established a role as watchdog over both governmental and religious institutions, and the colonies had their own *Spie*–Isaiah Thomas's *Massachusetts Spy* exposed those who trafficked with the enemy.

- The revolutionary press gave way to a nation-building press in which the issues of the shape and character of the new government were reported. Federalists and anti-federalists each created their own newspapers to inform and encourage the public debate over the fundamental principles on which the new country would be built. One of the most important roles of this partisan press was to serve as a watchdog over the opposition party, a process of discovery and disclosure that at times became so virulent that the government with limited success tried to legislate against the practice.[12]

- At the dawn of the twentieth century, a new generation of journalists dubbed "muckrakers" gave voice to reform at the local, state, and federal levels. Their detailed investigation and exposure of corrupt power, ranging from child labor abuses to urban political machines and railroad and oil trusts, led to a progressive movement in national politics.

- As a fledgling effort at nonprofit journalism began to flower at organizations such as the Center for Public Integrity and its International Consortium of Investigative Journalists, one of the most successful was dedicated to investigative reporting, with an annual budget of $10 million. ProPublica, started by *Wall Street Journal* editors

Paul Steiger and Richard Tofel, recognized a powerful reality: While it might be difficult to cover a major metropolitan city with such resources, that amount of reporting talent could powerfully augment the investigative might of partner news organizations around the country and serve as a signal reminder to those in power that while the press itself was scaling back, as an investigative force it was still here.

As the practice of investigative journalism has matured, several forms have emerged. Today three main forms can be identified: original investigative reporting, interpretative investigative reporting, and reporting on investigations. Each bears some examination.

ORIGINAL INVESTIGATIVE REPORTING

Original investigative reporting involves reporters themselves uncovering and documenting activities that have been previously unknown to the public. This is the kind of investigative reporting that often results in official public investigations about the subject or activity exposed, a classic example of the press pushing public institutions on behalf of the public. It may involve tactics similar to police work, such as basic shoe-leather reporting, public records searches, use of informants, and even, in special circumstances, undercover work or surreptitious monitoring of activities.

Original investigative reporting would include the work of muckrakers like Lincoln Steffens, whose *Shame of the Cities* series in 1904 led to wide-ranging reforms in local government, or Rachel Carson, whose revelations of the effects of pesticide poisoning in her 1962 book *Silent Spring* launched an international movement to protect the environment.

It would also include the reporting of Marcus Stern and Jerry Kammer, whose Pulitzer Prize–winning investigation in 2005 and 2006 for the *San Diego Union-Tribune* led to the resignation from office and eventual criminal conviction on corruption charges of Congressman Randy "Duke" Cunningham.[13] Using his own unique system that he called a "lifestyle audit," Stern became suspicious of relationships between some of the congressman's travel and his style of living. Digging into campaign contributions from defense contractors, Stern uncovered other suspicious financial exchanges. He enlisted Kammer's help, and the two eventually pulled on these strings to unravel what was later described by the U.S. Attorney's Office in San Diego as "the most audacious bribery scheme" in congressional history.

In modern original investigative reporting, the power of computer analysis often replaces the personal observation of the reporter. In 2010, as an example, the *Las Vegas Sun* produced a series called "Do No Harm," which through the use of computer-assisted techniques analyzed millions of hospital billing records to identify thousands of preventable injuries and mistakes. Such empirical proof would have been impossible years earlier. Following the series, the Nevada legislature passed six health care reform and transparency bills.

INTERPRETATIVE INVESTIGATIVE REPORTING

The second form of investigative reporting is interpretative reporting, which often involves the same original enterprise skills but takes the interpretation to a different level. The fundamental difference between the two is that original investigative reporting uncovers information never before gathered by others in order to inform the public of events or circumstances that might affect their lives. Interpretative reporting develops as the result of careful thought and analysis of an idea as well as dogged pursuit of facts to bring together information in a new, more complete context that provides deeper public understanding. It usually involves more complex issues or sets of facts than a classic exposé. It reveals a new way of looking at something as well as new information about it.

One early example is the *New York Times* publication of the Pentagon Papers in 1971. The Papers themselves were a secret study of American involvement in Vietnam written by the government. Reporter Neil Sheehan went to great lengths to track down a copy.

Then a team of *New York Times* reporters and editors expert in foreign policy and the Vietnam War interpreted and organized the documents into a dramatic account of public deception. Without this synthesis and interpretation, the Pentagon Papers would have meant little to most of the public.

A more recent example is a ten-part series on social class that the *New York Times* published in 2005. Using available demographic and socioeconomic data, a team of reporters explored "ways that class—defined as a combination of income, education, wealth and occupation—influences destiny in a society that likes to think of itself as a land of unbounded opportunity."[14]

Some journalists have pushed the boundaries of interpretative investigative work to higher levels. Airliners and many other public spaces today have heart defibrillators because journalist John Crewdson while at the *Chicago Tribune* established conclusively that they would save lives—at a time when U.S. airlines resisted the idea because they feared the liability of putting the equipment in the planes. At the *Philadelphia Inquirer* and, later, *Time* magazine, Donald Barlett and James Steele ambitiously explored the roots of elaborate social and economic conditions in America in projects such as "America: What Went Wrong" and "America: Who Stole the Dream?" Both of these multi-part series probed how the U.S. economic-political system had failed lower-income citizens. Both were the result of years of reporting, an intense examination of economic data, and hundreds of interviews. Both series operated under the premise that the country was leaving its poor behind.

The pieces were so interpretative that some journalists condemned them as polemics rather than journalism—suggesting the authors had abandoned the role of engaged, independent observer to become activists. *Newsweek*'s Bob Samuelson called "America: Who Stole the Dream?" "junk journalism" because it "does not seek a balanced picture of the economy—strengths as well as shortcomings."[15]

The critics are right that these pieces were not balanced in the sense of giving both sides equal space. Barlett and Steele were attempting to expose an aspect of economic trends that had gone largely unnoticed and unreported by others, who were recording the impact on those at the top of the economic ladder, active players in the economic boom. Even some journalists who praised the work believed the first series, "What Went Wrong," had more documentary evidence than the second. Evidence that the disclosures in the first series were a revelation to many people was the lines in the *Inquirer* lobby of people waiting for reprints, and that the paper received some ninety thousand calls in the first week. "We've never seen anything like it," said then *Inquirer* executive Arlene Morgan. People were more critical of the second series, and *Inquirer* editor Maxwell King turned the editorial pages into a public forum for critics on all sides. While the first series was better than the second because of the level of documentation, both succeeded in stirring public conversation about enormously important subjects.

Seen in retrospect, the series and the criticism about the work raise fascinating and important questions about the future of journalism in the twenty-first century. The criticisms point out how important it is for people engaged in this level of interpretive investigation to provide sufficient outlet for alternative views.[16] When they appeared, opening the opinion pages up of the host newspaper in this way was considered an innovative break with the norm–and one that increased public engagement. Today, the Web makes the potential for this level of public reaction and criticism easier, richer, more typical–even expected. The bigger question is what news organization, if any, would have the resources to or would allow two of its best reporters years to work on a single series. The answer is likely none. While Barlett and Steele were unusual even at the time, at the peak of their influence a number of top news organizations–the *New York Times,* the *Los Angeles Times,* and *CBS News* are just three examples–freed reporters for what today seem astonishingly long periods of time to dig into stories simply because they mattered. The expectation, assumed if not proven, was that such work would add to the "brand" of a news organization in the public mind. That notion has largely vanished today and stands as one clear loss to come from the fragmentation of audience and the democratization of news-providing sources.

At the same time, various people still produce journalism that amounts to what scholar Matthew Nisbet at American University has called "Knowledge Journalism," work of such depth, expertise, and interpretive force that it reshapes the public debate on issues in the way that Barlett and Steele or Crewdson did earlier. Writers such as Bill McKibben, Andrew Revkin, and Malcolm Gladwell and Jane Mayer at the *New Yorker* combine deep reporting with significant subject expertise and produce work that is designed to change public knowledge. These knowledge journalists stand apart not only in the depth of their reporting and the level of their interpretation but also in the nature of that interpretation, Nisbet argues. "Knowledge journalists employ a unique orientation in their writing towards an 'expert logic' that analyzes problems deductively and a 'political logic' that criticizes the status quo and often seeks support for policy solutions. Moreover, they often distance themselves from the 'media logic' of their peers, criticizing the tendency of journalists to define problems in terms of conflict, drama, and personalities, to falsely balance claims, or to present policy options in terms of just a few choices."[17]

The work may come in the form of books, e-books, magazine work, online projects, and more. In general, this work is highly personal. The commitment required involves a deep passion, expertise, and perseverance on the part of the writer, and often significant creativity about how to assemble the time and resources to do the work, whether it involves research grants, teaching positions, or other factors. McKibben, who writes about the environment, teaches at Middlebury College and lives in a place where his costs are much less. (McKibben also has engaged in advocacy work, operating a group called 350.org, trying to stop the Keystone oil pipeline, activity that pushes against the boundary of the committed observer.) Revkin left the *New York Times* in 2009 after fifteen years to become a senior fellow at Pace University and write a blog, Dot Earth, for the *Times* opinion pages. Gladwell has the rare advantage of working for the *New Yorker*.

What is less clear is how often, or whether, any community-based news operation has the wherewithal to finance and sponsor such work as the Pentagon Papers or "America: What Went Wrong," as the *New York Times,* the *Washington Post,* and the *Philadelphia Inquirer* once did. Will the handful of new news institutions that have grown in the twenty-first century, such as Bloomberg News (for which journalism is a sweetening element that distinguishes but is not fundamental to its real revenue source, financial and governmental data for business) engage in such deep and expensive journalism? Or will watchdog journalism increasingly be the province of outlets that depend on charitable dollars, such as ProPublica and InsideClimate News? The answer is not yet clear, but the trends suggest the answer leans toward nonprofits.

REPORTING ON INVESTIGATIONS

The third investigative category is reporting on investigations, a development that has become more common in recent years. In this case the reporting develops from a discovery or leak of information from an official investigation already under way or in preparation by others, usually government agencies. It is a staple of journalism in Washington, a city where the government often talks to itself through the press. But reporting on investigations is found wherever official investigators are at work. Government investigators actively cooperate with reporters in these cases for many reasons: to affect budget appropriations, to influence potential witnesses, and to shape public opinion.

Most of the reporting on President Clinton's affair with Monica Lewinsky was actually reporting on the investigation of Independent Prosecutor Kenneth Starr's office, augmented by counterinformation leaked by the White House or lawyers for those going before the grand jury. The reporting that security guard Richard Jewell had planted the bomb at the 1996 Atlanta Olympics was similarly based on anonymous leaks from police and FBI sources and proved to be mistaken. In contrast, most of the work on Watergate, especially in the early critical months, was original investigative work in which the journalists were talking directly with principal sources about what had happened, not with investigators about what they theorized had happened.

Reporting on investigations proliferated after the 1970s. In part, this was because the number of investigations had grown, particularly in Congress, where investigating the misdeeds of the rival party became common, particularly if one of the congressional chambers was controlled by a different party than the White House. In part, this was because after Watergate, federal and state governments passed new ethics laws and created special offices to monitor government behavior. But it also spread because over time journalists came to depend on unidentified sources to the point where the practice became a concern both among journalists and a suspicious public. Relying on government officials to do the investigating seemed safer for some news organizations than cultivating unofficial anonymous sources.

In an article about the secretive National Security Agency (NSA), the primary collector of electronic intelligence for the U.S. government, reporter Seymour Hersh, writing in the *New Yorker,* quoted anonymous intelligence officers about how the deteriorating quality of the NSA's work left it unable to meet the threats of sophisticated terrorist groups and rogue states. Whitfield Diffie, an encryption expert at Sun Microsystems, was quick to seize on the vulnerability of Hersh's anonymous methods: "What bothers me is that you are saying what the agency wants us to believe–[that] they used to be great, but these days they have trouble reading the newspaper, the Internet is too complicated for them, there is too much traffic and they can't find what they want. It may be true, but it is what they have been 'saying' for years. It's convenient for NSA to have its targets believe it is in trouble. That doesn't mean it isn't in trouble, but it is a reason to view what spooky inside informants say with skepticism."[18]

The risk of this reporting, as Diffie pointed out, is that its value is largely dependent on the rigor and skepticism of the reporter involved. The reporter is granting the interview subject a powerful forum in which to air an allegation or float a suggestion without public accountability. This does not mean that reporting on investigations is inherently wrong. But it is fraught with sometimes unforeseeable risks. The reporters here usually are privy to only part of the investigation, rather than in charge of it.

The *New York Times* learned that lesson when it broke a story on nuclear espionage drawn from a secret congressional report. The *Times* story picked up the alarming language of the report and said that China was catching up with American nuclear technology because it had obtained data on building warheads from a Chinese-American scientist, Wen Ho Lee. The *Times* did not name Lee, but it did allow authorities to characterize the scandal as the biggest in recent history. The story led investigators to rush into getting an indictment against Lee, who was eventually jailed for one year. Out of the fifty-nine counts brought against him, he pleaded guilty to one: illegally gathering and retaining national security information. He was sentenced to time served by a judge who issued a profound apology from the bench. The *Times* also printed a lengthy correction apologizing for taking so much of the report for granted and not giving Lee the benefit of the doubt.[19]

The chance of being manipulated by investigatory sources is high. Instead of being a watchdog of powerful institutions, the press is vulnerable to becoming their tool. Reporting on investigations requires enormous due diligence. Paradoxically, news outlets often think just the opposite—that they can more freely report the suspicions or allegations because they are quoting official sources rather than carrying out the investigation themselves.

Tom Patterson, the Benjamin C. Bradlee professor at the John F. Kennedy School of Government at Harvard, documented the shifting standards that gave rise to this new category of investigative journalism. "What we see in the studies," he told us, "is that by the late 1970s we find a substitute for careful, deep investigative reporting—allegations that surface in the news based on claims by sources that are not combined with factual digging on the reporters' part. That tendency increased in the 1980s, increased again in the 1990s, and the mix began to change. The use of unnamed and anonymous sources becomes a larger proportion of the total."[20]

Investigative reporter and author Jim Risen has argued that most investigative reporting involves elements of all three forms. Woodward and Bernstein, for instance, regularly checked in with government investigators as they worked on their own inquiry. Yet there are distinctions between whether a reporter's work is fundamentally original, interpretative, or about someone else's investigation, and it is important to recognize them—particularly for those engaged in the work. Each type of reporting carries its own distinct responsibilities and risks. Too often, though, journalists have not been sufficiently mindful of or careful about the differences.

THE WATCHDOG ROLE WEAKENED

In the ebb and flow of the watchdog role over the last two centuries, we also reached a moment of diminution by dilution. The celebrity of Woodward and Bernstein was followed by the success of *60 Minutes,* in which correspondents Mike Wallace, Morley Safer, Harry Reasoner, and Ed Bradley, succeeded by later generations, became stars in their own reports. People tuned in to see who Mike, Morley, Harry, and Ed would catch this week. Investigative journalism, particularly on television, thus became a means both for public good and for commercial ratings. In the nearly thirty years since, the proliferation of outlets for news and information has been accompanied by a torrent of investigative reportage. With most local news stations in America now featuring an "I-team" and prime time newsmagazines offering the promise of nightly exposés, we have created a permanent infrastructure of news devoted to exposure.

Much of this reportage has the earmarks of watchdog reporting, but too often the stories focus on risks to personal safety or consumer pocketbooks, not to citizens' freedoms. Among some popular topics of local television I-teams over the years have been: crooked car mechanics, poor swimming pool lifeguarding, sex slave rings, housecleaning scams, and dangerous teenage drivers.

At the peak of network prime time newsmagazines in the late 1990s, for instance, a study revealed a genre of investigative reporting that ignored most of the matters typically associated with the watchdog role of the press. Fewer than one in ten stories on these programs concerned the combined topics of education, economics, foreign affairs, the military, national security, politics, and social welfare—or any of the areas where most public money was spent. More than half the stories, rather, focused on lifestyle, behavior, consumerism, health, or celebrity entertainment.[21] Victor Neufeld, then executive producer of ABC's *20/20,* told us, "Our obligation is not to deliver the news. Our obligation is to do good programming."[22]

Safety can often be an important target for intense and critical watchdog reporting. Yet too much of the new "investigative" reporting is tabloid treatment of everyday circumstances. Local television news often employs its I-teams in such stories as "dangerous doors"—reporting on the hazards of opening and closing doors; or "inside your washing machine"—a look at how dirt and bacteria on the clothes consumers put in their washers get on other clothes. Consider the Los Angeles TV station that rented a house for two months and wired it with a raft of hidden cameras to expose that you really can't get all the carpeting in your house cleaned for $7.95. Or the series of reports, popular in the mid-1990s, about a bra whose metal wires could poke the owner.

While this reporting frequently is presented in a way that makes it look like original investigative work, it often is not. First, much of it is what TV reporter Liz Leamy called "just add water" investigative reporting. These reports come from TV news consultants who literally offer stations the scripts, the shots, and the experts to interview, or the interviews themselves already on tape, and are specifically designed to generate ratings during sweeps periods. Some TV news producers call such exposés "stunting," an acknowledgment that they are playing tricks with viewers' appreciation of investigative work without actually doing the legwork required to deliver it. Another problem is that exposing what is readily understood or simply common sense belittles investigative journalism. The press becomes the boy who cried wolf. It is squandering its ability to demand the public's attention because it has done so too many times about trivial matters. It has turned watchdogism into a form of amusement.

The significance of this shift should not be underestimated. On television, which is still the most popular medium for news, I-team segments and prime time magazines effectively replaced the documentary or any other long-form investigative reportage. As a consequence, some journalists began to question the expanded role of investigative journalism. Patty Calhoun, editor of *Westword*, an alternative newspaper in Denver, Colorado, wondered about the impact on a public that had no way of discerning between gossip and fact when she observed: "Talk radio ... puts out rumors and now thinks they're doing investigative reporting–which is novel–but unfortunately, their listeners can't tell any better than the radio DJs that they're not."[23]

Public perceptions of the watchdog role tend to be complex. For years, the survey work of Andrew Kohut for the Pew Research Center for the People & the Press found public support of the watchdog role remaining stable while the press in general began to become more unpopular. But the support was not unreserved. By 1997, Kohut found the public objecting to techniques such as having reporters not identify themselves as reporters, paying informers for information, and using hidden cameras or microphones.[24] Over two decades, similarly, the public developed more doubts about press criticism of the military. The number of people who believed such reportage weakened the nation's defenses rose from 28 percent in 1985 to 47 percent in 2005. Yet as questions arose about the government's handling of the war in Iraq, public support began to rise for watchdog journalism that covered political leaders. By 2005, 60 percent of Americans thought news organizations kept political leaders from doing things they shouldn't, up from 54 percent in 2003.[25] In short, despite enormous misgivings about how the people engaged in journalism go about their work, and doubts about nearly every other dimension of press behavior, support for the watchdog role of the press remains remarkably high, if not unqualified.

INVESTIGATIVE REPORTING AS PROSECUTION

Although all reporting involves investigation, investigative journalism adds a moral dimension. It engages the public to make a judgment about the information disclosed, and implies that the news organization considers it important—worthy of special effort. In that sense, investigative reporting usually involves not simply casting light on a subject but also making a more prosecutorial case, based on an observation that something is wrong. Here, journalists should be careful that they have enough evidence to do so, especially since pieces can be structured as either exposés or news stories. Playing fast and loose with the claim of exposing wrongdoing without the evidence to support the claim is an abuse of the audience for your work. This is particularly important in an age when various actors, from think tanks, nonprofits, and independent websites, have entered into the realm of investigative reporting that does not apply journalistic standards of verification and transparency.

The prosecutorial dimension of investigative reporting requires a higher level of proof, and this can be best seen by examining stories that fell short of that level. When questions arose about a state medical examiner who failed to thoroughly investigate the conduct of President Clinton's mother in a wrongful-death case (she was a nurse), the *Los Angeles Times* wrote the story as an exposé. The story suggested that when Clinton was governor of Arkansas, he "refused for several years to dismiss a state medical examiner whose controversial decrees included a ruling that helped Clinton's mother ... avoid scrutiny in the death of a patient." The problem was the story was inherently confusing and technical. Clinton, for instance, having been defeated for reelection as governor, was out of office at the time of the incident involving his mother. A good many reporters at the *Times,* even some involved in reporting it, believed the whole controversy could have been avoided if the paper had simply written the story as a feature about a curious piece out of Clinton's past, instead of as an exposé. The *Times* failed to understand that an exposé is in effect a prosecutor's brief, and the case it sets forth must be unambiguous; if the story does not meet this test, it should be written as something else.

The incident points out an important issue that arises with the investigative model: The news outlet is taking an implied stance on the issue that some wrongdoing has occurred. That is why investigative journalism has been called advocacy reporting, or as journalist

Les Whitten said, "reporting with a sense of outrage," and why the acronym for the professional association called Investigative Reporters and Editors spells out the word *ire*.

To fulfill the watchdog principle responsibly, Bob Woodward has said, one key is to keep an open mind. "You might start a story thinking you are going to look at how the city health department administers vaccines, but ... find that the story's really about the city's mismanagement in general.... Look at as much as you can in every direction." To do so, "some of the things I do are build a chronology, try to talk to everybody and interview them repeatedly."

Pulitzer Prize winner Loretta Tofani relied on the power of talking to potential sources face-to-face and spending a lot of time with them. In a story about a pattern of widespread rape inside a Maryland jail, which she wrote while at the *Washington Post,* she uncovered crimes that were occurring literally under the nose of law officers–crimes widely known to the police and judges. To get the story, she spent months of her own time in the evenings after work doggedly knocking on doors in order to convince some of the most reluctant possible witnesses to talk to her, and she was able to produce a series of stories that documented the prevalence of rape inside the Prince George's Detention Center in Maryland. In the end, Tofani produced what her editors thought impossible: a story documenting the crimes by quoting, by name and on the record, the perpetrators, the victims, and the responsible officials who should have acted to prevent the crimes from ever taking place.

As Tofani said, when the articles were published, all the needed documentation was "given to the government basically on a silver platter.... It had everything. It had medical records. It had the victims' names. It had the rapists' names."[26] Public disclosure of the information forced the government to change the system that allowed the rapes to occur. In the end, the government convicted all the rapists.

Investigative reporter Susan Kelleher also said that, before a source agrees to an interview, she tells the source up front everything that is involved in an investigative report. "I tell them how I work," she says. "I tell them they have to go on the record. I tell them I am going to be asking other people about them, that even though I find them really nice people, I am going to have to check them out. . . . I say to them, 'Once you agree to talk to me, that's it. You don't really have control, but you do have control to the degree you want to participate. And once you are on the record, if there's something you don't want me to know, then don't tell me because it's going to be on the record.'"[27]

This level of honesty with sources allowed Kelleher to uncover some remarkable stories. One exposed abuses at an infertility clinic where some doctors were secretly, and illegally, taking extra eggs from their patients and selling them to other patients. Kelleher's story was meticulously documented with medical records and on-the-record information by people involved in the process. And, like Tofani's report, this one won a Pulitzer Prize.

As the twenty-first-century revolutions in technology and economic organization create new opportunities, they also threaten an independent watchdog press in two different, seemingly contradictory ways. One way is that as news itself struggles to generate revenue, newsrooms are shrinking and the resources available for watchdog reporting—and the time it takes to do it well—have become scarcer. Large newsrooms whose leaders value expensive, long-form investigative work because of the prestige it adds to a news brand are disappearing. Work that cannot be justified by an increasingly challenged bottom line becomes harder to produce.

At the same time, digital communications that allow information to move more easily and quickly have led to the creation of large national and international financial combines in which journalism plays a small part in a large financial portfolio. In some cases these are publicly traded corporations such as Disney (owner of ABC News) or Comcast (NBC News, and its related parts), or large privately held newspaper chains such as Digital First (which is owned by the private hedge fund investment firm Alden Global Capital and controls by one count 77 dailies and more than 130 non-dailies).

One of the important and often overlooked elements of journalistic independence in America is that, historically, news was produced by companies whose primary business was journalism. The smaller part of any company balance sheet or owner portfolio that news is, the more difficult it is, inevitably and by degrees, for those who work there to claim journalistic independence. It becomes more difficult for an ABC News producer to cover not only Disney, but also any other Web, e-commerce, entertainment, cable, or tele-communications company that might be a competitor with ABC's owner.

The theory of a free press as we know it—that there should be an independent voice that can monitor the influence of powerful institutions in society—is put into question. "[These] mergers in the media business matter in ways that other takeovers don't," Rifka Rosenwein wrote in 2000, in an article examining a wave of media mergers prior to the first burst in the tech bubble. "Having five or six major widget companies may be enough to safeguard the price and product competition with which traditional economic theory and antitrust law have been concerned. But concentrating much of the power to create and distribute news and ideas in five or six media conglomerates with a vast array of interests raises all kinds of other issues. There is, after all, a virtue in diversity, lots of it, when it comes to expression that transcends widget economic theory."[28] Some of those first mergers, such as Time Warner AOL, failed, but they were replaced a decade later by another wave, as new owners sought the refuge of bigness.

History promises that a market economy in an open society has the capacity to correct its mistakes organically. And there are signs of a market response to concerns about the loss of independence in American journalism. Consider that in 2013, the Pulitzer Prize Board awarded the coveted prize for national reporting to InsideClimate News, a seven-person website based in Brooklyn that relies on foun-dations and individual donations to fund its work. And a 2013 Pew Research Center study of nonprofit news organizations found that almost every state has a nonprofit newsroom and that, of those sur-veyed, a solid majority expected to hire more staff in the coming year and believed they would continue to be financially solvent five years down the road.[29]

As interesting as these new efforts are, though, they are fragile and embryonic, especially when compared with mainstream journalism. The support of private philanthropy can disappear as quickly as it can be given, and these outlets' ability to draw an audience depends on getting the attention of for-profit media to air their research.

The rise of new independent journalism outlets shows how the new technology could reorganize the way news is produced and communicated. Potentially, it suggests that if the old media abandon the watchdog role in any serious sense, others might take it up. Even a lone hacker rummaging through the databases now has the ability to shape or even dictate the flow of news, if what the hacker unearths is important enough (Edward Snowden and the NSA).

But there are more practical economic questions still unanswered. Investigative journalism is distinct from the witness-bearing role of the press we outlined earlier, in chapter 1. It tends to require special reporting skills, experience, and temperament. More often than not, revelation comes not from a single document suddenly found, but from discoveries slowly earned–winning the trust of sources, noticing a fragment of information, recognizing its possibilities, triangulating that with fragments from other information, fitting the pieces together, and establishing proof to a level that will satisfy lawyers. This work usually requires access, significant commitments of time and resources, independence from other interests, and also libel insurance. All of these special characteristics of investigative reporting combine to make it likely that it will remain primarily the product of organized professional journalism–not the random or lone whistleblower.

In that sense, digital start-ups populated by professional journalists, such as ProPublica or InsideClimate News, seem more likely to be the new model for investigative reporting than crowd-sourced models such as WikiLeaks. It is too soon to know whether ProPublica and InsideClimate News, which depend on charitable donations, will sustain themselves, or at what level.

But it is no accident that the rise of investigative modern reporting in the 1960s coincided with the growing financial strength of news organizations in print and television. The collapse of that model raises substantial questions about whether investigative journalism will continue on the level that we have come to know.

One positive sign is that more enlightened legacy news organizations such as the *New York Times*, the *Washington Post*, and the *Guardian* have begun to incorporate the public as part of their information-gathering staff in organized ways. It may be only a matter of time before some of these hurdles can be overcome and verified investigative reporting will become more diverse. We will discuss this more in the next chapter.

The strongest possibilities lie in the new approach to journalism we have described, one in which the community plays a significant role as partner, not substitute, to the professional investigative journalist. The community also has a significant role as sentinel over journalistic integrity. For that to happen, however, established news organizations must learn how to work with the worldwide audience with which they can now interact, extract from its guidance on matters that need to be brought to light, and distill its expertise in developing their professional reporting. At the same time they need to help develop among that audience a deeper understanding of what constitutes journalistic integrity. If either the news organization or the participating audience confuses independent investigative reporting with propagandistic activism masquerading as investigation, then our new and deeper public discourse will inevitably slide toward endless argument. Facts, instead of helping form the foundation of our public discourse, will become elements that combatants use to confuse issues and create uncertainty rather than understanding.

Journalism as
a Public Forum

C ody Shearer had just returned from a trip to Europe when he sat down one Tuesday night to watch television. The Washington freelance journalist cruised across channels, stopping on a cable news channel, and watched a few minutes of the talk show *Hardball* with host Chris Matthews.

The year was 1999, and the story dominating Washington was the potential impeachment of President Bill Clinton. At the center of the impeachment scandal, at least legally, was whether Clinton had lied to special prosecutor Kenneth Starr during a deposition probing whether the President had had sexual relations in the White House with an intern named Monica Lewinsky.

Matthews's guest on his talk show that night was Kathleen Willey, a woman who claimed President Clinton had groped her in the White House. They were discussing Willey's claim that someone had tried to silence her by threatening her.

As he watched, Shearer suddenly realized that the topic of the interview was not the President or Willey's allegation–it was Shearer himself.

CHRIS MATTHEWS: When this man came up to you in–at dawn that morning, in Richmond five years after this incident, who was that guy? I'm gonna ask you again, because I think you know who it was.

KATHLEEN WILLEY: I do know. I think I know.

MATTHEWS: Why don't you tell me who it was? This is an important part of the story here, why would you want—come out and—on this program tonight on live television and not tell us who you think that person was? . . . Let me ask you a more careful way. Were you ever led to believe who it might be, and who led you to believe it and what did they lead you to believe?

WILLEY: I was shown a picture and—

MATTHEWS: And who was in the picture?

WILLEY: I can't tell you. I'm not trying to be coy—

MATTHEWS: Would I recognize the picture?

WILLEY: Yes.

MATTHEWS: Is it someone in the President's family, friends? Is it somebody related to Strobe Talbott? Is it a Shearer?

WILLEY: I've been asked not to dis—

MATTHEWS: You've been asked not to admit that?

WILLEY: Yes, by—

MATTHEWS: OK.

With a sinking stomach, Shearer knew what Matthews was getting at. A rumor had been floating around Washington that it was Shearer who had approached Willey while she was jogging and that he had threatened her if she didn't drop her case against the President. The rumor was unsubstantiated. It was also untrue. Shearer had been in California when the encounter had supposedly taken place, but no one had bothered to check out that part of the story. Now he could only watch as Matthews made the false rumor public knowledge and sound like fact.

MATTHEWS: Let's go back to the jogger, one of the most colorful and frightening aspects of this story. You were confronted as you were out walking. You couldn't sleep, your neck was hurting—this guy came upon you you never met before—You never met him before.

WILLEY: No.

MATTHEWS: And tell me about that—what he said, finish up that whole story.

WILLEY: Well, he mentioned my children by name. He asked how they were and, at the—at this point, I started asking him who he was and what he wanted. And he just looked me right in the eye and he said, "You're just not getting the message, are you?" And I turned around and—and ran. I had no business running, and probably ran about 100 yards, I was so frightened, and I turned around and he was gone.

MATTHEWS: Who showed you the picture of the person you think might have been him?

WILLEY: Jackie Judd.

MATTHEWS: From ABC?

WILLEY: Yes.

MATTHEWS: And did you identify it positively?

WILLEY: Yes.

MATTHEWS: So it's Cody Shearer.

WILLEY: I can't tell you.

MATTHEWS: OK. But you identified it pos—Let's talk about a couple of other things just to tie up the loose ends here.[1]

The show had been over for only a few minutes when the first phone call came. It was an anonymous deep voice, and it was threatening Shearer's life. Shearer was shaken by the call, but he figured it was only a crank who had gotten charged up by the *Hardball* show. Then, however, came a second call. And a third. Shearer began to grow concerned.

The next day conservative talk radio host Rush Limbaugh broadcast the rumor: "She says Ken Starr asked her not to reveal the identity of the man who she says threatened her two days before her testimony in the Paula Jones case. . . . Here's who it is: It's Cody Shearer, S-H-E-A-R-E-R."[2]

Limbaugh had an even greater impact. Call after call came in that day to Shearer's house, nearly a hundred, nearly all of them threatening death or physical harm. Though the story was demonstrably untrue, that night on *Hardball* Matthews reprised some of the Willey interview and played a clip of his "scoop" for his panel of guests.

Shearer left town for a few days and tried to forget the incident. Washington was a town with attention deficit disorder, he figured. In a week or so, no one would care about this.

He was wrong. Sunday morning, back in Washington, Shearer was taking a shower when a houseguest ran into his bathroom and said there was a man in his yard with a gun claiming he had come to kill Shearer. Shearer thought it was a joke, until he came out and saw the man, with a gun aimed directly at another friend and demanding to see him.

Suddenly, inexplicably, the gunman ran to his car and fled. Shearer and his friends copied down the license plate number and called the police. An hour later the police delivered the weird incident's even weirder denouement. The crazed gunman was Hank Buchanan, the brother of Patrick Buchanan, the former talk show host and GOP and Reform Party presidential candidate. Hank Buchanan had a history of mental illness.

Most of all, Shearer was appalled by Chris Matthews. "If I made a mistake like that, I would have sat down and written a letter explaining I was on a tight deadline and apologizing," Shearer said. "But I got nothing, not even from the producer.... And the most amazing thing is that nothing happened to him. He was back on the air the next night."[3]

The two met on a train a few days after the broadcast but before the Buchanan incident. They argued heatedly, according to Shearer, and he thought Matthews was unapologetic. After receiving letters from Shearer's attorney, Matthews made an on-air apology that included the attorney's assertion that Shearer "had nothing whatever to do with the events described by Ms. Willey."

"I now regret having spoken–not spoken–beforehand with him [Shearer] before I mentioned his name on the air. I should have never brought his name up till we had vetted it," Matthews said on his program. The words, however, were something less than a correction. They also failed to acknowledge that the story was untrue.

The case of Chris Matthews and Cody Shearer offers a caution for understanding the next element of journalism. From its origins in the Greek marketplace to the colonial American taverns, journalism has always been a forum for public discourse. As far back as 1947, the Hutchins Commission placed this mission as an essential obligation of the craft, second only to telling the truth. "The great agencies of mass communication should regard themselves as common carriers of public discussion," the commission wrote.[4]

This is the sixth principle or duty of a free press:

Journalism must provide a forum for public criticism and compromise.

New technology has made the forum more robust and journalism less paternal. But as the Shearer incident suggested even in the earliest days of the Web's influence, a time when things moved far slower than today, the forum's greater speed and velocity today also bring with them an increased power to distort, mislead, and overwhelm the other functions of a free press. And this tension between the forum's ability to self-correct and the speed with which false information can spread has only increased with the expansion of social media. Inevitably, as citizen involvement grows, more of our media culture is concerned with talking about news, instead of focusing on original reporting and the vetting of it.

In chapter 2, on truth, we examined the natural forum the first periodicals provided and its relationship to the creation of public opinion. With the reporting of details of events, the disclosure of wrongdoing, or the outlining of a developing trend, news sets people to wondering. A modern media culture re-creates over long distances something akin to the face-to-face forum in the Athenian agora and Roman markets where the world's earliest democracies were formed.

Today, the forum is so pervasive that it informs almost every aspect of gathering and reporting news. At the *Guardian* in England, reporters and editors are expected to keep Twitter open as they work so that they can track what others are delivering on the subject each reporter and editor is covering and so that they can know what people are saying about it. The conversation about news and its gathering has become simultaneous and public. The discussion about implications, meaning, and next steps begins before many members of the public have heard the initial report. During a breaking news event such as the hunt for bombers at the Boston Marathon in April 2013, the analysis of reporting mistakes by CNN and the AP, or false rumors on the social media site Reddit, were cycling through parts of the news ecosystem well before many in the public or even in some newsrooms knew such mistakes had been made.

In many ways the notion that there is something that can be called a general news cycle has become impossible. The real issue is not that the news cycle is continuous but that it is asynchronous. We do not learn at the same time. Each of us has a personal news cycle, and it may change day to day, based on our own behavior, our personal community of friends, the network of people we follow, and some element of randomness. And while that was to a lesser degree always true, now the speed and variation of our digital media culture mean we never catch up. The concept of taking stock, of determining what facts are in evidence, established and vetted, is complex to the point of seeming obsolete. Everything is in motion, since each of us is learning in a different individualized space and at a different time. Any stock taking must be personal and individualized as well. Our asynchrony is constant.

None of this is lost on advocacy groups or political parties, which want to exploit this new political *Rashomon*. Every year millions of dollars are spent trying to sway public opinion, often with half-truths, sometimes with outright lies. That makes it all the more crucial that the news media play the role of honest broker and referee as they carry the common discussion. In the new age of media, it is more incumbent on those who aspire to provide us with a responsible journalism that serves the public interest that they decipher the spin and lies of commercialized argument, lobbying, and political propaganda—that they vet what is true and attempt to take stock, rather than simply inflame or hitchhike on controversy to attract a crowd. The editorial pages of the newspaper, the opinion columnist, the talk show, the point-of-view magazine essay, bloggers, any of us who engage in social media, and anyone else have every right to be opinionated. But if the authors of this intelligence want to call their work journalism, then it follows that they should not misrepresent the facts–that they should hold to the highest standards of truthfulness and allegiance to public interest.

So journalism must provide a forum for public criticism, and in a new age, it is more important, not less, that this public discussion be built on the same principles as the rest of journalism–starting with truthfulness, facts, and verification. A forum without regard for facts fails to inform, and a debate steeped in prejudice and supposition only inflames.

Just as important, this forum must be available to all parts of the community, not just those who are most vocal and thus most present in social media, or those who are demographically attractive to those selling goods and services.

Finally, there is another element to understand about the public forum that news creates: A debate focused only on the extremes of argument does not serve the public but instead leaves most citizens out. Even as our news media and public discourse give air to the wide variation of opinions that reflects a society as pluralist as ours, we must not lose sight of the fact that democracies are, in the end, built on compromise. The public forum must include the broad areas of agreement where most of the public resides and where the solutions to society's problems are found.

Some people might consider this argument for stewardship anachronistic–and more than a little elitist–a leftover from an era when only a few outlets controlled public access to information. In a new century, with its new communications technologies, isn't it enough for Matthews to let Willey speak and then let Shearer respond? Why not get the journalist mediator out of the way and let the debate occur in the genuine public square, not the artificial one defined by NBC or CBS News? The Web is a self-cleaning oven. You need not worry about it. This is where the technology-versus-journalism debate comes to its clearest philosophical divide.

It is true that we have the potential today for a more open debate than in the past. And it is appealing to think that technology will do the fact-checking for us, that we can trust the larger market-place of facts and ideas, not journalists, to sort out the truth. Each one of us can now simply pass along what we have heard without checking it. If it's wrong, it will get found out somehow. The promise of social media, and its extraordinary ability to help us learn quickly from many sources, seemingly adds to the promise. The limits of a few flawed gatekeepers, the problems of group think, establishment bias, cultural blinders, and false consensus are now overcome, it should seem, by mathematical progression.

There is a problem, however, with this notion of automatic fact-checking. It is a form of passing the buck. It increases the likelihood that people will be misled, even if things are later corrected. And it is based on the theoretical hope in the network.

But does the hope that mistakes will be quickly noticed and corrected in an open forum absolve publishers of responsibility for passing along false information? How will the media system self-correct if everyone feels they are absolved of fact-checking? By what criteria, for instance, is a host of Public Broadcasting's *NewsHour*, such as Gwen Ifill, freed of the obligation to engage in the discipline of verification as she conducts a live interview with someone making unchecked allegations? More channels? Interactivity? The prospect of infinite links? While this notion might seem liberating—why do the hard work when technology will do it for me, especially when newsroom resources have shrunk and I have less time to report?—in the real-world marketplace of communication and political culture, it isn't true. Social science research on how information is shared in social networks makes clear that there are still influencers, those with more followers and more impact, and that their influence is often ideological and based on information that may or may not have been thoroughly vetted. We are beginning to discover that while old oligarchies are being displaced, newer ones are rising to take their place.

The danger is that by assuming technology will replace responsibility, we will create a public square with a diminished regard for fact, fairness, and responsibility. Spin will replace verification. Right will become a matter of who has the greatest might, wattage, or rhetorical skill.

Already the public forum presented on television and radio has begun abdicating its responsibility to verify, relying on live interviews as their primary method of news delivery. The live interview format, as any newsmaker will happily acknowledge, cedes power to the interviewee. The guests control what they say, with broad power to mislead, talk over the host, or even lie. The journalist host, for all intents and purposes, has a limited ability to check or correct all but the most obvious deceptions. Although TV journalists may not realize it, they have structured their programs in such a way that facts are effectively vulnerable to whatever the guests on these programs feel they can sell.

THE FIRST SOCIAL MEDIA

Public discourse lies at the heart of, and actually predates, formal American journalism. Before the printing press, as we have said, "news" was something exchanged over a pint of ale in publick houses. News accounts weren't static printed words, and they didn't exist in a void; they were part of conversation. And though conversations obviously involved the exchange of information, much of the point was the exchange of ideas and opinions.

With the arrival of the printing press, this tradition did not disappear but was carried forward into the essays that filled the earliest newspapers. Noah Webster (whose dictionary first defined the term *editorial*) described this function in an "ADDRESS to the PUBLIC," published in the inaugural issue of his *American Minerva* (December 9, 1793): "Newspapers are not only the vehicles of what is called news; they are the common instruments of social intercourse, by which the Citizens of this vast Republic constantly discourse and debate with each other on subjects of public concern."[5]

In the eras that followed, journalism worked to keep alive the idea of an open forum with the public. When newspapers began to hire reporters and had more "news" to deliver, the editorial page became a place for community discussion through published letters to the editor and later the page opposite the editorials, usually written by readers. Publishers also kept the forum concept alive in more elementary ways. In 1840 the *Houston Star* was among the first newspapers to make its lobby more than an entryway into the newsroom; it became an open salon for the public. Residents were encouraged not only to come by but also to help themselves to "a good glass, an interesting paper and a pleasant cigar." In many cities, the tradition of the newspaper lobby as an inviting public reading room and salon continued for more than another hundred years. The newspaper was not only part of the community but also in a very concrete way a place for the community to gather and talk.[6]

Arguably, at its peak of power and sense of responsibility, the industrialized press grew too restrained. Newspaper editorial pages in the latter part of the twentieth century tended to be tweedy spaces better known for their earnestness than their passion. The conservative *Wall Street Journal* editorial pages of the 1980s and 1990s stood out most of all because they were staunch when most were dull.

Tom Winship, the editor of the *Boston Globe* from the 1960s to the 1980s, decided that at one point he had confused being restrained with being responsible. The *Globe* won a Pulitzer Prize for distinguished public service in 1973 for its coverage of the school busing crisis in Boston. Later, Winship concluded that he had made a critical mistake during the crisis when, out of fear that they would inflame the situation, he asked his columnists to refrain for two weeks from discussing the controversy. In retrospect, he concluded that the *Globe*'s columnists might have made constructive suggestions regarding details of the implementation of the plan. "Why didn't we question more vigorously the details of the busing plan?" he asked. "I think we became overwhelmed by the street demonstrations and the opposition assaults on the paper. . . . I have been plagued by my censorship of the paper's columnists."[7] What troubled Winship most, he explained, was that he failed to see the columnists as a tool for outreach, through which the paper could have helped some citizens work through the problem.

In the years since, of course, the public forum around the news has grown more robust. That early period of growing argument brought with it other lessons.

By the 1990s, the media had helped develop what linguist and author Deborah Tannen described as the "Argument Culture." It was led by television programs such as *Crossfire* on CNN, *The McLaughlin Group* on commercial television, and talk radio, but it reflected deeper changes that were occurring in culture and politics.

By 2000, in an average twenty-four-hour period, there were 178 hours of news and public affairs programming on television. About 40 percent of these hours were devoted to talk shows, many of them involving staged debates.[8]

Scholarly experiments at the time affirmed that if the same ideas were conveyed through heated argument and, on the other hand, more civil and dispassionate exchange, audiences preferred the drama of the argument.

But the rise of the Argument Culture was not grounded on social science research. It owed more to the fact that, quite literally, talk is cheap. The cost of producing a talk show is only a fraction of the cost of building a reporting infrastructure and delivering news.

Then there was the nature of the discussion itself that dominated the Argument Culture. The media's penchant for talk increasingly grew into a penchant for polarization and alarmism, instead of for journalism's mission of enlightening. On the theory that everyone likes a good fight, all problems began to be seen as unsolvable. Compromise was not presented as a legitimate option.

As far back as 1993, the late novelist Michael Crichton deconstructed the nature of the Argument Culture discourse: "We are all assumed these days to reside at one extreme of the opinion spectrum or another. We are pro-abortion, anti-abortion. We are free traders or protectionist. We are pro–private sector or pro–big government. We are feminists or chauvinists. But in the real world, few of us hold these extreme views. There is instead a spectrum of opinion."[9]

For all its pyrotechnic appeal, the Argument Culture didn't expand the scope of public discussion. It narrowed it. The Argument Culture tended to limit itself to subjects where there was a good fight to be had. And as the Web began to replace cable news as a venue for breaking news, cable talk shows began to narrow their focus even further, dealing increasingly with a single subject: politics. The reason for this is the paradox of fragmentation. As the public forum grows, the tendency at any one destination is toward specialization.

The social consequences of this fragmentation are obvious. The more time we spend in specialized forums, the more the public commons shrinks. This is the concept of the digital "filter bubble," the idea that with more diverse choices, we tend to dive into channels that we prefer, and the range of our learning shrinks. The reluctance of TV networks to broadcast key moments of public life, such as political conventions, and instead leaving that job to cable television, is only one sign. Yet the result is that the mass media no longer help identify a common set of issues. One of the most distinguishing features of American culture—the nation's ability to summon itself to face great challenges, as we did facing fascism or the Depression—becomes more doubtful. Dysfunctional breakdowns of government, such as the government shutdown of 2013, become more common and even accepted, since many of us are paying scant attention anyway.

The ironic effect of these characteristics of the new larger public—the diminished level of verification, the tendency of the filter bubble, the emphasis on an oversimplified, polarized debate—is that they tend to prevent journalism from accomplishing its most important purpose: providing people with the information they need to self-govern.

"Democracy is based on a fundamental compromise between the majority and the minority," Robert Berdahl, the former chancellor of the University of California at Berkeley, noted at the height of the Argument Culture era.[10] "Compromise, however, becomes impossible if every issue is raised to the level of a moral imperative" or "framed in a way to produce ultimate shock value." This, however, is what the press now typically does.

"I don't think for a moment that the media and newspapers are the sole source of cynicism in our society," Berdahl added. "But a wave of cynicism is upon us, and it is very damaging to the institutions of civil society.... For the kind of corrosive cynicism we are witnessing leads to apathy and indifference. It leads to withdrawal. It leads to the focus on the individual at the expense of concern for the larger community.... Cynicism, I believe, is corroding the quality of civil discourse in America and threatening the basis for democratic institutions."

By 2006, the Argument Culture was giving way to something new. The media forum in legacy media was moving away from staging polarized debates and toward content that produced reassuring comfort and therefore a predictable and loyal audience size. The Argument Culture, in which talk shows invited antagonists from both sides to argue, was giving way to the Answer Culture, in which the appeal of the host was to provide affirming answers to an ideologically more uniform audience.

There was a discernible tipping point moment in the transition. It came on October 15, 2004, with the appearance of comedian Jon Stewart on the CNN program *Crossfire*, the iconic example of Argument Culture media, which by then had been on the air for more than a decade.

Stewart, host of *The Daily Show* on Comedy Central, which had become wildly popular especially with young audiences, had become a critic of *Crossfire* and the argumentative way it dealt with political figures—particularly Democratic presidential candidate Senator John Kerry. Stewart was invited to the show by cohosts Paul Begala, representing the political Left, and Tucker Carlson, representing the Right of the political spectrum.[11]

"Well, he's been called the most trusted name in fake news," Carlson said with a broad smile that suggested the relish with which he looked forward to the conversation with Stewart and "his one-of-a-kind take on politics, the press and America." But it became obvious almost immediately that Stewart had not come on to the show to trade jokes.

STEWART: Why do you argue, the two of you? I hate to see it.
CARLSON: We enjoy it.

STEWART: Let me ask you a question.

CARLSON: Well, let me ask you a question first.

STEWART: All right.

CARLSON: Is John Kerry—is John Kerry really the best? I mean, John Kerry has . . .

STEWART: Is he the best? I thought Lincoln was good.

CARLSON: Is he the best the Democrats can do?

STEWART: Is he the best the Democrats can do?

CARLSON: Yes, this year of the whole field.

STEWART: I had always thought, in a democracy—and again, I don't know—I've only lived in this country—that there's a process. They call them primaries.

CARLSON: Right.

STEWART: And they don't always go with the best, but they go with whoever won. So is he the best? According to the process.

CARLSON: Right. But of the nine guys running, who do you think was the best? Do you think he was the best, the most impressive?

STEWART: The most impressive?

CARLSON: Yes.

STEWART: I thought Al Sharpton was very impressive. I enjoyed his way of speaking. I think, oftentimes, the person that knows they can't win is allowed to speak the most freely, because otherwise shows with titles, such as *Crossfire* . . .

BEGALA: *Crossfire*.

STEWART: Or *Hardball* or "I'm Going to Kick Your Ass," or . . . will jump on it. In many ways, it's funny. And I made a special effort to come on the show today, because I have privately, amongst my friends and also in occasional newspaper and television shows, mentioned this show as being bad.

BEGALA: We've noticed.

STEWART: And I wanted to . . . I felt that that wasn't fair and I should come here and tell you that I don't—it's not so much that it's bad, as it's hurting America. But I wanted to come here today and say . . . Stop, stop, stop, stop hurting America.

Carlson, sensing that he was no longer in control of the conversation, tried to regain it by challenging how Stewart had interviewed Kerry on *The Daily Show*.

CARLSON: Don't you feel like ... you got the chance to interview the guy. Why not ask him a real question, instead of just suck up to him?

STEWART: Yes. "How are you holding up?" is a real suck-up. And I'm actually giving him a hot stone massage as we are doing it.

CARLSON: It sounded that way. It did.

STEWART: You know, it's interesting to hear you talk about my responsibility.

CARLSON: I felt the sparks between you.

STEWART: I didn't realize that ... and maybe this explains quite a bit.

CARLSON: No, the opportunity to ...

STEWART: ... is that the news organizations look to Comedy Central for their cues on integrity ... So what I would suggest is, when you talk about you're holding politicians' feet to the fire, I think that's disingenuous. I think you're ...

[Crosstalk]

STEWART: But my point is this. If your idea of confronting me is that I don't ask hard-hitting enough news questions, we're in bad shape, fellows.

There was more crosstalk, and then Stewart got quite serious.

STEWART: You know, the interesting thing I have is, you have a responsibility to the public discourse, and you fail miserably.

CARLSON: You need to get a job at a journalism school, I think.

STEWART: You need to go to one. The thing that I want to say is, when you have people on for just knee-jerk, reactionary talk ...

CARLSON: Wait. I thought you were going to be funny. Come on. Be funny.

STEWART: No. No. I'm not going to be your monkey.

BEGALA: Go ahead. Go ahead.

STEWART: I watch your show every day. And it kills me.

CARLSON: I can tell you love it.

STEWART: It's so ... oh, it's so painful to watch. You know, because we need what you do. This is such a great opportunity you have here to actually get politicians off their marketing and strategy.

CARLSON: Is this really Jon Stewart? What is this, anyway?

STEWART: Yes, it's someone who watches your show and cannot take it anymore. I just can't.

CARLSON: What's it like to have dinner with you? It must be excoriating. Do you, like, lecture people like this or do you come over to their house and sit and lecture them: they're not doing the right thing, that they're missing their opportunities, evading their responsibilities?

STEWART: If I think they are.

CARLSON: I wouldn't want to eat with you, man. That's horrible.

STEWART: I know. And you won't ... Why can't we just talk ... please, I beg of you guys, please.

CARLSON: I think you watch too much *Crossfire*. We're going to take a quick break.

STEWART: No, no, no. Please.

CARLSON: No, no, hold on. We've got commercials.

STEWART: Please, please stop.

In January 2005, CNN President Jonathan Klein announced he was canceling the show. Announcing its demise, he told the press, "I guess I come down more firmly in the Jon Stewart camp."[12]

By then, Klein was hardly alone. Talk hosts like Rush Limbaugh on radio or Bill O'Reilly or Rachel Maddow on cable, websites like Free Republic on the Right or Talking Points Memo on the Left were offering ammunition for devoted followers, instead of outlining the parameters of civic argument.

The Answer Culture, in effect, contained a new view of journalists' responsibility toward the public forum. No one destination need accommodate the full range of opinions. The Web that now allowed aggregators to provide essentially unlimited sources of information on sites such as The Huffington Post, Google Reader, or Bloglines could do it better.

The Web, in effect, was the setting for the new Argument Culture. (In 2013, CNN, struggling for ratings, would resurrect *Crossfire*, but by then more argument was seemingly everywhere.)

If the era of Argument Culture in media narrowed our public discourse by appealing to extremism, the Answer Culture fractured it further by targeting an infinite number of specialized channels, each with its own niche appeal.

Put aside the fact that in many instances the motive is commercial, not intellectual. The other problem is that a news institution that sets out only to please its audience is not serving the larger public need for compromise or understanding. It is engaged in pandering.

Jack Fuller, who rose from reporter, to editorial page editor, editor, publisher, and eventually president of the newspaper division of the Tribune Company, eloquently explained how this kind of pandering by news operations wears itself out. He was discussing print, but the concepts apply across media: "Here is the tension," Fuller told us. "A newspaper that fails to reflect its community deeply will not succeed. But a newspaper that does not challenge its community's values and preconceptions will lose respect for failing to provide the honesty and leadership that newspapers are expected to offer."[13]

To be at once the enabler and the goad of community action is a great challenge, but it is one that journalism has always embraced. It is a challenge that can be met by accepting the obligation to provide the members of the community not only with the knowledge and insights they need but with the forum within which to engage in building a community.

In effect, not meeting this obligation is a variant of the same mistake Tom Winship made at the *Boston Globe* forty years earlier—failing to challenge the community for its own good.

At the end of the day, the issue is what happens to our understanding if there is no space for civil discourse, for common ground.

And as rich and diverse as the new forums of a networked media culture may be, their passion cannot substitute the need for fact and context that the journalism of verification supplies. If those who gather and then deliver the news no longer spend time and money to report, verify, and synthesize—if they fear that applying judgment is an act of elitism, or that the technology now frees them from these old burdens of vetting, and of identifying points of consensus that define the public commons—then argument, magnified by the wide reach of the Web, is all we are left with.

Who will find out which assertions in the public conversation are true and which are not? Who will explore the backgrounds and motives of the various factions? Who will answer the questions that need to be answered?

In the future, we may well rely more on citizens to be sentinels for one another and in the process take on a watchdog role over their own exchanges and discussions. No doubt this will expand the public forum and enrich the range of voices. But unless the forum is based on a foundation of fact and context, the questions citizens ask will become simply rhetorical. The debate will cease to educate; it will only reinforce the preconceptions people arrive with, and the public will be less able to participate in solutions. And public discourse, instead of being something we can learn from, will dissolve into noise, which the majority of the public will tune out.

So first, the journalistic forum should adhere to all the other journalistic principles, and, second, it should relate directly to Madison's recognition of the central role of compromise in democratic society. But if the primary role of the forum, then, is to illuminate rather than agitate, how is it that journalists engage an audience? This is the next element of journalism.

8

Engagement
and Relevance

Most people would have thought Lara Setrakian had it made. She was a young foreign correspondent based in Dubai for ABC and Bloomberg Television, and she had the story of a lifetime to cover—the unfolding Arab Spring in the Middle East.

She loved her job. But in 2012, as she spent more of her time focused on the devolving civil war in Syria, she grew more worried about her ability to accurately tell the story.

The Syrian civil war is "excruciatingly opaque ... and fundamentally complex," she would later write.[1] Foreign journalists were heavily restricted on the ground. The crosscurrents of history, centuries-old conflicts, decades of party politics, the multiple aspects of a story in which many Syrians were sympathetic to rebellion but also fearful of it—these subtleties were difficult to portray. Traditional television newscasts were constrained by time. The conventional news article, even online, didn't accommodate smaller pieces of information and context, or the flow of content coming from so many places. Journalists could not really fully share what they knew in the ways that were most useful. In any familiar mainstream news report it was asking a lot for the average person to grasp "context, history, or much depth."

She began to imagine a better way. On a page in her reporter's notebook she started to sketch the idea, almost a map, of a new Web experience. The website she imagined was a portal into a single subject–using the power of design as a storytelling concept. It involved different kinds of content modules, which together combined the strengths of original reporting, data journalism, social media, maps, photos, video, and more. She would call the site Syria Deeply.

"I wanted to fundamentally redesign the user experience for news," Setrakian said. With a team of designers and developers, "we worked to create digital journalism as advanced sensemaking," to blend different kinds of content, design, headlines, look, and feel "to help our audience understand this very complex story."

Users could pick what kind of content they wanted and how they wanted to learn–from eyewitness conversation on Twitter to the latest breaking news, conventional news narrative, or timelines of national history. There were photo sequences, a breakdown of the main players in the Syrian government and the opposition, as well as personal stories of Syrians on the ground, and more. A constantly updated banner at the top of the page offered a sense of the latest development. Another module was dedicated to staff hosting discussions with experts and journalists, a place for newspeople to be more transparent and to "share their notes" with the audience, Setrakian said.[2]

On Syria Deeply, the unit of news, in a sense, is not the latest article, but the Syrian story itself.

Roughly a quarter of the site is original reporting. The rest is curated, automated, or background material, a good deal of it material that remains static–essential knowledge that does not have to be repeated each day the way it is in conventional reporting–and thus becomes richly designed history and context rather than compressed boilerplate mashed into a narrative.

To a significant degree, Syria Deeply solves the problem of audiences being baffled by a news story they have not followed from the start. The website is a multi–entry point destination for a story that most might find inaccessible. What Setrakian has conceived with Syria Deeply also translates into the seventh journalistic principle:

Journalism must make the significant interesting and relevant.

When people talk about making the news engaging and relevant, the discussion often becomes an unhelpful dichotomy–engaging versus relevant. Should we emphasize news that is fun and fascinating, and plays on our sensations? Or should we stick to the news that is the most important? Should journalists give people what they need or what they want? The supposed dilemma may seem magnified a thousandfold in the digital era–when the traffic to each story is counted in real time and the appeal of cat pictures and teenage pop stars seem to automatically trump news with civic value.

This classic way of posing the question of engagement–as information versus storytelling, or what people need versus what people want–is a distortion. This is not how journalism is practiced. Nor is it, we believe, how people come to the news. The evidence suggests that most people want both: they read the sports and the business pages, the *New Yorker*'s long stories and its cartoons, the book review and the crossword puzzle. The *New York Times* supports some twenty-plus foreign bureaus, its Washington bureau, and covers city council meetings, but it also has fashion, lifestyle, and food sections. BuzzFeed has made a science out of predicting the viral potential of photos of basset hounds running, but it also has found its appeal widens with political coverage, breaking exclusive stories, and even long-form content it has dubbed BuzzReads.

Storytelling and information are not contradictory. They are better understood as points on a continuum of communication. At one end, perhaps, is the bedtime story you make up to tell your children, which may have no point other than intimate and comforting time spent together. On the other end is raw data–databases, sports statistics, community bulletin boards, or stock tables–that contain no narrative at all. Most journalism, like most communication, exists somewhere in the middle. Writing teachers Roy Peter Clark and Chip Scanlan say that effective writing about news can be found at the intersection of civic clarity, the information citizens need to function, and literary grace.

This is a far cry from writing news stories and surrounding them with a few "bells and whistles." It is an entirely new kind of narrative storytelling that recognizes the strengths of other forms of content–from startling data visuals that users can control and that reveal the impact of economic projection, to puzzle-like interactive games that allow users to try to balance the state budget, or a curated Twitter conversation in Syria that feels like being invited to an amazing dinner table conversation.

Understood this way, the best work–that which rises above its subject matter–pushes a story further toward the middle of that continuum than the audience would expect. It does so through superior reporting, thinking, narrative, design, and presentation of data, in a way that helps readers make sense of what's going on in the world. Quality, in short, has less to do with the seriousness of the topic than its treatment. It can be found in the Hollywood profile that says something deeper about filmmaking; the investigative exposé that also reveals the human condition; the treatment of demographic data that brings a neighborhood to life. The task of those engaged in journalism–whether they are professionals who make a living at it or community members who find themselves trying to explain what it was like to survive a disaster–is to find a way to make the significant parts of each story interesting for the reader. For those trying to offer a full record of the day, it also involves finding the right mix of the serious and the less serious that reflects what real life is like.

Perhaps it is best understood this way: Journalism is storytelling with a purpose. That purpose is to provide people with information they need to understand the world. The first challenge is finding the information that people need to live their lives. The second is to make it meaningful, relevant, and engaging.

Engagement should be seen as being part of journalism's commitment to the citizenry. As one reporter interviewed by our academic research partners put it years ago, "If you are the kind of person who, once you have found out something, find that you are not satisfied about knowing it until you figure out a way to tell somebody else, then you're a journalist."[3]

Part of journalism's responsibility is not just providing information but also providing it in such a way that people will be inclined to listen. And one of the extraordinary dimensions of digital presentation is that journalists are no longer limited to a conventional palette of news writing, or even traditional narrative.

But this responsibility also implies, as it always has, choosing, selecting, deciding what is important and what is not, knowing what to highlight and what to leave out, and understanding which tools to place in the hands of citizens to help them discover the threads of a story on their own. Put another way, storytelling involves more than words. But whatever form of presentation it takes, its main purpose is distillation—critical analytical thinking that illuminates the matter under consideration.

"At one end of the spectrum it is what is most important—is there going to be war or peace, are taxes going up, are they going down?" said Howard Rheingold, an author, critic, teacher, and former executive editor of the online magazine *HotWired*. "The other end of the spectrum is just what's purely interesting.... And most stories are something of a mix of the two."[4]

So how does the question of making news engaging get so distorted, as if there were no way to balance engagement and significance of information? If people do not basically want their news one way or the other, why does the news so often fall short?

A litany of problems stands in the way of news being delivered compellingly: habit, haste, ignorance, laziness, formula, bias, cultural blinders, a shallow grasp of the topic, lack of skill. It takes time to write a story well, if you're not using a ready-made template like the inverted pyramid style in print, the intro/sound bite/bridge/sound bite/close in TV, or the static bar chart representation of data. It is, in the end, a strategic exercise that involves more than just plugging facts into short, declarative sentences, writing code, or pulling data from an Excel spreadsheet.

Unfortunately, at a time when the public has ever more exciting and interesting alternatives to the news and is more skeptical of journalism, cutbacks in traditional newsrooms have put more pressure on time and resources. Some news organizations, too, are convinced that ever-shortening attention spans require ever-shorter stories, further challenging the ability of journalists to comprehensively understand the events they are trying to cover.

And engagement requires that journalists understand a new, deeper structural reality: In the old order, audiences had to adapt their behavior to fit the rhythms of the news media. They had to be home at 6:30 to see the newscast, or be sure to read the morning paper to be current with the news others had seen. Now the news media must adapt to fit the behavior and curiosity of the community that new technology has created. A survey of AP audiences done by Deloitte in 2013 in the UK for example found that with the advent of handheld devices 89 percent of those surveyed now accessed news online frequently, and half of those looked for videos because they improved their understanding of the stories. One-third said they would go to another site if no video was available. Now that audiences can go elsewhere with ease, they will increasingly demand that journalists make the best choices about how much and what kind of information to provide and not provide, given that arbitrary space limits are not an issue. Time has become the only scarcity. All of this demands that journalists research and understand, in a way they only guessed at before, the real needs and habits of the people they serve.

Rethinking is required in part because some of the conventional wisdom about shortened attention spans was misguided and has hurt, not helped, journalism. A multiyear study of local television news we designed at the Project for Excellence in Journalism, for instance, found that stations that ran more short stories—under forty-five seconds—tended to lose audiences. Stations that did more stories over two minutes, on the other hand, tend to gain viewership.[5]

Similarly, many early studies of the Internet suggested that people would never read long-form material on digital screens. The average time people spent on Web pages tended toward about thirty seconds, according to eye tracking studies by the Poynter Institute. The advent of the smartphone and then the tablet and the e-reader began to dispel this illusion. (Not only do people read books digitally, but 61 percent of mobile news consumers read long-form articles on smart phones and 73 percent on tablets).[6] The short attention span found on computer screens had less to do with anything inherent about the screens than it did with the fact that the people observed in earlier studies were using desktop computers, and often in their offices.

The good news is that the same technology that devastated the economic foundation of commercial news in the beginning of the new century has also unleashed a profound new wave of creativity. The tools include new ways of using data, graphics, and technology, involving the community, and more. The level of experimentation is probably unprecedented in at least a century, and while dizzying to many older hands, it offers the potential to make journalism more engaging, more relevant, and more empowering than in generations.

There are countless examples of innovators who defied conventional wisdom about what audiences want. Watch young people who have never read a newspaper talk about protests in Turkey called Occupy Gezi, because they saw a friend mention it on Twitter and then Googled it and went to a curated report on BuzzFeed, which was easier for them to grasp than the write-up in the *New York Times*. Ira Glass, host of the radio program *This American Life*, which broadcasts "stories that are like movies for radio," says the average listener tunes in for forty-eight out of the sixty minutes of the show. *This American Life* reaches around 1.7 million people a week and usually runs three stories per episode, ranging from extended reports, to essays, to found audio material.[7] It is only one example that contradicts the conventional wisdom about the limited attention spans in an increasingly crowded media environment.

It's hardly certain whether the success of *This American Life* can be replicated on an industry-wide scale. Many conventional news operations lack the will, resources, and strategic vision to embrace the storytelling potential that technology holds, and many of the technology companies that have the ability to employ these tools have little interest in producing journalism. Many of the pioneers who do care work outside conventional settings, lack scale or impact, and have seen slow adoption of their ideas.

Change is being held back not only by the absence of a robust revenue model. It is also hindered by an underlying cultural divide between journalism innovators, whose embrace of new tools sometimes seems a repudiation of all that came before, and nervous stewards of journalism's legacy skills, many of whom fought for quality against commercialism and now are struggling to adapt again.

The sweet spot for innovation is the convergence point where technology is viewed as a way to fulfill the public interest mission that has always animated our best journalism.

Plenty of journalists are applying this type of creative thinking to their coverage, from innovative individuals such as Setrakian and her colleagues, to those launching efforts at institutions such as NPR, the *New York Times*, and the *Seattle Times*. It is that embrace of exploration–tied with the civic values required of news–that will occupy us here.

There is also, however, the risk of a new kind of digital sensationalism: the possibility that people will react to the new metrics of the Web by abandoning their faith that quality will build a loyal and deeply engaged audience, much as some in television did a generation ago. This is the path of chasing cheap page views, cat videos, and celebrity slide shows.

THE LURE OF INFOTAINMENT AND SENSATIONALISM

In the first two decades of technological disruption, when cable television began to lure the audiences away from broadcast, and twenty-four-hour cable news took audiences away from traditional network evening and morning newscasts, one reaction was to make news more like entertainment. This was the age of infotainment, a late-twentieth-century version of tabloid sensationalism. It reached its peak in the late 1990s, right before Americans and their media were jolted by the terrorist attacks of 2001 (and is finding new form to a degree in social media platforms). Before the era of cheap-to-produce reality shows, the television schedule was punctuated instead by prime time journalism magazines devoted to celebrity and true crime. Stories like the murder of child beauty contestant

JonBenet Ramsey dominated not just on the front pages of tawdry supermarket tabloid newspapers but also the once hyper-selective network evening newscasts.

In the summer before the attacks of September 11, 2001, the biggest story in the nation's capital was not the growing unease in intelligence circles that the overseas communications they monitored suggested a growing threat to America itself. Nor was it the implications of the weakening economy in the wake of the tech bubble bursting, although the lessons not learned would drastically affect the nation's economic landscape a few years later. The big story was the disappearance of a young female intern in Washington named Chandra Levy. Levy had had an affair with her congressman, Gary Condit, who had helped her get her internship at the Federal Bureau of Prisons. Although there was little proof, other than assumed motive and the fact that Levy was missing, the press speculated pointedly that Condit had murdered Levy to cover up their affair.

It was explosive stuff. The only problem was the speculation was unfounded. Levy had been murdered. Her remains would be found in Rock Creek Park the following year. But Levy, it would turn out, had been killed in a random assault and robbery.

The journalism of the infotainment era shared some common characteristics.

Leo Braudy, the author of *The Frenzy of Renown*, has argued that a key feature of infotainment journalism was to "somehow present the story as a secret. You have to be the knowing reporter and to let the audience in on it. And unfortunately, more and more as time goes on, the secret is something scandalous or salacious." This, in turn, creates "an audience that likes to think of itself as being in the know"–that needs the next salacious fix.[8]

There were other elements to this cycle of news as a hidden secret revealed. They included the titillation of forbidden or even violent sex, the lure of the innocent by an unscrupulous predator or a powerful manipulator, or the tragedy, downfall, or perhaps even redemption of a celebrity. The Condit story had many of the elements. So did the progenitor Washington scandal that preceded it two years earlier, the Clinton-Lewinsky scandal. Such stories have hardly vanished. The saga of Congressman Anthony Weiner's sexting, or the fascination with the royal birth in 2013, are a reminder that infotainment, celebrity, and scandal will always provide easy ways to catch audiences' attention.

But to a significant degree, the age of infotainment that dominated the end of the twentieth century media culture seems to have faded. The shift almost certainly owes something to digital technology: Citizens whose choices drive more of our public dialogue share in a different kind of discourse; there are other kinds of content, from slide shows to quizzes to interactivity, that drive engagement, all of which do so more effectively than manipulation of sources or material for dramatic impact. History suggests the change in tone also owes something to cultural and economic change—a nation more troubled by war, recession, terror, political polarization, and loss of international status.

We have seen tabloid cycles come and go before with economic booms, cultural shifts, and political crisis. As the immigrants of the 1890s moved into the middle class in the twentieth century, the sensationalism of yellow journalism gave way to the more sober approach of the *New York Times*. As the delirium of the Roaring Twenties gave way to the severity of the Depression, the celebrity age of the tabloids and gossipmongers like celebrity radio and newspaper columnist Walter Winchell gave way to a new seriousness that lasted through the Cold War. The survivors of the great newspaper wars of the 1960s, which saw most cities become one-newspaper towns, were not the mass-circulation tabloids but the serious papers in each city—the *Washington Post*, the *New York Times*, the *Los Angeles Times*, the *Philadelphia Inquirer*, the *Boston Globe*, and countless others. It was true in television as well. The dominant television network news operation was generally the one with the largest number of bureaus and greatest commitment to delivering serious news, whether it was the *Huntley-Brinkley Report* in the 1960s, the *CBS Evening News* with Walter Cronkite in the 1970s, *World News Tonight* with Peter Jennings from the mid-1980s to the mid-1990s, or NBC News' multi-platform approach in the late 1990s and into the new century.[9]

Some websites, such as TMZ, or even some of the more whimsical viral material on BuzzFeed—which is also doing significantly innovative work in journalism—are the digital reminder that infotainment is not far away. Indeed, the Web poses its own potential for a new kind of infotainment or sensationalism. There is a temptation for editorial staffs to take Web metrics and follow the same mistakes that television made with ratings—assume that the path to the largest audience is to fill a publication with popular bits of diversion that people will want to share with friends. (We will discuss this in greater depth in the next chapter.) Investing in quality reporting, after all, is more expensive and newsrooms are shrinking.

Yet history offers three reasons to believe that attracting audiences by being merely amusing is not a lasting business strategy.

The first is that if you feed people only trivia and entertainment, you will wither the appetite and expectations of some people for anything else. This is especially true of those people who, due to inclination, time, or resources, are less likely to seek alternatives. This is the dilemma now faced by so much local television news. "Of those who do watch local news, more than half those surveyed no longer care which station they watch," Insite Research, a leading television audience research firm in California, declared more than a decade ago.[10] The problem of local TV news losing audience would only intensify in the years since, as the infotainment on the air failed to translate into useful news online.

The second long-term problem with the strategy of infotainment is that it destroys the news organization's authority to deliver more serious news and drives away those audiences who want it. This, too, has happened in local television news. A survey by Indiana University researchers for the nonprofit research group NewsLab, for instance, found that five of the top seven reasons that people stopped watching local TV news were different ways of saying that it lacked substance (the other two top reasons were that people were not home or too busy).[11] This research is backed up not only by the intuition of many local newspeople but also by other survey research. "Avoidance of local news has doubled in the past ten years," say other data from Insite Research. One reason given was: "More than half of those surveyed feel that most stations spend too much time covering the same stories over and over again."[12]

Finally, the infotainment strategy is faulty as a business plan because when you turn your news into entertainment, you are playing to the strengths of other media rather than your own. How can the news ever compete with entertainment on entertainment's terms? Why would it want to? The value and allure of news is that it is different. It is based on relevance. The strategy of infotainment, though it may attract an audience in the short run and may be cheap to produce, will build a shallow audience because it is built on form, not substance. Such an audience will switch to the next "most exciting" thing because that audience was built on the spongy ground of excitement.

These challenges, like a distracted public, do not make journalism impossible, only more difficult. They separate successful journalism from lazy, good from bad, the complete from the overly sensationalized.

Perhaps most important, winning back audience through better forms of storytelling is hard. It takes imagination. Experimentation. And faith in the audience.

When the Web began to take audience from print, those qualities were largely missing online. Because of this, journalists initially tended to consider the Web an inferior platform, and glorified the virtues of thumbing through the print paper, hoping audiences would share their nostalgia rather than turn to the convenience of the Web.

In time, journalists began to use the Internet as a place for posting the same material produced in print or on television rather than as a distinct platform with its own potential. This was the era in which leaders such as Arthur Sulzberger Jr., the publisher of the *New York Times*, would assert that they were "platform agnostic."[13]

The problem with agnosticism is that it reflects ambivalence and uncertainty. The innovators of the digital age, however, weren't platform agnostic. They were "platform orthodox": They believed in, and wanted to exploit, the Web's unique potential to tell stories in new ways and engage the audience community in their news gathering.

By the second decade of the twenty-first century, the situation had begun to change. Organizations that believe in journalism, both in legacy media and online, have begun to emerge as Web innovators, from the *New York Times* to ProPublica to upstarts like Syria Deeply. They have eschewed the lure of digital sensationalism and are exploring the potential of new storytelling and engagement. With digital tools, this means moving from seeing news as a static product–something an audience receives–and instead seeing it as a service that can help people live their lives better. That service involves imagining new and better ways to perform the different functions of journalism outlined in chapter 1, from authentication and sense making to empowerment.

We cannot pretend to offer here an encyclopedia of methods for doing this. That is a different book. But we want to look at some more conceptual issues that may help citizens, citizen journalists, and professional journalists begin to think differently.

This starts with understanding what so often was lacking in some traditional journalistic writing. Forms such as the inverted pyramid for news stories were so formulaic that, although the stories modeled on them were filled with facts and detail, they failed to engage readers. Much of this news writing may have taken the form of stories, but it did not come alive in the way that good storytelling can. The inverted pyramid and other forms in which news was too often written fell victim to some common flaws:

Character is missing—sources become templates, not real people.

Time is frozen and lacks movement. Everything happened yesterday or this evening.

Information is designed for a single audience, not multiple ones.

The news is presented as a conversation among insiders.

Stories don't illuminate a greater meaning.

There is little attempt to globalize the local or localize the global.

Storytelling is predictable and formulaic.

The Web is used as a new platform, but the material remains in the legacy platform and fails to take advantage of technology with new possibilities.

SOME INNOVATIVE APPROACHES

If the journalism industry did seek out its most talented members, collate their thinking, and search for uncommon ideas from across all media, it would discover some compelling new thinking about content. What follows here are concepts, some of which have to do with storytelling, but many of which apply to any kind of content—from curated content, to photos, graphics, and videos, to telling stories with data.

First, better storytelling doesn't begin after one sits down to edit a story on video, begins to write a script, or pulls up to an empty screen to draft a story. It begins before someone ever goes out to report. And it involves reporting differently, talking to different sources, and asking different questions.

WHO IS THE AUDIENCE AND WHAT DO THEY NEED TO KNOW?

Often journalists begin a story by gathering what was reported up until now and then reporting on the newest development. This incremental adding of the newest development, however, can limit the story.

Some of the most creative people in news advocate a different approach. When taking on a story, or thinking about engaging a topic, one should ask (and audiences should be able to detect) the following questions:

1. What is this story really about? (What do the facts we know so far, or the data we have seen, suggest?)
2. Who does this story or these facts affect, and how? What information do these people need to know to make up their own minds about the subject?
3. Who has the information, and who can put it in context?
4. What's the best way to tell this story? Is it even a narrative, or is it better told other ways?

These simple questions can make a big difference. They direct coverage toward the citizen—the audience first, away from interest groups, insiders, and other direct participants. They also may lead the journalism to a new set of sources not found in the previous coverage. These questions pull the coverage away from the routines of the old, which may already have limited the audience rather than expanded it.

THE STAKEHOLDER WHEEL

Pulitzer Prize–winning writer Jacqui Banaszynski teaches people to make coverage of issues more engaging by thinking about "stakeholders"–the people who are invested in or affected by events.

To do this, she has people draw a circle on a piece of paper with the event or issue written inside the circle. Then, they draw "spokes" radiating from the hub, one for every group of people or even a particular person who has a stake in the issue. Such an individual could be someone involved in, interested in, affected by, or even just curious about the event or subject. Initially people reacting to the exercise make only a few spokes on the wheel. Then Banaszynski gets them to think more broadly.

Take a subject like education, for instance, or the first day of school, and people usually name initially:

* Students
* Parents
* Teachers

Then Banaszynski tells people to think more broadly. They do so, and then begin to add new stakeholders to the list, such as school bus drivers, crossing guards, cafeteria workers, school administrators, janitors, school nurses, guidance counselors, even truant officers.

Banaszynski then advises to think wider still. Soon the spokes point to siblings, grandparents, teachers' unions, legislators, school boards, commuters, day-care and after-care operators, retailers that sell school supplies, companies that make and sell children's clothes, employers who have kids, universities, researchers, taxpayers who pay for schools, parents of kids with special needs, young people thinking of becoming teachers. Not every story, or piece of content, connects to all of them. Yet each of the spokes poses a host of questions that might prompt a good story, or alters the way to tell a story or what content modules (in Lara Setrakian's model at Syria Deeply) should be included. Suddenly, in other words, the story-teller, whatever his or her tools, has focused on the audience and the community.

A NEW DEFINITION OF WHO, WHAT, WHEN, WHERE, WHY, AND HOW

Journalists can rethink the basic elements of news—who, what, when, where, why, and how. Roy Peter Clark, writing professor at the Poynter Institute in St. Petersburg, Florida, has done just that. He took the five w's and an h and turned them into reminders of how to create a story through storytelling. Years ago, Clark was struck by the ideas of Seattle writer and editor Rick Zahler, who argued that news writing took dynamic events and froze them. Time sequences become simply yesterday. Place becomes a dateline. Zahler wanted to "thaw out" the news and put things in motion. Building on his ideas, Clark now talks often about how this can be done.

"Who becomes character. What becomes scene. Where be-comes setting. When is chronology. Why becomes motivation or causation." Finally, "how becomes narrative," or the way all the ele-ments fit together, Clark says.[14] At the beginning of *Romeo and Juliet*, Shakespeare tells in the first eight lines of a sonnet all the facts of the story, including the ending, Clark points out. So what's left to tell? As he explains it, the next two hours of the play fill in all that miss-ing detail. "We often give the news, but you still want to know how it happened. Narrative is the way we answer the question 'How did that happen?'" says Clark.

If we think of *who* as character, *when* as chronology, *where* as setting, and *how* as narrative, we can blend information and story-telling. Quotes become dialogue. News becomes not just informa-tion but also meaning. Doing this, not so incidentally, requires more reporting and more curiosity on the part of the reporter. Jack Hart, a writing coach at the *Oregonian*, said fifteen to thirty inches is a reasonable length for a narrative that can be produced in a day. The idea is to follow a character through a complication and show how he or she resolves it. This can be done in a five-part narrative arc. First comes the exposition, in which the character and the complication are introduced. Then the rising action, which is the bulk of the piece, showing the obstacles on the way to solving the complication. What follows are the point of insight, or the moment when the character has a revelation, and the resolution, when the complication is resolved. The ending is the denouement, a chance to tie up loose ends.[15]

TAKE RESPONSIBILITY FOR WHAT THE AUDIENCE UNDERSTANDS— NOT JUST WHAT IT SEES

Ezra Klein at the *Washington Post* is a new kind of journalist. While some readers wonder whether his work crosses a line between that of a columnist and a reporter, Klein's intelligent analysis of economics and public policy is serious and substantive, and it resonates with readers. He is part policy analyst, part researcher, part blogger, part reporter, part explanatory journalist.

Some of what distinguishes Klein's work is how he communicates with his audience. Too much of traditional journalism, he says, was about making information available to the public–and too little was concerned with taking responsibility for creating understanding– worrying about what readers really knew and thought.[16]

He strives, he says, to give the readers the "feeling of a key turning in a lock," to create the sense that new knowledge is being revealed.

To do this, Klein argues, first one must genuinely understand the substance of what one is trying to convey. This means, he says, sitting down to read the academic scholarship and research reports. And then take readers on the same journey that you took, while omitting the parts that didn't lead anywhere.

He also tries to eliminate "the cognitive anxiety of the reader," the sense that things are dull, or hard to follow. (In other words, make the significant interesting.) One way to do this is to think about lifting the heavy cargo of data and putting in charts and graphs– merging data visualization and narrative. Another is to think often about relying on understandable forms of discourse, such as bullet lists and Q&A. Whatever it is, your first concern should be whether your method for conveying the story will lead the reader to a greater understanding of the issue at hand.

EXPERIMENT WITH NEW STORYTELLING TECHNIQUES

The most common narrative structure traditionally used in journalism–the inverted pyramid–is remarkably limited. In the inverted pyramid, every news event is told as a narrative, with the facts considered most important put at the top of the story. As journalism grew more complex and the topics more vast, many of the best journalists increasingly felt that conventional structure inadequate. "Sometimes just starting at A and going through to Z is not the best way to do it," William Whitaker of CBS News told our academic research partners more than a decade ago. "Sometimes you grab L, M, N, O, P out of the middle and put it at the top because that's the point that makes the most sense and that's what's easiest for people to understand and that puts it in perspective."[17]

Jim Brady, the executive editor of Digital First, argues that on many breaking news stories that people want to read immediately, a running account with the latest news on top may make more sense–given that most readers already have heard something and are coming to know what's new. Todd Hanson, head writer at the weekly humor periodical the *Onion*, told the *Online Journalism Review* that much of his magazine's humor arises from the anachronistic quality that characterizes newspapers like the *New York Times* or the *Washington Post*. The magazine features such headlines as CONGRESS APPROVES $4 BILLION FOR BREAD and CIRCUSES AND FAIRY PRINCESS RANKS DEPLETING AS GIRLS ASPIRE TO BE DOCTORS, LAWYERS.[18] Look at the *Onion* in 2013. The parodies are not just of news stories. They spoof exchanges in social media, the use of graphics, and the seemingly endless range of new story elements.

THE MULTIPLE PATHS TO STORY

Jacqui Banaszynski, who developed the stakeholder wheel, also notes that any piece of news–whether an event, idea, issue, press release, calendar listing, trend, agenda item, dinner conversation, billboard, church bulletin–has potential for new forms of engagement beyond what is obvious or traditional. That potential plays out in two dimensions:

> What stories to pursue
> How best to tell those stories (what platform to use)

Banaszynski talks about seven concepts to think about when deciding how to convey a story. We have added two more:

1. *Issues or trend.* Ask if there is a larger picture to explore. Does the event tie to some larger context? How has it developed over time? Is it a window of opportunity to revisit a bigger issue the public needs to know about, or to reveal how that issue plays out in specific ways?

2. *Explanatory piece.* Does the news offer an opportunity to dig inside to explain why something happened or how something works? More than just identifying an issue or trend, this approach explains how it evolved, and in so doing sheds some refracted light on how the world works.

3. *Profile.* Is there a relatable character at the center of an event or issue, or affected by it? Is there a "tour guide" to help your audience see/understand an issue? Profiles need not be about people, nor do they have to be narrative. They could be about a place or even a building. But they must, Banaszynski says, be about character.

4. *Voices.* Are there people who can speak to the event or issue in a way that illuminates it and how it affects people? This may be the video of a subject of the story talking, or it may dictate the way a story is structured. It may lead to a social media stream, or a Storify treatment. It can make content speak to audiences in powerful ways.

5. *Descriptive.* Give the story a vivid setting. Re-create what it feels like, what it looks like, what it smells like to be present at the event or issue.

6. *Investigative.* Look into wrongdoing, "follow the money," analyze power struggles, and make use of available documents.

7. *Narrative.* Can the story hold together, with a beginning, middle, and end? Does it follow a central character through plot, action and forward motion, tension, conflict, and resolution?

8. *Visual.* Is the story better told without much text, through photographs, graphics, illustrations?

9. *Data.* Is the essence of the story told with numbers? Data visualization and data journalism, however, are still storytelling. And what is left out is as important as what is left in.

Each of these concepts, and others you might fashion for yourself based on your own approach to writing, is a tool that should be kept in mind as you gather information and as you begin to organize your information prior to deciding which form of storytelling will most effectively serve to engage and inform the ultimate consumer of the information. The critical point here is to keep in mind what form your story might take so that you gather the information needed to best shape the story that way. For example, can the profile you are preparing be best told visually? If so, what visuals will best serve to profile the person? Or can the person best be profiled by a specific event or action? In that case, you'll need meticulous detail in order that the profile will emerge from the powerful detail of the event or action.

THE HOURGLASS

In the early 1990s, Roy Clark noticed what he called the "hourglass" structure. "It isn't purely narrative. It isn't just the inverted pyramid. . . . It is a form in which you begin by telling the news, telling what happened, and then there is a break in the pyramid, and a line that begins a narrative, often chronologically, as in, 'The incident began when . . .'" At that point, the news is thawed out and put in more dramatic form to create an engagement with the information.

Q&A

New York University journalism professor Jay Rosen has long thought about how to orient news more toward the interests of citizens rather than needs of the journalists' traditional formats.

Some methods are deceptively simple. Rosen considers the Q&A story form (reframed online as FAQ) to be a powerful but underused method. It forces the journalist to frame the material around things that citizens might ask. It also allows audiences to scan a story and enter it wherever they want, rather than having to read it from the top down.

BUTCH WARD'S DINING TABLE

Butch Ward at the Poynter Institute has a way to make people producing journalism think like citizens as they conceive of, and then imagine conveying, stories. He tells people they are no longer journalists but a group of neighbors gathered for dinner on Saturday night. Put a subject on the table (health care, public safety, our children) and go around the table. Each "neighbor" must share a personal (true) story about a recent experience with that topic. When was your last encounter with the health care system? Or the government? What happened? Take twenty minutes to retell your personal stories. Then take ten minutes to make a list of these stories as journalism. Turning them first into storytellers is what made the resulting list look so much different than it would have if Ward had given journalists thirty minutes to sit down and develop a list of stories.

STORY AS EXPERIENCE

Michael Herr, whose book *Dispatches* is considered one of the best to come out of the Vietnam War, added a new dimension to war reporting by carrying Gay Talese's "fly on the wall" technique a step further. Not only did Herr gather the copious detail that kind of reporting entailed, but he also let the soldiers speak for themselves, selecting his material not only to tell their story but also to capture their state of mind and their thoughts. As Alfred Kazin wrote in a review of the book in *Esquire,* "Herr caught better than anyone else the ... desperate code in which the men in the field showed that they were well and truly shit."[19]

BEING ON THE NOSE

The late Doug Marlette, a Pulitzer Prize–winning editorial cartoon-
ist, said that the reason so much of news is boring is that it's not
surprising enough.

"When you're bored," Marlette said, "you stop learning and
communication fails."[20] The principal reason is that "you're never
surprised." In the theater, there is a term for this boredom. It's called
"being on the nose," which "is when you tell people what they already know."

In news, it is "telling not showing; lecturing; didacticism," Marlette said. "It is the moment in TV news when the correspondent
tells the audience what they are already seeing." It is the moment a
newspaper story belabors a point rather than moving on.

How do we keep news from being on the nose?

PICTURES OF THE MIND

One way is to help people build their own pictures in their minds,
rather than drawing them for them. Annie Lang, who teaches tele-
communications and runs the Institute for Communications Research
at Indiana University, says academic research has clearly established
the power of mental pictures, including metaphor. "There is nothing
more scary than to say to someone, 'There is a snake behind you.'
That is so much more powerful than to show them the snake."[21]

CONNECTING THE STORY TO DEEPER THEMES: THE REVEAL

Former NBC News correspondent John Larson has suggested that
surprise is key to storytelling. But, he adds, "surprise them in a meaningful way. Not just shock them and stun them."[22] Some in television call this "the reveal." In Larson's mind, the best kind of reveal
is when a story connects to some deeper unexpected themes. It's
when stories "reach us on some elemental level. They talk about
a mother's love for her children, a husband's pride in his country.
Ambition. Avarice. Greed. There's something very important that's
always going on in a very simple way in good stories."

These themes are not stated by the journalist but are shown, or
revealed, in how the journalist treats the material—using the right

quote, showing the right camera shot on TV, or describing the look two people give each other when they are not talking. "Good stories lead you to the truth; they don't tell you the truth," as Larson puts it.

Robert Caro, the National Book Award–winning biographer of President Lyndon Johnson and New York power broker Robert Moses, says this notion has guided his life's work. When writing about Moses, a little-known bureaucrat who transformed New York City, Caro wanted to do something more than an exposé. "I was a reporter and I was covering politics, and I felt that I wasn't really explaining what I had gone into the newspaper business to explain, which was how political power worked, and a lot of it led back to this man, Robert Moses, a lot of what I didn't understand. Now, here was a guy who was never elected to anything, and I was coming to realize that he had more power than anyone who was governor or mayor."[23]

CHARACTER AND DETAIL IN NEWS

Other journalists believe character is the key to pulling people into stories. Good characterization often is found in the minor details that make someone human and real. When the father of the ship-wrecked boy Elián Gonzalez came to America in 2000 to retrieve his son and take him back to Cuba, KARE-TV correspondent Boyd Huppert was struck most of all that in his interview with immigration officials, "the father knew [the son's] shoe size." For Huppert, this "put a whole new light on the man," revealing something about the father's relationship with the child, his involvement, and his character.[24]

Too much journalism fails to develop character in this way. The people are cardboard; they are names and faces fit into a journalistic template—the investigating officer, the pro-life protester, the angry minority spokesman, the aggrieved mother. A major reason for this is that the journalist doesn't allow the interview subjects to speak the way people do in real life. Quotes are too often used as tools, instead of being cast as part of a deeper conversation between the subjects of a story and the audience. The way interviews are shot on TV is another major factor in this depth. Often people do not even look like real people when shot against artificial backgrounds in perfect light, or standing in front of a building surrounded by microphones. They exist in an artificial world—the world of news—and seem more caricature than character.

To call someone "the investigating officer" is to describe a source. But "Detective Lewis, a second-generation homicide cop, whose father had a case like this twenty years earlier," is a character. The first makes homicide investigator Lewis fit a fairly rigid template, one that is passable for journalistic purposes but shallow, and that turns him into a stick figure who is indistinguishable from any other investigating officer.

"The second-ranking Republican member of the House Ways and Means Committee" is a template. "The thirty-year veteran of the House, who has opposed nearly every tax cut except for mental health after becoming the grandfather to a disabled child," is already more engaging to the reader. Yet turning sources into people involves thinking ahead about character. It involves asking different questions of the officer, looking more for images, mannerisms, and being curious about him as a potential character rather than merely a source. It may take more time, but not as much time as one might think. "Have you ever had any cases like this? Do you have any special style or method for investigating?" Most important, this process involves looking at the officer as a person rather than merely looking for quotes or facts, and never forgetting that there is no person from whom you cannot learn something you never knew before.

In a television context, this deepening of character may also mean thinking differently about the way stories and segments are filmed. David Turecamo, a filmmaker who shoots, interviews, writes, and edits his own pieces, always tries to photograph his subjects as they actually live—shopkeepers while behind the counter, salesmen while driving in their cars, businessmen while walking to meetings— usually in long takes. His pieces are small character studies, and the audience members' view of the issue is changed because they suddenly see real people, businesspeople, and no longer "advocates" or parts of a "lobby."

FINDING THE METAPHOR OR HIDDEN STRUCTURE IN EACH STORY

Perhaps no American journalist in radio and television has been more involved in making important topics interesting than Robert Krulwich, who over the course of his career has covered economics for NPR, science for ABC, and other supposedly dry topics in ways that were anything but. Krulwich has always tried to find in each story the hidden material that makes it memorable and genuine. This means avoiding formulas, treating each story as unique, and letting the material suggest its own structure. "I do a lot of abstract stories, so you have to find a metaphor that people will remember. It's like a hook in the sense of a hook where you hang your coat. If you have the hook, then, 'Well, that was the story about the chicken who sang, right? What was he talking about? Oh, yeah, currency devaluations.'"

Krulwich's metaphors are often quite unexpected. To reinforce the idea of the slowing Japanese economy, he slows down the video. To reinforce that people cannot spell the word *millennium,* he shows a stern schoolteacher slowly spelling the word.

UNLEASH THE POWER OF THE WEB

The Web has probably done more to inspire new methods of storytelling than years of writing coaching.

Print, television, and radio are largely based on narrative, each having different tendencies or strengths (television is more easily emotional, print informational, and radio a blend that is also more intimate). Yet the options of any one of those mediums is limited. A print treatment of an event, we've noticed, generally involves just seven key elements—a narrative, a headline, a photo, an illustration, a graphic table or chart, and perhaps some design elements such as pull-quotes. Online, the list of storytelling tools and elements explodes—from data to hyperlinks to interactive graphics. In combination, as sites such as Syria Deeply reveal, storytelling becomes something self-directed, and the potential for engagement expands.

We can identify more than sixty such elements that can be combined (albeit more easily for a single running story, such as Syria, than on unrelated event news). Still, the list grows every month. "It's time to rethink the unit of journalism,"says Bill Adair, the creator of PolitiFact. It no longer needs to be the narrative story. But on any given story, the form or element employed should be driven by the goal of creating understanding, creating public insight, not just creating new forms for the sake of being new.

Here are a couple of conceptual approaches to doing so.

NEWS AS STRUCTURED DATA

The rich new wealth of data made possible by the Web can be rendered in ways that go beyond narratives about data (traditional "data reporting") or even the largely visual representations of numbers ("data visualizations"). One of these alternatives is to structure the information into new constructed data points that tell the story. This is data that is organized and analyzed into points of meaning beyond raw data.

PolitiFact, a website run by the *Tampa Times*, the focus of which is political "fact checking," is an example. Rather than write stories, the site rates the veracity of statements by political figures on a meter, from true to utterly false. Each rating, in effect, is a data point. These data points, in turn, can be combined to tell other stories over time, like charting the overall truthfulness of Barack Obama's statements and comparing his to other officials'.

Homicide Watch, a website that tracks crime in cities at the street level, does something similar. Information is logged as data points, not just narrative, and that data can be sorted, mapped, filtered, and analyzed in a comprehensive way over time.

This notion of data points is akin to the way raw baseball statistics, such as hits and bases-on percentage, can be divided into new statistical units, such as slugging percentage (OPS) or the overall performance of a player versus others at his position (replacement value).

The potential here is far greater than most news organizations realize. When print publications went digital, every story necessarily transformed from words on a page into a data record in a CMS database. Generally, however, few of these stories were treated as data that could be related to one another and analyzed program-matically. As an example, when newspapers posted to the Web real estate transactions that were printed in the paper, the different data points about location, price, and buyer could have been entered into different data fields, such as school districts, tax assessments, access to public transportation. If they had been, the potential for under-standing and analyzing that data would have grown exponentially. The paper would no longer just have stories archived. It would have knowledge about the community that could be used in different ways.

Turning news into data opens up profound new potential for creating a more deeply informed and engaged audience. Even news operations with fairly limited resources can analyze the data to do more insightful, efficient reporting. The data can be made sortable and interactive, for users to manipulate. News organizations can build news apps and mobile apps that leverage the data, and news coded and treated as data can be leveraged into new revenue. Both PolitiFact and Homicide Watch, for example, are making money by licensing their technology platform to other news organizations.

This notion of taking the information that news organizations gather and converting it into sortable data, rather than just narrative, is a mind shift. "A lot of what we do in journalism is counting.... Our devices can now do that for us," says Adair.[25] And, actually, our devices can do the simple counting better than we can.

MULTIMEDIA THAT'S ACTUALLY MULTI-MEDIA

A growing number of places are experimenting with Web-native sto-rytelling forms that blend video, audio, images, text, animations, and interactive graphics into one integrated narrative. This is somewhat different than the modular approach of Syria Deeply, which brings many content types to bear on a running story.

In this new form of storytelling, each piece of content involves multimedia dimensions. It's not a text story with a video embedded, or slide shows with text. Rather, these are new kinds of narratives that can't be clearly defined by their components, or even, admit-tedly, described here with words.

Zeega.com, for instance, is a website that enables anyone to easily combine animated GIFs, audio, images, text, and video from across the Web. Cowbird is another site that does something similar. Explore them and you will find video of the space race, narrated by astronaut Frank Borman, which users control by clicking, and collages of images with written text in different fonts, and animations with audio narration. There are no set norms, and most visitors will find some stories stimulating and others flat. Whether it's work by professionals such as Alex Madigral of the *Atlantic* or work by amateurs of all ages, there is only a single common denominator on Cowbird: creativity.

The *New York Times* received wide praise for its 2013 blending of elements in telling the story of the avalanche at Tunnel Creek in Washington State's Cascade Mountain range. The rich and skilled rendering of the incident that trapped and killed experienced skiers indicates the promise of this kind of new definition of multimedia, but it is hardly alone. Prison Valley is the interactive Web story of a town in the middle of Colorado with thirteen thousand people—and thirteen prisons—that is almost the meeting of television documentary and video game. NPR's Picture Show, a daily curation of photos from around the Web, produced a special report called "Lost and Found" that blended rare color photographs shot by amateur photographer Charles Cushman in 1938 with audio narration and the story of how Cushman's lost photos were discovered.

NARRATIVE IN SERVICE OF TRUTH

Finally, a caution. At times, narrative news writing has come to be viewed by editors as "writing with attitude." This is writing in which the journalist interjects his or her own feelings or opinions like a stage whisper, as is evident in self-referential lines like "There was an audible groan from the reporters when the candidate began to speak."

In some cases, an attitude can evolve that plays itself out in story after story, reporter after reporter, and even across different publications—a kind of running meta-narrative that journalists share. Politicians are in it only for power. Newt Gingrich is a little crazy.

George W. Bush was a puppet of Vice President Dick Cheney, or a lost son motivated to go to war in Iraq out of a Freudian need to one-up his father. Barack Obama is a professorial wonk, who, though elected twice to the presidency, doesn't really understand politics. The meta-narrative can become so powerful that it clouds the truth by oversimplifying it, although it lingers because it has strains of truth within it.

As we discuss technique, it is vital to take care to remember that form never determines substance. Technique should never alter the facts–the journalist's use of narrative forms must always be governed by the principles of accuracy and truthfulness, outlined earlier. Regardless of the form of presentation, the most engaging thing of all must be kept in mind: The story is true.

We have emphasized public affairs reporting in this discussion, but there is no subject for which the need for journalism that is engaging and relevant does not apply. In many ways, a story that helps the audience understand how the marketing strategy of Bill Gates affects their lives is as important as one that discusses a presidential candidate's position on Internet policy. The celebrity profile that shows why Hollywood makes the films it does can be a major work illuminating American culture–or it can be press agent promotion. It depends on the treatment, not the subject matter. Thus citizens can use the principle of engagement and relevance to judge the value of any journalism they encounter.

The next principle puts engagement and relevance in a broader context: How do we decide which stories get covered in the first place?

Make the News Comprehensive and Proportional

When she ran a company called Research Communications Limited, in Florida, Valerie Crane liked to tell a story about how *not* to study audiences. It's about the head of market research at a major cable television network who was asked to include this question in a round of focus groups with young viewers: "What will be the next big trend for young people?"

The researcher felt that you could use tools such as survey research, psychographics, and focus groups to see how people react to things. You could even use them to learn more about how audiences live their lives and how they use the media. But they couldn't be used, or at least they shouldn't, to replace professional judgment.

The bosses wanted the question asked, however, so the researcher watched glumly as the focus group leader put the question to the teenagers gathered around a table on the other side of the one-way mirror: "What do you think the next trend will be?" To his delight the response came: "What do you mean, what will the next trend be? We rely on you to tell us what the next big trend will be."[1]

If the principle of engagement and relevance helps explain how journalists can more effectively approach their stories, the principle that follows informs what stories to cover.

What is news? Given the limits of space, time, and resources, what is important and what isn't, what is to be left in and what is to be left out? And in the age of Internet infinity, who is to say? These questions inform the eighth principle citizens require from their press:

Journalism should keep the news comprehensive and in proportion.

But how? In the age of exploration, cartography was as much art as science. The men who sat over parchment and drafted the pictures of the expanding world were able to do a fairly accurate job of drawing Europe and even the neighboring seas. As they moved west to the New World, however, to the regions that were so inflaming people's imaginations, they mostly made guesses. What was there? Gold? Fountains of youth? The end of the earth? Demons? The size of distant continents they sketched would swell and shrink according to which audience they thought might be purchasing their charts. In the faraway Pacific, they painted sea monsters, dragons, or giant whales to fill in what they did not know. The more fanciful and frightening their monsters, the more exotic the gold mines and Indians they depicted, the more their maps might sell, and the greater their reputations as cartographers might grow. Sensation made for popular maps, even if they were poor guides for exploration or understanding.

Journalism is our modern cartography. It creates a map for citizens to navigate society. That is its utility and its economic reason for being. This concept of cartography helps clarify the question of what journalists should cover. As with any map, journalism's value depends on its completeness and proportionality. Journalists who devote more time and space to a sensational trial or celebrity scandal than they know it deserves—because they think it will sell—are like the cartographers who drew England or Spain the size of Greenland because doing so was popular. It may make short-term economic sense, but it misleads the traveler and eventually destroys the credibility of the mapmaker. The journalist who writes what he or she "just knows to be true," without really checking first, is like the artist who drew sea monsters in the distant corners of the New World. A journalist who leaves out so much of the other news in the process is like the mapmaker who failed to tell the traveler of all the other roads along the way.

Thinking of journalism as mapmaking helps us see that proportion and comprehensiveness are key to accuracy. This goes beyond individual stories. A front page, a Web page, or a newscast that is fun and interesting but by no reasonable definition contains anything significant is a distortion. At the same time, an account of the day that contains only the earnest and momentous, without anything light or human, is equally out of balance. The metaphor works for niche outlets or those focused on a single subject as well. Within the parameters of any subject, the concepts of proportionality and comprehensiveness still apply.

Obviously the limits of time and resources mean no institutional newsroom—let alone a small community website—can cover everything. One of the great challenges to commercial news production in the last decade has been shrinking resources. The notion of covering the waterfront has become harder and harder. Newsrooms with vision have had to decide which parts of the waterfront were most important, and which parts could get by with only an occasional stroll by the watchman.

Still, as citizens, we can ask these questions: Can I see the whole community represented in the coverage? Do I see myself? Does the report include a fair mix of what most people would consider either interesting or significant?

THE FALLACY OF TARGETED DEMOGRAPHICS

The mapmaker concept also helps us better understand the idea of diversity in news. If we think of journalism as social cartography, the map should include news from all our communities, not just those with demographics that are attractive to advertisers.

Unfortunately, this has proven a difficult principle to uphold. As we outlined in chapter 3, on loyalty to citizens, news organizations in the latter part of the twentieth century tended to focus on targeting–particularly on more affluent readers at newspapers and women in television news–because it served the needs of advertisers. There were several reasons for the strategy. After twenty-five years of losing audience and advertisers to television and other media, newspapers decided that there were structural limits to how much circulation they could have in the video age. Newspapers, in effect, decided they were a niche medium for the better educated. A second major reason had to do with costs. Newspapers sold each paper at a loss. The twenty-five cents, or even a dollar, paid covered only a fraction of what it cost to report, print, and deliver each copy. The rest–at one time roughly 75 percent–was made up in advertising revenue. Every copy of the paper sold to readers who didn't attract advertisers, in effect, cost money. The advertising business also decided to use newspapers mainly to reach the upper classes. Other media, especially television and radio, would be left to reach blue-collar audiences. In time, newspaper business strategists rationalized that targeting circulation on the affluent was not only a necessity but also a virtue. Calculating cost per copy and revenue per subscriber could justify not appealing to the whole community, in the name of economic efficiency. Writing off certain neighborhoods also meant not having to invest heavily to cover them.

It became difficult to argue with the economics, or even–given the loss of readership to television–the idea that lower-income readers were not coming back. Bucking that trend would have meant believing in a long-term strategy that Wall Street and most conventional thinking disagreed with. The problem was the path of narrowing ambitions for efficiency and profit made news outlets defensive, margin-oriented, and woefully ill-equipped to innovate when the technology of the Web suddenly made audience growth not only a possibility but a business imperative. In other words, while abdicating journalistic responsibility looked attractive in the short term, it proved to be a bad business strategy in the long term.

Television in time also began to think about targeted demographics–caring more about younger viewers who had not yet developed brand loyalty and women who were considered the commercial decision makers, particularly after more stations began to produce news coverage, shrinking everyone's share of the pie. The pressure was intensified by the fact that stations, and Wall Street, were accustomed to enormous operating profit margins from news at local television stations–usually more than 40 percent. To sustain the margins, stations kept fewer reporters on staff, and required most to produce at least a story a day.[2] Covering the whole community was impossible. The news was aimed instead at the most desirable segment–younger women.

The passage of time makes it possible to see serious problems with the economic logic of targeting demographics. One is that the audiences that started to be ignored in the late 1970s were the rising immigrant communities that were changing America's cities–precisely the population that had served as the backbone of journalism's success one hundred years earlier. Pulitzer, Scripps, and the rest of the penny-press barons made immigrants their core audience. Their prose was simple so immigrants could puzzle it out, and the editorial pages taught them how to be citizens. New Americans would gather after work to talk about what was in the papers, or to read to one another and discuss the highlights of the day.

As the immigrants of the 1880s and 1890s became more Americanized, the papers changed with them, becoming more middle class and more literary. The *New York World* of 1910 was a far more sober paper than the *World* of twenty years before. Eighty years later, the journalism industry, now obsessed with economic efficiency, did not make that same investment in establishing a relationship with the newest Americans, as it had done a century before.

Nor, as journalism targeted itself to just the most profitable demographics, did it make much investment in the youngest Americans. Stories were long, sophisticated, and often required a college degree to follow. Critics such as Stephen Hess of the Brookings Institution began to talk about journalists writing for their sources.[3] On television, the emphasis on crime, and also titillation, transformed television news from something that families would gather to watch into something from which parents would shield children.[4] In the name of efficiency and profit margins, we did nothing to help a new generation become interested in news. Today, audience data from the Internet show that young people are interested in news, but not in any of the old forms of presentation from older technologies.[5] While the news business cannot take all the blame, it had in fact a business strategy that helped create non-news consumers.

Could it have been otherwise? Could journalism have avoided this disconnect with the broader audience and reached out successfully to a more diverse audience and a younger one? This is difficult to answer definitively. But as journalism companies aimed at elite demographics and cost efficiency, the industry as a general rule did not try. Or by the time some publishers did, it was very late. The concept of the mapmaker makes the error clear. We created a map for certain neighborhoods and not others. Those who were unable to navigate where they lived gave it up.

The newscasts and newspapers that ignored whole communities also created problems for those they did serve. First, they left its audiences poorly informed because so much was left out. This left citizens vulnerable to making poor decisions about contemporary trends and about their needs. Ultimately, the strategy threatened the livelihood of the news organization, the institution with the greatest need for an interested citizenry. In the memorable phrase of Wall Street analyst John Morton, we had "eaten our seed corn."[6]

With whole communities left out, there was also the reverse problem of offering too much detail to the demographic group journalism was serving. Stories became longer and more copious, but aimed at a narrower segment of the population. The papers were sometimes more than a hundred pages a day and could take a full day to read. In television, targeting had a similar effect. The daily health segments on local TV today, for instance, which cover every new medical study no matter how preliminary, tend more to confuse citizens about health than inform them.

The mistake may be repairable. The Web makes possible new levels of engagement with audiences in ways inconceivable when news was limited to legacy platforms. Even with the disruption, the

Web has made news audiences younger and increased the level of news people consume. Consider just a few numbers. The average age of a print newspaper reader in 2013 was fifty-four. The average age of consumers of newspaper content on mobile devices was thirty-seven. A quarter of people also said they now consumed more news than they used to thanks to digital technology, versus 10 percent who said less. Among those that used mobile devices, 32 percent said they consumed more, with 8 percent saying less.[7]

One challenge is the question of the public commons. Creating a viable public commons where solutions can be found to community issues is not only a journalistic responsibility; it may be a path to financial viability. Thus those interested in journalism of community must act quickly to find ways to serve diverse populations–but to serve them as part of a whole community. There is also evidence that citizens agree. For several years, the Project for Excellence in Journalism has studied what kind of local TV news builds ratings. A design team of local news professionals rated covering the whole community as the most important responsibility of a TV news station. The data found that viewers concurred. Stations that covered a wider range of topics were more likely to be building or holding on to their audience than those that did not.[8]

THE LIMITS OF METAPHOR

As with all metaphors, the mapmaking comparison has its limits. Cartography is scientific, but journalism is not. You can plot the exact location of a road and measure the size of a country, or even an ocean. The proportions of a news story are another matter. A big story for some is unimportant to others.

Proportion and comprehensiveness in news are subjective. Their elusiveness, however, does not mean they are any less important than the more objective road and river features of maps. To the contrary, striving for them is essential to journalism's popularity–and financial health. It is also possible–not just an abstract notion–to pursue proportion and comprehensiveness despite their being subjective. Honest people can disagree about a story's importance, but citizens and journalists alike know when a story is being hyped disproportionately. They may disagree on precisely when the line was crossed, but at a certain point they know it has happened. In an era of more competition for people's attention, it tends to happen more.

As news has become atomized—as increasingly we get information from aggregators, RSS feeds, or delivery platforms such as Twitter in which we assemble our own news from disparate sources—the responsibility for proportionality and comprehensiveness shifts from the news provider to the individual. To the degree that we now rely on these self-styled systems and less on gatekeepers, we become both consumers and editors of our own news—and to an even greater degree, captains of our own civic awareness. The question is not "Is there anything I should know?" It is "Am I checking all the places I need to in order to inform myself?" We have become, in effect, the watchmen who must decide which parts of the waterfront to check.

Some assume that if there is anything worth knowing, someone will tell us. We will know it by osmosis. In reality, we won't. We increasingly will be left behind. Civic awareness will slip away from us, like physical fitness, from disuse.

THE PRESSURE TO HYPE

At moments when the news media culture is undergoing disruption, there is usually more pressure to hype and sensationalize. You might call it the principle of "the naked body and the guitar."

If you want to attract an audience, you could go down to a street corner, do a striptease, and get naked. You would probably attract a crowd in a hurry. The problem is, how do you keep people? Why should they stay once they have seen you naked? How do you avoid audience turnover? There is another approach. Suppose you went to the same street corner and played the guitar. A few people might listen on the first day. Perhaps a few more on the second. Depending on how good a guitar player you are, and how diverse and intriguing your repertoire is, the audience might grow each day. You would not, if you were good, have to keep churning the crowd by moving to new places, getting new people to replace those who grew tired of repetition. You would, to the contrary, benefit from staying on the same corner.

This is the choice, in effect, that the news media face at a time when new technology expands the number of outlets and each organization watches its audience shrink. When the future is uncertain, and it is unclear how long you can stay in business unless you generate audience fast, which approach should you pursue? To some extent, a news publisher has to operate according to a faith or philosophy, since empirical models of the past may not work in the future. Then add to this the new complexity of having real-time metrics that show how certain kinds of content can draw a quick crowd.

Some news organizations, even those with fairly serious legacies, have resorted to the path of the naked. Consider the websites of newspapers that display slide shows about celebrity starlets prominently on the home page. In part, this is driven by the idea that news has become a commodity that is in oversupply. As one Wall Street analyst, James M. Marsh Jr. of Prudential Securities, told us when we talked with him about television, "There is currently an overabundance of news programming, with supply easily outstripping demand."[9] In part, too, this path of the naked is driven by the fact that producing a lot of original reporting is expensive and requires a web of correspondents, camera crews, and bureaus in different parts of the world.

As noted earlier, in the chapter on engagement, television news employed a variety of techniques to try to lure audiences as cable disrupted its monopoly. Morning news programs put a heavy focus on celebrity, entertainment, lifestyle, and product cross-promotion. Nightly newscasts for a time shifted to showing less coverage of civic institutions in order to offer more entertainment and the attraction of celebrities, although that changed measurably after the terrorist attacks of September 11, 2001.[10] (By 2012, the three networks had developed fairly distinct personalities. CBS News offered measurably more coverage of so-called hard news topics such as government and foreign affairs, ABC News was more oriented to lifestyle coverage, and NBC News was in between.)[11]

Another technique is for TV newscasters to try to connect with audiences by telling people how they should feel about the news. They do this by lacing stories with emotional code words, words like "stunning ... horrifying ... horrific ..." and phrases such as "a serious warning every parent needs to hear." On one randomly selected morning, for instance, the three network shows used such words thirty times in introducing the first five stories alone, often in the anchor introduction or close, but sometimes by selecting sound bites in which sources used these words.[12]

Demonstrating emotion and even outrage can be a career booster for individual journalists, connecting them with audiences and demonstrating their humanity, in the vein of fictional anchorman Howard Beale of the Paddy Chayefsky film *Network*, who became more popular after he began declaring on the air, "I'm mad as hell, and I'm not going to take this anymore." These bursts of emotion may be honest at first, but they can also be exploited. After he evinced a powerful sense of outrage over and empathy with the victims of Hurricane Katrina in 2005, CNN host Anderson Cooper was promoted to become the news channel's main prime time host, complete with an ad campaign showing him in moments of emotional reaction to the news.

Various observers have lauded signs of the newfound passion of the fourth estate, and some have even wondered whether it might be a sign of a newfound aggressiveness. The praise, however, has by no means been unanimous. Many have questioned whether a hundred-year journalistic commitment to reporting the facts dispassionately was in jeopardy.

The issue cuts to the heart of what it means to be a journalist. In a profession that promises to suppress self-interest to assure credibility, when are emotionalism and outrage appropriate? It would be difficult to argue that emotions coming from journalists who are witnessing human suffering are always out of place. So if emotionalism seems appropriate in some cases but not in others, where is the line?

The first sensible rule of thumb would seem to be that it should come at those moments when any other reaction would seem forced—when emotion is the only organic response. When anchorman Walter Cronkite wiped his eyes after John Kennedy's assassination in 1963, or showed the sense of awe he felt over the space shots a few years later, it struck Americans as appropriate.

The second point is that emotionalism should disappear between the moment of discovery of a problem and the subsequent search for information meant to put the event into a broader and deeper context. Once journalists have reacted in a human way to what they have seen, they must compose themselves to search for answers, and that requires professionalism, skepticism, and intellectual independence. Human emotion is at the heart of what makes something news. But once you try to manufacture it, or use it to bring attention to yourself, you have crossed the line into something there is already enough of–reality entertainment. At that point, emotionalism becomes a shtick to exploit the news, not a genuine and helpful reaction to it.

THE ANALYTICS OF METRICS

The Web introduces another dimension to all of this, one that is not as unprecedented as some in news believe. In theory, the Web allows publishers to know how many people read or watch a particular piece of content, where they go on a page, and how long they stay on it.

There are two major problems with metrics that hinder publishers from using these data to accurately assess their work. The first is that the metrics themselves are confused. What is the right thing to measure? Is it unique visitors–a proxy for the overall size of the audience? Scholars such as Matthew Hindman at George Washington University point out that the unique visitor is muddled by the fact that the same person accessing a site on different devices is counted multiple times. Or is engagement measured better by time spent on the site, or length of visit? Or are page views the right measure? And all of these questions are confused by the fact that there is no standard way of measuring. Data from comScore can vary widely from that supplied by Nielsen, or Omniture, or Google Analytics. Emerging data also show that many of the page views may not actually be from people at all, but from bots, automated clicks designed to make traffic look higher. What are publishers to make, for instance, of the fact that one month comScore gave the *Washington Post* 17 million unique visitors while Nielsen counted 10 million, or that the two firms' calculations of Yahoo's audience in a given month varied by 34 million uniques, a difference equivalent to the population of Canada?[13]

The second problem with Web metrics is newspeople's traditional resistance to using data to drive their editorial decisions. Even if the data were reliable, should news organizations that built their reputations on depth and quality in their legacy platforms build their online operations by chasing page views in the hope of selling more cheap banner ads? The metrics only repeated a familiar and predictable lesson: Wire stories about Justin Bieber would always blow away enterprise policy stories about Mississippi politician Haley Barbour. Those celebrity slide shows atop the home page of papers like the *San Francisco Chronicle* may drive traffic, but they also brand the paper as having to rely on gimmicks to survive.

If the experience of television, which has had real-time data for years, is a guide, there are reasons to be concerned that the news industry will struggle to make sense of it all.

Using minute-to-minute ratings, a television news manager can tell at what point in certain stories people began to click away. So the medium began to tailor newscasts to ensure that every story had a wide viewership. But the strategy did little to forestall the declining audience—and it may have encouraged it.

"News organizations have been hoist on their own petard," explained John Carey, an audience researcher who worked with NBC and other media clients.[14] "Over time they have followed those ratings numbers, doing more and more of those stories that get high numbers, and they get stuck in those patterns." As a consequence, prime time newsmagazines were "stuck with an older audience, a more sentimental one and a more sensational one" while the bulk of viewers fled. "In a sense, the people at the network know it, but they don't know how to get out of it," Carey said at the height of the prime time magazine craze. He was right.[15]

In local TV news, meanwhile, managers tended to operate by

a set of conventional ideas about what drove viewership, which imagined that the audience was fairly dumb and needed to be manipulated. Among those myths was the idea that stimulating visuals would hook viewers at the top of the broadcast and keep them watching. Another related idea was that crime and public safety stories that lent themselves to such visuals worked, and that stories about civic affairs, or information-dense stories about policy and government, would drive viewers away.

Managers often saw confirmation of these preconceptions in the way they interpreted their ratings data—and also in inexpensive market research designed by TV consultants that almost unwittingly reinforced conventional industry wisdom.

When more rigorous research was conducted, it repudiated much of this conventional thinking. Probably the most detailed effort was conducted over several years by the Project for Excellence in Journalism, in collaboration with scholars from the Shorenstein Center at Harvard and the University of Hawaii. Their effort involved several steps. Rather than simply identifying each story by its topic, their research deconstructed each story by the level and quality of the reporting. Rather than look at ratings minute by minute, the research looked at ratings over time to reveal deeper trends. And rather than look at how audiences reacted at one station, the research examined the relationship between content and long-term ratings across many stations, providing a more robust sample.

The analysis of 33,000 stories, from 2,419 newscasts on 150 stations over five years, found that how a story is gathered and reported—the number, balance, and expertise of sources, whether its relevancy to the audience and importance to the community is established, whether the story is more complete—are *twice* as important as topic in determining audience ratings.[16]

This finding is especially important in a digital age when increasingly the story—rather than the newscast—becomes the essential unit consumers will seek out.

The research revealed something basic but often overlooked. TV stations that found poor audience response to their civic affairs reporting were misunderstanding what they were hearing. People were not expressing disinterest in civic affairs. They were reacting to the fact that too much reporting of it wasn't very good. And it wasn't good because programmers thought viewers wouldn't be interested.

The research conducted, in turn, expected this and subtly reinforced it. We discovered that self-fulfilling prophecy when we worked with the Pew Research Center for the People & the Press to conduct an experiment that compared the wording in a survey from a popular TV market researcher with different question wording Pew researchers considered more objective. The questions were probing the public appetite for news about government. The TV market research survey asked simply whether people wanted to see more stories about state and local government. Only 29 percent said they would be very interested in that kind of reporting. When Pew connected government to the problems it was focused on solving, the numbers changed dramatically. When people were asked whether they'd be interested in "news reports about what government can do to improve the performance of local schools," the percentage of "very interested" jumped to 59 percent. And when participants were asked whether they would be interested in reports on what government could do to ensure that public places were safe from terrorism, the percentage of "very interested" rose even further, to 67 percent.[17] Similar interest-level percentages were tallied for stories about reducing health care costs. All of these topics, from schools to health care to public safety, have everything to do with politics and government.

The same challenge–of how to create a better journalism with data rather than confirm the worst expectations about the audience–now faces publishers as they grapple with the emerging Web metrics.

MARKETING VS. MARKETING

So, as journalism moves ahead in an age of more data, what should we keep in mind from the research of the past–and particularly television–to avoid the mistake of misguided self-fulfilling prophecies and attention-seeking gimmicks that may in the long run prove self-destructive?

The first step is that those engaged in reporting news cannot isolate themselves and ignore the ways in which data can help them produce a richer and more rewarding content. To the contrary, in an age when audiences are in control of their own media consumption, the survival of a journalism that serves the public depends on a new deeper and sophisticated understanding of that public. As we have said elsewhere, citizens no longer have to change their behavior to suit the delivery patterns of the news media. From now on, the media must change its behavior to match the needs of the audience.

Some believe that the news industry should coalesce around a standardized set of metrics that will illuminate which stories and trends are worthy of coverage. We disagree. This may help in setting prices for advertising or e-commerce, but the metrics of news also have to reflect civic and editorial judgments such as significance, relevance, and quality. As we noted before, the maximum audience is not always achieved by focusing only on popular stories. It is actually achieved by understanding your community better and then by presenting a range of stories so diverse that there is something there for everyone. Television has had unified metrics for years, and while it has helped advertisers agree on where to spend their dollars, it has been inadequate for creating a more valuable and engaging journalism.

The answer to deeper engagement will be found in a new kind of audience research, and a different way of analyzing Web metrics about traffic.

That starts with moving away from the sort of market research used in other industries that doesn't take into account the realities of the news business. Conventional market research asks consumers to choose between predictable alternatives. Do you prefer this sneaker in orange or blue? Your toothpaste in a squeeze bottle or tube? Paste or gel? "[People tend] to choose from a limited spectrum of options. You already have defined for people what the range of choices will be," explained Lee Ann Brady, who for years did media analysis for Princeton Survey Research Associates. "So they are not telling you what they like. They tend to be reacting to your limited choices and giving you a hierarchy."[18]

Consider a typical survey, which lasts for twenty minutes and is comprised of maybe twenty or twenty-five questions. Usually only two of these questions allow the interviewee to come up with an independent answer. The rest either are multiple-choice or yes-or-no, asking the respondent whether he or she agrees or disagrees with statements offered by the survey.

But because news changes every day, it defies much of traditional market research, which tests a static universe of options. News is what hasn't happened yet, so it's difficult for people to know in advance what type of coverage they want to receive.

Conventional market research, when applied to news, also tends to focus on determining what kind of news people want more of and less of. This kind of approach makes the mistake of asking citizens to play the role of editor or executive producer, a role that they have not really thought about and thus are not well equipped to play. In this scenario, the answers researchers get back are guesses, often influenced by what respondents think they should say, and usually asking for more of everything, something that cannot be delivered. Any research that results in people providing answers that are not deeply felt is flawed.

Focus groups—one of the cheapest and most common forms of market research—allow for more open-ended questions, and they are popular because they allow the client to observe audiences talking about their products. "Occasionally, you will get a voice or thought from a focus group that had never occurred to you," said Brady. "So they can be helpful if you have a blank slate."[19]

But anyone who has monitored a focus-group session can readily see its limitations as a means of probing the news. To begin, focus groups are not scientific samples approximating the population at large. It is enormously difficult to make focus groups representative, or to have two focus groups replicate each other, a basic definition of objectivity. One or two people can sway the discussion, or the focus-group leader can unconsciously lead the group toward a predetermined answer.

Probably most important, though, is that organizations often misuse focus groups to test hypotheses or options they are already considering, instead of probing for open-ended ideas. "Focus groups first entered the scene as a way of evoking ideas that could then be taken out and examined in a properly done open survey and applied to a larger population," said the late Leo Bogart, one of the pioneers who first tried to bring rigorous data analysis to media. "There was no expectation that anyone would draw conclusions or make projections from what a handful of people said." In most contemporary media usage, however, "they are greatly misused," Bogart had concluded by the end of his life.[20]

But what if we return to the idea of the "interlocking public," to a news report that A. M. Rosenthal called "the smorgasbord of news and information" when he was executive editor of the *New York Times?* Or, as newspaper editor Dave Burgin used to say about how a page in a newspaper should be laid out: If no story may attract more than 15 percent of the audience, make sure there are enough stories so that everyone will want to read one of them. By choosing content this way, a news organization can be more assured of putting the news in proportion.

Or go back to the mapmaker analogy. If journalism provides people only with information they say in advance that they want to know about, we are telling them only about the part of the community they already know about.

A NEW MARKET RESEARCH FOR JOURNALISM

So what kind of audience research and metrics analysis would have more value and lead to a fuller approach to news?

First, it should be designed to help journalists make judgments—not to eliminate their need to make them in the first place. Rather than asking people to be surrogate editors or producers, a better research method would approach the person surveyed as a citizen and ask that person to talk about his or her life. How do you spend your time? Walk us through your day. How long is your commute? What are you worried about? What do you hope and fear for your kids? These kinds of questions are helpful because they probe broad trends of interest—the kinds of questions that will allow journalists to understand citizens better and then create a journalism that is comprehensive and proportional to their community and their needs.

This was the kind of research conducted by Valerie Crane at Research Communications Limited. Crane's research involved two broad approaches, neither of them strictly traditional. The first identified through in-depth interviews and then larger survey samples what basic needs in people's lives are met by the news they get—a quantitative way of going back to the function of news. "For some people it is about connecting to community," Crane said. "For some it is about making their life better [healthier, safer, more comfortable]. For others it's about making up their own mind. For others it is a way of winning social acceptance." Crane identified a range of needs that vary depending on the type of media, the way news categories are defined, and the kind of audience that is studied.[21] Instead of asking directly what kinds of topics people are interested in, Crane quantified for news companies the purposes for which people use news. "Too rarely do people [in news companies] think about what citizens' needs are," she said of her clients.

Second, Crane studied how people in a given community are living their lives, using a version of what some people call lifestyle and trends research. This type of research tends to group populations into clusters based not just on demographics but on attitudes and behavior. She studied fifteen different areas, from health, to religion, work, consumerism, family relations, education, and more, and identifies the top concerns and trends in a given place. Taken together, her research into why people use the news and her study of the deeper concerns and trends in their lives gave journalists insight into how to apply their own professional judgment. But the research, she said, should augment, not supplant, that judgment.

Al Tompkins, a former news director who teaches broadcasting at the Poynter Institute, believes Crane's research told journalists "how communities live, where their loyalties are, and not just what are they watching, but why are they watching."[22] Crane's work, Tompkins said, "guides the presentation of news but doesn't determine what stories you do." For instance, although a lot of research suggests people don't like politics, Tompkins said, "Crane's research shows us they do care about their community, but they don't trust the political institutions. . . . It wasn't the topic they were sick of, it was the approach to the topic."

Researcher John Carey conducted ethnographic research at Greystone Communication. Ethnography, which is an outgrowth of anthropology, works through direct on-site observation. Carey sat in people's houses and watched how they interact with media and technology. He sat in people's houses through mealtimes, at breakfast, dinner, early in the morning, and even late at night.

Carey's findings turned many of the conventional ideas about television on their head. For instance, although a good deal of social science research suggests what some academics have called "the supremacy of the visual"–the notion that pictures are more powerful than words in television–Carey's work found that "very often people are not watching but listening to television news. Many people are actually reading a newspaper while the news plays on their living room TV, and they tend to turn their attention to the television when they hear something that they think will have important pictures." Carey's research suggested that it would be a mistake to focus on the visuals of a TV news program at the expense of having engaging verbal content.

Carey's research also suggested that the concept of teasers, or tempting people to stay tuned a little longer for an important upcoming report, may be ineffective. "A big mistake is thinking that people are watching over a length of time. Teasers are a huge mistake. People don't wait." Those items that say, "Will it rain tomorrow? Well, tonight will be cold, and Jim will be back in seven minutes with the complete forecast"–those tend to drive people away. Carey's observations show that any time there is a commercial, most viewers immediately switch channels.[23] A better alternative, Carey believed, would be to provide key information like weather constantly, to pack information all over your newscast, even to scroll it during commercials. "You would grab people by the constancy of your information."

The late Carole Kneeland, a news director in Austin, Texas, in the late 1990s who was also known for defying conventional wisdom, followed the approach. She repeated the weather forecast throughout the newscast on the assumption that people wouldn't stay for the whole half hour, but if you could inform more people quickly, over time you would command the most loyal and the largest audience. "I think in the future we will have to break away from thirty-minute and sixty-minute content," Carey suggested. "You could have programming that is five minutes long in cycles," with longer pieces at certain times, much like radio programs with news and weather repeating every eight or twelve minutes, or NPR's broadcasts, in which repeating headlines are intermixed with longer stories.

Carey's ideas are even more powerful now, when citizens have so much control over their own news consumption, and better options are only a click away. His ideas adapt journalism to the needs of the citizen—rather than seeing the citizen as someone whose attention should be manipulated on behalf of an advertiser. Ultimately, this will make the journalism more valuable and more popular. It turns us toward a journalism that fulfills the promise of a digital age, one that is a service on behalf of the public—something that helps people improve their lives, rather than a static product designed for another era. That mind shift, from product to service, is one of the underlying ideas of this book.

Yet these are concepts so far beyond the realm of traditional market research, or even traditional ratings and circulation data, that they require journalists to reinvent the nature of research and the formats of journalism.

THE REAL METRICS OF THE WEB

To fulfill journalism's potential in the digital age, there are two more steps to take with regard to research and data. The next one, after understanding how citizens live their lives, involves doing a better job of analyzing Web metrics. Journalists must begin to analyze their Web metrics in a way that sustains journalistic values and doesn't overwhelm them. This means digging more deeply into the metrics, instead of abandoning them or reading them at face value.

The conventional approach to metrics is to look at them as a way of finding out which stories or content are most popular. As we have noted, there are debates over which metrics matter most—is it page views, time with a story, number of visitors? Some publishers use companies that match time of day and location of stories on a site (although the growing use of multiple devices complicates that). All of this information is fine, but it does little to solve the riddle that some stories—and, to a degree, some topics—are naturally going to be more popular than others, in ways that are usually predictable.

One publisher, Deseret Media, led by former Harvard Business School professor Clark Gilbert, has tried to crack this problem by trying to compare similar categories of stories to one another. His company compares the performance of its enterprise stories (those pieces that it has put the most effort into producing), for instance, to the performance of other enterprise stories, and sports stories to other sports stories. This allows his managers to make sure that certain kinds of journalism, whose value is not easily quantifiable, are measured fairly. The long enterprise series that is significant but not necessarily popular is not measured against the story about the college football championship that almost everyone will read.

Deseret is onto something important here. Not everything that matters can be counted, and not everything that can be counted matters. To avoid the trap of counting the wrong thing, or missing what's important, publishers need to build their analytics around their news values. In the same way that stories can be turned into data, stories can also be tagged online for journalism values. Stories (or any content) can be rated for their level of enterprise, the quality of the execution, the public importance or impact of the piece.

This involves combining two sciences. The first is content auditing, or the science of creating variables that identify each story by different values. The second is then using metrics in new ways, correlating these values to one another and to traffic. It is an emerging area, but it approximates the detailed research we did at the Project for Excellence in Journalism in the past on local television, which unlocked what kind of journalism really connected with the public and got beyond the surface of driving managers toward a reliance on blockbuster content.

This kind of research obviously depends first on understanding the community. But if the news organization's sense of values resonates with its community, that will reveal itself over time in the data–though not necessarily instantly. Yet if the thinking and the execution are right, providing the public with a diverse mix of content that puts effort into significant topics and issues, it should result in a larger audience over a longer period.

Recently, a movement has begun to form around the idea of "impact," or the social good of stories. While a promising development, we believe it is too limited. Social good misses the more fulsome definition of journalism's purpose, which includes discovery of the new and unusual and may in the long run be more important than presently suspected. But the concept of imagining characteristics of content that go beyond content is the right idea.

THE NEW NEWS CONSUMER

The third and final step toward a better, more useful understanding of audience and metrics is to learn how audiences are beginning to consume news in new ways. This is slightly different from asking people in a given market how they live their lives, the first component of a better approach. And it is different from harnessing online metrics. Understanding the new news consumer involves research at a national level that discovers how people behave in acquiring news, now that they no longer have to adapt their behavior to the delivery cycles of the news media. This involves understanding how time of day influences the way people interact with news and how that, in turn, influences device choice. It involves understanding how setting–office versus home versus commuting, or weekends versus workday–influences news behavior. It also involves beginning to discover what we call the personal news cycle, or the path to learning about news. People no longer rely primarily on one medium for news. They tend to hear stories initially via word of mouth and television, and then tend to go to a second source, and often a different platform, to learn more. They also choose different media for different kinds of stories and questions they want to answer. Now that publishers are no longer limited by format, device, or style of content, knowledge of these differences is critical to making journalism that serves the citizen.

The *New York Times* has done some of the most rigorous work in using data to understand its audience, as it led the way in charging for online content, against the doubts of many critics. By 2013, the company had a team of two hundred people working on its subscription system, twenty-five of whom were engaged in audience research and testing of content, pricing, and market strategies. The company relied heavily on involving readers in giving feedback on new designs, content, and marketing. Nearly every idea, from new content to sales approaches, went through A-B testing, the system of trying two different approaches to innovations and measuring the audience response.

This relentlessly empirical approach helped the paper succeed in introducing a paywall when virtually no consumers were used to paying for online content and there was no previously successful model to follow. Mistakes would have been easy to make, and almost all outsiders expected the *New York Times* to fail at this. Indeed, after the paper succeeded, many dismissed that success as evidence that the *Times*, as a national paper aimed at elites, was unique. In reality, what was unique was that the paper had studied the audience and listened to them while creating its new pricing model.

The lesson, said Tim Griggs, is "test, test, test, even things you think are a given."[24] It is a drastic change from a few years earlier. The paper learned, for instance, not to charge print subscribers more, which would exploit its most loyal readers rather than reward them. It also learned that when introducing the new plan, it needed to explain the pay meter to its readers, instead of annoying them by relentlessly promoting it. Thus, as readers get closer to reaching the ceiling on free articles, they see a counter at the bottom of the screen—not an ad or a promotion. The *Times* experience probably stands as the most dramatic example we know of a quality news organization that ran toward research, not away from it, in making informed and innovative decisions, and this has affected not just its understanding of its audience but the process that informs its editorial decision making. The *Times* has come to see empiricism and research as a genuine tool for understanding the audience rather than something that would distort editorial values and amount to pandering.

As with taking command of metrics, the field here is just emerging. But it will be critical going forward.

An embrace of data on behalf of better journalism is a significant shift for those who aspire to produce news in the public interest. The traditional resistance to research in newsrooms was often based on an urge to protect journalistic independence or, more specifically, to avoid allowing advertising and sales to make news decisions. Research tended to be controlled by the marketing and sales departments. For the most part, it was designed, particularly at print organizations, to inform advertisers.

"It's what I call the myth of the golden gut," Crane told us. That view was always self-defeating, even if it was an understandable response to bad data. It made newspeople seem like incurious know-nothings resistant to learning or to change. That view now is even more suicidal. It will likely be the difference between success and failure. Those who fail to study and understand the new news audience will almost certainly lose out to those who do. Ironically, journalists have more of the skills needed to do the kind of observational research about people's lives that might be best suited for journalism. Journalists, however, have not developed any tradition of doing it. Nor do they appear close to trying.

If journalism lost its way, the reason in large part is that it lost meaning in people's lives, not only with its traditional audience but with the next generation as well. We have shown, we hope, that a major reason for this is that journalists no longer have the self-confidence to try to make the news comprehensive and proportional. Like the ancient maps that left much of the world terra incognita, journalism confronts contemporary audiences with similar blank spaces in place of uninteresting demographic groups or topics too difficult to pursue.

If journalists are nimble and creative enough to use it, the interactive nature of the Web offers opportunities to take dramatic steps in overcoming the problems created by shortsighted use of market research and demographic data. Using these new tools can create a journalism that truly meets the needs of communities, and create the kind of understanding that would allow the public itself to continuously fill in some of the blanks in the coverage of their world and to provide knowledge based on their own peculiar experiences that give them unique insights.

The answer is not to return to a day when journalists operate purely by instinct. We hope we have spotlighted a group of new cartographers who are developing tools to chart the way people live their lives today and the needs for news these lives create. They are providing one of the most important tools a news organization needs to design a more comprehensive and proportional news report that attracts rather than repels the audience. Now it is up to journalists to try.

With all this, there is still another element that ties all the others together. It relates to what goes on in the newsroom itself.

Journalists Have
a Responsibility
to Conscience

For three weeks in October 2002, Washington, DC, was paralyzed by fear. With cunning stealth and deadly efficiency, someone stalked thirteen men, women, and children in the city and its Maryland and Virginia suburbs, shooting to death nine and seriously wounding four. The victims included a twelve-year-old boy who was shot while walking up to his school.

A nationwide manhunt ensued, with city, county, state, and federal law enforcement officials taunted by notes left at the murder scenes, including one that warned "your children are not safe anywhere, anytime." The murders seemed frighteningly like the opening of a guerilla phase in the shadowy ill-defined "war against terror" declared by President George W. Bush thirteen months after hijacked jetliners became suicide bombs, killing thousands when they obliterated the World Trade Center buildings in New York City and destroyed a section of the Pentagon in Washington. Press coverage of the murders pushed other news—including that of American troops fighting in Afghanistan—off the front page as the world focused on the fear that gripped America's capital community.

For Howell Raines, executive editor of the *New York Times*, the

Washington story presented another opportunity to send a message to his staff. Under Raines, the paper's strategy was to "flood the zone" of a big story and dominate everybody else. Raines had been promoted to the top job in 2001, a few weeks before the September 11 attacks, and he had mobilized the staff to cover that historic event so well that it won the paper a record five Pulitzer Prizes. The Washington story was his opportunity to take on the *Washington Post* in its hometown and try to erase the hurt many *Times* staffers still nursed over the way the *Post* had out-reported them on the Watergate scandal thirty years earlier.

Although the *Times* had the largest bureau in Washington, with a cluster of a half dozen of the paper's best investigative reporters, Raines kept direction of the coverage in New York. Among the people he dispatched to Washington was Jayson Blair, a twenty-seven-year-old former intern who had been a reporter for only twenty-one months. Within days the addition of Blair seemed an inspired choice. The new reporter was producing front-page stories with tantalizing details that other Washington-area reporters were unable to match.

But soon, experienced reporters in Washington began raising questions about "this guy Blair," whose name kept appearing in the paper but whom none of them saw in the bureau or in the field. One of those reporters, Eric Lichtblau, who covered the Department of Justice for the *Times*, became concerned when stories by Blair were routinely questioned by officials he had come to trust in the Department of Justice. Other reporters were raising questions as well, and when one source in exasperation told Lichtblau he "didn't know who the anonymous sources this guy Blair is depending on was, but much of what he was writing is just not true," Lichtblau went to Rick Berke, the bureau's news editor. Berke reported his concerns to New York, where he said he was "brushed off" with suggestions that the complaints were prompted by jealousy. Raines, Berke was told, "had already decided Blair was a great shoe-leather reporter."[1]

What none of the people in the Washington bureau knew was that complaints about Blair's work had infected the newsroom in New York for months before Blair was sent to Washington. Somehow, as Blair was moved from one supervising editor to another, the doubts about the quality of his work didn't travel with him. It was as if the editors worked on different continents instead of a few yards or miles from one another.

Washington reporters were considering filing an organized complaint to New York when two suspects were arrested and charged in the sniper shootings case. Coverage was reduced, and the tension and doubts began to ease as Blair was reassigned to other stories. The dateline on his stories was no longer Washington; they began to appear from Maryland, West Virginia, Ohio, even Texas, where Robert Rivard, the editor of the *San Antonio Express-News,* saw something in a Blair story that troubled him. It concerned him enough to send an e-mail message to Raines and *Times* managing editor Gerald Boyd, telling them he had found an article written by Blair to be "disturbingly similar" to one his newspaper had published eight days earlier.

This outside complaint from the editor of another newspaper couldn't be ignored, and Raines and Boyd confronted Blair with it. The young reporter tried to explain himself but quickly became caught up in a web of contradictions. After two days, it became clear that he had never visited the Texas home he wrote about, and his "eyewitness" detail had come from pictures in the *Times* photo archives. The rest of his information came from stories by other reporters. On May 1, 2003, Blair resigned. News of his resignation had the effect of blasting open closed lines of communication inside the *Times.* One after the other, staff members realized that they were not the only ones who had been suspicious of Blair's behavior and his work.

A full-scale investigation revealed what many on the staff had suspected: Blair was not an aggressive, dedicated reporter but a troubled young man relying on deceit, plagiarism, and fiction to further his career at the expense of everyone around him. Staffers started to air long-repressed feelings of resentment, even betrayal, about the paper, feelings they had thought they were alone in having. For the next two weeks Raines and Boyd met with individuals and groups in the newsroom and tried to reassure them that the paper's values hadn't changed. The people they heard in those meetings were reporters and junior editors who believed such basic violations of standards and values threatened to destroy their own credibility, and that of the newspaper.

Instead of being reassured, staff discontent only became more intense and aggressive, and publisher Arthur Sulzberger Jr. announced that he and Raines and Boyd would meet with the newsroom in a "town hall" meeting to address questions and concerns. The meeting, which was closed to other journalists, was held in a nearby theater. The depth of suspicion and anger that focused on senior management during the session would later be described as "unusually raw, emotional, and candid." Some of those who took part not only described the confrontation to reporters from other news organizations but also sent e-mail messages to journalism watch sites like Romenesko, where they were posted for everybody to see. Their messages began to build a public bill of particulars against the leadership of Raines and Boyd.

The picture these messages painted was of a newsroom in which internal communications had become so dysfunctional that five years of warnings about the quality and reliability of Blair's work were ignored, as he was assigned to more and more important stories, until his byline appeared on stories of national–even international– interest. Before the Blair episode concluded, both Raines and Boyd were forced out,[2] and more than two dozen newsroom employees engaged in a long-term reorganization of the newsroom's standards, structure, and operations.

By June the internal investigation had documented Blair's "frequent acts of journalistic fraud ... widespread fabrication and plagiarism [that] represent a profound betrayal of trust and a low point in the 152-year history of the newspaper." As more information surfaced, it became clear to the staff that it had taken an outside voice to break open the dysfunctional lines of internal communication.

Much of the impetus for the collapse of the top newsroom managers was credited to the Internet, on which many of the *Times* employees posted the complaints that previously had been ignored. Staff members who used the open architecture of the new medium to become "the outside voice" provided a check on internal behavior. Along with others, they realized that the Web had assumed an important role in opening new channels through which values and standards could be questioned and judged by the larger community, which depends on the integrity of the press.

In the end, journalism is an act of character. Given that there are no laws, no regulations, no licensing, and no formal self-policing practices governing journalism's production—and because journalism by its nature can be exploitative—a heavy burden rests on the ethics and judgment of the individual news gatherer, and the organization that publishes the work. And this is even truer in an age when publishing can be an individual act.

This would be a difficult challenge for any profession. But for journalism there is the added tension between its public service mission—the aspect of the work that justifies its intrusiveness—and the interests that finance the work. Today, to a greater degree than before, more of the work of journalism occurs in or is underwritten by think tanks, issue advocacy groups, donors, political organizations, and other organizations for whom journalism is a new and ancillary activity.

At the same time, the rise of the Web and the democratization of content production have given voice to citizens who are monitoring politics, society, and the press, creating a new broad cohort of media pundits and critics. Some operate independently; others express their views at a host of more formal settings that have grown up to watch the press—places such as Media Matters on the Left or NewsBusters on the Right. Together, they represent an unprecedented network of media watchdogs. Today, if trouble is brewing inside a newsroom, it will almost certainly leak. If the organization is skirting responsibilities, somebody will point it out. The tension and fear of having organizational issues discussed outside the newsroom have prompted some editors to stop sending memos or putting decisions down on paper.

Some of these new monitors have not only increased demands for transparency in newsrooms but, as was the case with Jayson Blair, also have helped expose ethical lapses and flaws in the hierarchical structure of organizations like the *New York Times*. It's true that a good deal of the new expanded digital public discourse about media does not rise above ideological accusations of the press being too conservative or too liberal. When it does, however, and when it brings up serious issues, the credibility of that journalistic product can be greatly affected. For all the vitriol, we believe the public discourse about media has made those who produce news more thoughtful, more reflective, more searching about their work. After a decade of turmoil, criticism and epochal financial disruption have forced journalists to become better at their jobs.

It's important to keep this consequence in mind because, whether or not we are conscious of its importance, when all is said and done, what we are choosing when we download an app, follow a media voice in social media, click a digital magazine, choose a TV news program, or read a newspaper or its website is the authority, honesty, and judgment of the journalists who produce it. And it's part of journalists' responsibility, in whatever setting they work, to encourage a transparent and open culture that won't lead critics to call the credibility of the product into question.

As a consequence, there is one more principle that those engaged in journalism have come to understand about their work, and that we as citizens should recognize when we make our media choices. It is the most elusive of the principles, yet it ties all the others together:

Journalists have an obligation to exercise their personal conscience.

Every journalist, from the occasional citizen sentinel or freelancer to the newsroom, to the manager who visits the boardroom, must have a personal sense of ethics and responsibility–a moral compass. What's more, journalists have a responsibility to voice their personal conscience out loud and allow others around them to do so as well.

Especially for journalists in institutional settings, the exercise of this conscience requires that managers and owners create an open newsroom. Such an environment is essential to fulfilling the principles outlined in this book.

Innumerable hurdles make it difficult to produce news that is accurate, fair, balanced, citizen focused, independent minded, and courageous. But the effort is smothered in its crib without an open atmosphere that allows people to challenge one another's assumptions, perceptions, and prejudices. We need our journalists to feel free, even encouraged, to speak out and say, "This story idea strikes me as racist," or "You're making the wrong decision," or "I want to raise a concern about something on the site." Only in a setting in which all can bring their diverse viewpoints to bear can the news have any chance of accurately anticipating and reflecting the increasingly diverse perspectives and needs of American culture.

Simply put, those engaged in news must recognize a personal obligation to differ with or challenge editors, owners, donors, advertisers, and even citizens and established authority if fairness and accuracy require they do so. That engagement must be constructive in order to be effective, not self-serving, egoistic, or designed to create pyrotechnics.

In turn, those who run news organizations, whether large institutions or small Web experiments, must encourage and allow staff to exercise this personal obligation. It would be naïve to assume that journalists' individual commitment is enough, in an age of uncertainty about the future of the press. Many journalists are so worried that they might be swept away by the next wave of layoffs that challenging authority and a flawed organizational culture is the last thing on their minds. So news publishers need to build a culture that nurtures individual responsibility. And then managers have to be willing to listen, not simply manage problems and concerns away.

There is no separate section in this book on ethics. That is because this moral dimension, this quality of judgment, tone, taste, and character, is implicit in why we choose one magazine, newscast, or website over another. Ethics are woven into every element of journalism and every critical decision that journalists make. As citizens engaging with media, we sense this often more acutely than do journalists themselves, who sometimes cordon off ethics as an isolated topic.

As Chicago newscaster Carol Marin told us when we created the Committee of Concerned Journalists some sixteen years ago, "I think a journalist is someone who believes in something that they would be willing to quit over."[3]

In 1993, as NBC's *Dateline* was preparing a segment called "Waiting to Explode?" alleging that the gas tanks in General Motors trucks had a tendency to rupture and ignite in crashes, the reporter of the piece voiced concern. Although correspondent Michele Gillen had collected footage of actual accidents in which drivers wound up trapped inside burning cars, she knew that crash tests NBC had conducted had not produced the same results. A small fire broke out, but it lasted only fifteen seconds before burning itself out. So when she learned that the network was setting up additional crash tests rigged to be more dramatic, Gillen did something she had not done in her seven months with the show. She called her boss, Jeff Diamond, at home and expressed her concerns. She wanted the new tests stopped.

Diamond told her that he thought the footage would be striking and would add to the report. The two went back and forth on the point for days, but Diamond in the end convinced Gillen to narrate the test crash when her producers assured her that her concerns would be noted in the final broadcast. The test would be labeled "unscientific" and any conclusions would be left to the experts.

The piece, however, didn't note all of Gillen's concerns. It never mentioned how long the fire lasted or that it went out on its own. In the end Gillen agreed to narrate the piece anyway, against her instinct, because, she said, "at some point, you have to have faith in your executive producer, and if he's telling me this is okay, and he's responsible for looking after my best interests and the show's best interests, then I'll trust him."[4] Gillen was wrong, and the embarrassment of the rigged explosions was the low point in the history of NBC News.

The incident shows how delicate the question of moral compass can be. Conscience is not something to be gotten past, as it was in the *Dateline* case. It is something to be revered. The burden of protecting conscience cannot be laid entirely on the individual, nor can it be suffocated, as Gillen's objections were. Had Gillen's objections been heeded, NBC News would have avoided the embarrassment that eventually led to the resignation of Michael Gartner as president of the news division.

Would NBC make the same mistake today? It is certainly possible. The Web has hardly eliminated ethical errors in news. The reaction, however, would have played out differently, and would have involved viewers and GM truck owners differently. The new press criticism and review made possible by the Internet also would have likely championed Gillen and skewered NBC more vehemently and more immediately.

The open review of journalism today is counterbalanced by the speed with which journalistic decision making now occurs. In early 2013, Fox News Channel aired live footage of a car chase that ended with the suspect leaving his car and shooting himself in the head. Anchor Shepard Smith immediately apologized to viewers–their video delay should have kicked in to prevent that being shown, he said. Within minutes, however, BuzzFeed posted on YouTube and on Twitter a clip of the footage for which Fox had just apologized. That generated criticism, but BuzzFeed defended its actions, arguing that the car chase and suicide constituted a news event, and thus merited sharing.

EXERCISING CONSCIENCE IS NOT EASY

Introducing the need for conscience into the journalistic process creates another tension. By necessity, newsrooms are not democracies–and that is even more the case in the age of layoffs, buyouts, and expanded use of low-paid or free contributors. The staffs who produce news have less leverage in that environment than before. By necessity, news operations also tend to be unruly dictatorships. Someone atop the chain of command has to make the ultimate decision–whether to publish, whether to stand by a piece of content, to leave in the damning quote or take it out, to pull down the controversial story or leave it up. Even in a setting where content is posted without much initial supervision, there are ultimately commands and controls.

And when revenue is scarce, and the business side is increasingly experimenting with ideas such as sponsored content (in effect advertising that looks more like editorial content), what formerly seemed hard ethical ground has become softer sand. Such factors are a significant issue facing journalism's future, and that issue must be carefully managed, and thought through. As Bob Woodward, who when he was a young reporter covering Watergate had many higher pressures against pursuing the story, has said: "The best journalism is often done in defiance of management."[5]

In a time when the existential crisis facing journalism seems largely financial, it is important to recognize that journalistic conscience is also at risk. Allowing individuals to voice their concerns makes running any news operation more difficult. But it makes the quality of the news better. And that, in the end, is the real existential crisis. The rest is tactics.

This notion of moral conscience is something many, if not most, of those engaged in news believe in deeply. "Each individual reporter has to set his own rules, his own standards, and model his career for himself," longtime television journalist Bill Kurtis told us a decade ago.[6] This is even truer now, when everyone who imagines him- or herself a journalist is more likely to be the entrepreneur of his or her own career and work through many different venues.

When he began doing media criticism, writer Jon Katz sensed this about being a journalist and even more so about being a critic of journalists. Katz felt compelled to sit down and write his own personal code of ethics. "I think you have to have a moral context in the work you do for it really to have any meaning," he told our research partners. "Whatever you do, I think you have to do it in a way that is morally satisfying to you."[7]

Most journalists are far less formal about it than Katz. They simply sense that journalism is a moral act and know that all of their background and values direct the choices they make when producing it. "My own instincts, and the way I was raised . . . and I suppose my own emotional and intellectual development, have led me to some pretty strong beliefs over the years, and I pay attention to them around here," Tom Brokaw told our research partners.[8]

Many engaged in journalism are drawn to it because of some of its basic elements—calling attention to inequities in the system, connecting people, creating community. In our survey of journalists with the Pew Research Center for the People & the Press, these factors outstripped all others by nearly two to one as distinguishing features of journalism.[9] In short, for those who practice it, the craft has a moral aspect.

One reason journalists feel strongly about the moral dimension of what they are doing is that without it they have so little to help them navigate the gray spaces of ethical decisions. As Carol Marin told us, since "there are no laws of news ... it ends up being sort of your own guiding compass that will determine what you do and don't do."[10]

As audiences we are guided by the decisions journalists make about what to report and how it is reported, and we are guided in our choice of news packages by a subtle combination of reasons, but this moral sense is part of it. We are looking for information, but we are also looking for authority, for honesty, and for a sense that the journalists have our interests at heart.

Consider the experience Marin herself encountered in Chicago. Early in 1997, she was the anchor at WMAQ, the NBC-owned-and-operated station in the city. The man in charge of the news at the station, Joel Cheatwood, had an idea to sweeten the ratings of the struggling 6 P.M. newscast. Cheatwood, who had made a name for himself in Miami by turning a Fox affiliate into the number one station by going to "All Crime All the Time," planned on upping the ante in Chicago. He hired Jerry Springer, the disgraced Cincinnati mayor turned talk show host, to do commentaries at the end of the news. Springer was local. He taped his syndicated TV show about bizarre love triangles and violent confrontations right from WMAQ's studios.

When Cheatwood's plan was announced, the word sent WMAQ staff into depression. Were they in the shock-show business? They thought they were doing something important, something that had a public service. Marin shared these concerns and decided, eventually, that enough was enough. She thought WMAQ was degenerating into sleaze. Management already had put her on probation once because she had refused to narrate health segments that had been a collaboration between the station and a local hospital, which was given airtime in exchange for buying ads on the station. Now came Springer. Marin had no illusions about herself. She was no saint. But journalists live and die by their reputation as people with ethics. It's all they have. She decided she would resign.

Marin's colleagues burst into loud applause when she announced her decision on camera. You could see them, right on the air. Many wept. It meant something that a public person would take such an ethical stand about her own job. Marin left for another station, and in the wake of her departure, WMAQ's viewers fled as well.

Afterward, Marin was "awestruck" by the response, especially the "quantity and the quality of the letters and e-mails. . . . People wrote long tracts, and they did three things in many of the letters. They explained their relationship to the news. . . . They described themselves in demographic terms. . . . They explained an ethical dilemma that had happened to them. . . . A lawyer that I know in Chicago wrote me and said, every one of us in our lives will face a so-called Springer decision. I talked to butchers who won't short-weigh meat, and one who got fired. A real estate banker who wouldn't pad assessments in Lake Forest and lost two critical accounts with Chicago banks."[11]

The questions of character that journalists face are not unfamiliar to us as we consume news, and we look for them in the judgments we make about who is credible and believable.

A CULTURE OF HONESTY

"The ability of journalists to exercise conscience is much more important than anything they believe or any beliefs they bring to their job," Linda Foley, the president of the Newspaper Guild, told us as we went around the country and talked to those engaged in news about what set the practice apart. "It's credibility, more than objectivity, that's important for us in our industry.... There has to be a culture in newsrooms that allows a journalist to have a free and open discussion."[12]

Some years ago, Donald Shriver, the president emeritus of Union Theological Seminary in New York City, reviewed four books on journalism ethics and offered this about the handbook on the subject prepared by the Poynter Institute in Florida: "The most useful piece of the Poynter schematic for journalistic ethics is its illustration of the transition from 'gut reaction' ethics to observation of rules to the maturity of reflection and reasoning. At the top of this hierarchy is their assertion that 'collaboration is essential.' That is, check the story with your colleagues. Given the rush to deadline and competition among reporters in most newsrooms, this is rare advice. Yet, if journalism is a medium of dialogue among citizens, it seems right for the dialogue to begin in the newsroom."[13]

Interestingly, some of the best and most difficult decisions in journalism history have come about through just the kind of elusive collaboration Shriver is talking about. When publisher Katharine Graham made the decision to publish the Pentagon Papers in 1971, the process was extraordinarily open. Graham had to decide whether the *Washington Post* should risk legal sanction by publishing secret Pentagon documents after the Justice Department had already gone to court to block the *New York Times* from making them public. Here is how Graham herself described it in her autobiography:

Ben [Bradlee] was beginning to feel squeezed between the editors and the reporters, who were solidly lined up for publishing and supporting the *Times* on the issue of freedom of the press, and the lawyers, who at one point suggested a compromise whereby the *Post* would not publish the Papers on Friday but would notify the attorney general of its intention to publish on Sunday. Howard Simons, who was one hundred percent for publishing, summoned the reporters to talk directly with the lawyers.

[Don] Oberdorfer said the compromise was "the shittiest idea I've ever heard." [Chalmers] Roberts said the *Post* would be "crawling on its belly" to the attorney general; if the *Post* didn't publish, he would move his retirement up two weeks, make it a resignation, and publicly accuse the *Post* of cowardice. Murrey Marder recalled saying, "If the *Post* doesn't publish, it will be in much worse shape as an institution than if it does," since the paper's "credibility would be destroyed journalistically for being gutless." [Ben] Bagdikian reminded the lawyers of the commitment to [Daniel] Ellsberg to publish the Papers and declared, "The only way to assert the right to publish is to publish." . . . Gene Patterson . . . gave me the first warning of what was to come, saying that he believed the decision on whether to print was going to be checked with me and that he "knew I fully recognized that the soul of the newspaper was at stake."

"God, do you think it's coming to that?" I asked. Yes, Gene said, he did. . . .

Frightened and tense, I took a big gulp and said, "Go ahead, go ahead, go ahead. Let's go. Let's publish."[14]

As Anthony Lewis, then an editorial columnist for the *New York Times*, noted seventeen years later:

Examining that episode afterward, a law review article by Professors Harold Edgar and Benno Schmidt Jr. of the Columbia University Law School said it marked the "passing of an era" for the American press. It was an era, they said, in which there was a "symbiotic relationship between politicians and the press." But now, by printing the secret history of the Vietnam War over strenuous objections, establishment newspapers had "demonstrated that much of the press was no longer willing to be merely an occasionally critical associate [of the Government], devoted to common aims, but intended to become an adversary."[15]

A year after the Pentagon Papers, the *Washington Post* began looking into Watergate.

INTELLECTUAL DIVERSITY IS THE REAL GOAL

This notion of open dialogue in the newsroom is what a growing number of people who think about news consider the key element in the question of diversity and in the pursuit of a journalism of proportion.

"Is there a culture of the newsroom?" television journalist Charles Gibson asked during a forum we held in the late 1990s. "Are you challenging each other, are you talking to each other, are you pushing each other?"[16]

"I'll tell you how it plays out for Christians in my newsroom," answered David Ashenfelder, a Pulitzer Prize winner at the *Detroit Free Press*, who is also a Christian and a member of a large weekly Bible study group in suburban Detroit. "They don't talk. They're afraid of being ridiculed. They're there. I know who a bunch of them are. We sort of have this little underground, and we talk to each other and we talk among ourselves. One thing we've been asking ourselves lately is, why are we just talking among ourselves?"[17]

Traditionally, the concept of newsroom diversity was defined largely in terms of numerical targets that related to ethnicity, race, and gender. The news industry belatedly recognized that its newsrooms should more closely resemble the culture at large. The American Society of Newspaper Editors in 1978 formally stated that the number of minorities working at American newspapers should reflect the percentage in the general population—a goal that has never been met. These targets, and the failure to meet them, are important. The numerical quotas are matters of justice as well as a necessary step to making journalism, and therefore citizenship and democracy, something available to everyone.[18]

Seen in the broader context of personal conscience, however, this conventional definition of diversity, important as it may be, is too limited. It risks confusing means with ends. Getting more minorities in the newsroom is a target, but not the goal, of diversity. The goal is a news organization that is more accurate and representative. Ethnic, gender, and racial quotas are a means of approaching that. But they will accomplish nothing by themselves if the newsroom culture then requires that these people from different backgrounds all adhere to a single mentality. The local newspaper or TV station may "look like America," as President Bill Clinton was fond of saying, but it won't think like the community and it won't understand it or be able to cover it.

The goal of diversity should be to assemble not only a newsroom that might resemble the community but also one that is as open and honest so that this diversity can function. This refers not just to racial or gender diversity. It is not just ideological diversity. It is not just social class or economic diversity. It is not just numerical diversity. It is what we call intellectual diversity, and it encompasses and gives meaning to all the other kinds.

Increasingly, people who have fought for diversity are coming to precisely this conclusion. "We have defined . . . diversity too often in gender and genetic terms as people who look a little different but basically sound the same," Mercedes de Uriarte, who teaches journalism at the University of Texas, told us. "We extend that too often to sources, who echo the thing that we're comfortable in hearing on both sides of a very narrow spectrum of debate." But, said de Uriarte, "it is intellectual diversity that we still have difficulty including in the news. Intellectual diversity is, according to scholars of American culture, among the most difficult for Americans to accept."[19]

Unfortunately, this concept of intellectual diversity is also difficult for managers to encourage. The tendency, for many reasons, is to create newsrooms that think like the boss.

THE PRESSURES AGAINST INDIVIDUAL CONSCIENCE

Various factors pull toward making a newsroom setting homogeneous—even in the networked era of the Web. One is simply human nature. "Editors have a tendency to create people in their own image. If the editor doesn't like you for some reason, you don't rise. So there's a self-selection process that goes on within the profession," Juan Gonzalez, a columnist at the *New York Daily News*, noted.[20]

"We have hiring systems in this country that make it very difficult to take risks on people. The people who are outside the mainstream as we would define it . . . are precisely the people who don't get a chance," Tom Bray, then a conservative columnist for the *Detroit News*, told us.[21]

Another problem is a kind of bureaucratic inertia that sets in at any organization—even new media start-ups that have only been around for a short time. Inertia causes people to take the easy route of doing in any circumstance whatever is normally done. Routines become safe havens. Even online collaborative virtual communities, such as Twitter or Reddit, begin to adopt their own nomenclature and norms of behavior.

Some journalists have always worked at the edge of such routines, even in the era of more institutional journalism. Guided only by their commitment to the truth, these individuals pursue stories with single-minded, sometimes idiosyncratic purpose and regularly reveal unpopular truths others have ignored, avoided, or simply did not see—people like Thomas Paine, George Seldes, I. F. Stone, or, more recently, David Burnham and Charles Lewis.

In an age when it is easier than ever before to publish first and check later, to retweet a startling post or statistic without first verifying it, to pass on what one has not read carefully, to phrase one's comment provocatively, the new norms tend toward action rather than contemplation, and overstatement rather than understatement. In this kind of environment, skepticism and deliberation—sometimes even civility—may be a form of personal conscience.

BUILDING A CULTURE WHERE CONSCIENCE AND DIVERSITY CAN THRIVE

Perhaps the biggest challenge for the people who produce the news is recognizing that their long-term health depends on the quality of the culture they create, and the degree to which it allows people to be different—whether in a physical workplace or a virtual community of users. As difficult as the obstacles are, the history of journalism is filled with cases where collaboration and confrontation occurred, and were even nurtured. Some engaged in news naturally gravitate to a culture where people feel free and encouraged to operate according to conscience. But when an industry is under pressure, particularly in its financial health, that may become far less true.

One model is to have this culture flow down in clear demonstrations from the top, in public, where managers set a tone for others to see. Maybe the best example is the story that the late journalist David Halberstam told of his first meeting with Orville Dryfoos, who had only recently been made publisher of the *New York Times*:

> It was in early 1962, maybe February. I had been in the Congo only since the previous July and had been called back to New York to receive an award. A man walked up to the desk where I was sitting and introduced himself as Orville Dryfoos. "I heard you were here," he said, "and I wanted to let you know how much I admire what you do, how much we are all aware of the risks you take. It is what makes this paper what it is." As much as anything else it was that attitude and the ease with which that conversation could occur between the publisher and a reporter that set that newsroom apart from any other.[22]

In the end, most journalists should feel that communicating to fellow citizens is a mission that transcends the institution where they work. That it is something of a calling, and everyone who works in a newsroom is a steward of that mission. For their part, managers need to help their journalists fulfill that mission to their best potential. Gregory Favre, former editor of the *Sacramento Bee*, vice president of news for the McClatchy chain, and later a faculty member at the Poynter Institute, often talked to journalists about this larger sense of mission.

> You help people whether it's a time of calm or whether it is a time of crisis. You help them speak to each other, allowing many voices to be heard, and providing them with information necessary to function as productive citizens. You help them build a bridge across their gulf of differences. And you have an obligation to question yourselves, just as you question others. An obligation to live and work by the same set of values that you ask of those you cover. An obligation to help bring

about a change in the culture throughout our business, a culture that
has a sense of caring, that demands diversity in our ranks, that has
a human touch, internally and externally, a culture that is wrapped
in a moral fabric that won't be ripped apart in the moments of tough
times.[23]

Indeed, Favre told people this mission is so significant that journalists have an obligation to preserve it and strengthen it, for both
those who came before and those who will come after.

THE ROLE OF CITIZENS

The final component in the equation is how the members of the
community, the citizens, become part of the process. What responsibilities do they have?

One frequent response of journalists is that if the press is failing—if it is overly sensational or biased toward infotainment—then
these are ultimately failures of the citizenry. If people wanted better
journalism, they say, the market would provide it. The problem with
this rationalization, as we have seen, is that journalism is not shaped
by a perfect market. The kind of local news we get in television, for
instance, owes a great deal to the level of profitability required by
Wall Street. The nature of a newspaper, we have learned from news
executives, is heavily influenced by the values of the ownership. The
quality of the decisions journalists make from day to day is heavily
influenced by editors and the culture of the newsroom. Newspapers
once were monopolies, but even that was not always so. Those monopoly papers of the millennium were the winners of the newspaper
wars of the 1960s and 1970s, and their sense of responsibility, and
their arrogance, were born of that history. TV stations, which are
licensed on the public airways, are largely oligarchies but in a highly
competitive business. At this point, the Internet is still too young to
predict what market reality it will come to represent.

The market does not, as it is so often said, provide citizens simply with the news they want. They also get the news that Wall Street,
ownership, journalism training, the cultural norms of each medium,

and the conventions of news dictate be made available to them. If this is to change and if the principle that the journalist's primary allegiance is to the citizens is to have meaning, a new relationship between the journalist and the citizen must evolve.

There is a mythical dimension to the idea of a free and open Internet. For a public that desires quality content, however, the new system brings with it new transaction costs. Advertising will finance a smaller share of the news that informs civic engagement. In its place, the highly engaged, through meters and subscription fees, will pay a growing proportion of the cost. In effect, the few increasingly will be subsidizing the whole to create informed publics. With this shift toward audience comes another more invisible transaction cost in the form of responsibility. The people formerly known as the audience will need to be more attentive and critical consumers of information than before. The public will also need to contribute to journalism itself, not by performing all of its functions but by supporting and engaging in more aspects of them. What those aspects are, and what growing responsibilities they convey, constitute the final element of journalism, one that has always been at play but that in the new century is becoming more palpable, and more vital. It is the role of the citizen.

11

The Rights and Responsibilities of Citizens

On the morning of July 7, 2005, three bombs exploded in the London subway, followed shortly by an explosion on a double-decker bus. The suicide bombings killed fifty-two people in an attack evocative of the 2004 train explosions in Madrid.

The British Broadcasting Corporation, or BBC, understood that this was an important story and threw its staff at it, trying to get information first and, as Richard Sambrook, director of the news division, wrote, "get things right."[1] On that day, the BBC received unprecedented help from London residents. Six hours after the attack, the organization counted more than one thousand photographs, twenty video clips, four thousand text messages, and twenty thousand e-mails—all of which had been sent in by citizens.

The BBC had always encouraged citizen involvement in the news, but this level of participation was new. "The quantity and quality of the public's contributions moved them beyond novelty, tokenism or the exceptional and raises major implications that we are still working through," recalled Sambrook.

The concept of "crowd sourcing," or using the public to help

gather the news, was only beginning to form in 2005. The notion that reporters should monitor the public conversation on their
beats every day, with a product like TweetDeck open on their
screens, was not yet widely accepted. Twitter did not yet exist.
Facebook was limited to a few college campuses. But in the wake
of the 2005 London bombings, the managers at the BBC made
good use of the material, even going so far as to open a newscast
with video footage received from citizens. Sambrook called the
reporting of the London story a partnership, and noted that his
organization learned that "when major events occur, the public
can offer us as much new information as we are able to broadcast
to them."

In less than a decade, it sometimes seems as if more has changed
than remains the same. In truth, the changes are in one sense bringing us back to the coffeehouse, to the news as a continuing conversation.

Sambrook, who now teaches journalism at Cardiff University,
was an early advocate of the new relationship between journalists
and citizens. By 2001, the BBC had started the Digital Storytelling
Project, which involved local workshops where BBC professionals
taught ten people at a time to craft scripts, record audio, and edit
stills and video. With the media corporation's help, local authorities
off the coast of Scotland had created a participatory media project
called Island Blogging, in which islanders were issued a personal
computer and a narrowband Web connection, which they put to
use posting pictures and stories, and sparking debate on numerous
community issues. The BBC Action Network had attempted to reconnect citizens with the political process by offering them a forum
to discuss issues relevant to them.

"As someone who supports this new direction, I don't suggest
the BBC staff abdicate their responsibility for accuracy, fairness or
objectivity," Sambrook wrote back then. "As we open up to contributions from the public, we must do so in a way that is consistent
with our editorial values. However, I believe that truth, accuracy,
impartiality and diversity of opinion are strengthened by being open

to a wider range of opinion and perspective, brought to us through the knowledge and understanding of our audience."[2]

Well into the second decade of the Web, journalism is only beginning to explore ways in which it can better involve the public. The process of finding how the public and the press combine to make this new journalism will take time and likely frustrate both the public and the journalists on occasion. As we noted in a more detailed discussion of the tensions in chapter 1, some advocates of the new have imagined that professional journalism is now, if not largely obsolete, an artifact of an industrial age, which plays a much diminished role. Others tend to doubt that citizens operating as occasional watchmen have the skills and organization to monitor events in a meaningful way. The community watch program may be helpful, but it is no substitute for a police force. Our view, reflected throughout this book, is that the two sides, citizen and professional journalist, are not in competition. They must work in combination. The new citizen sentinel will not replicate the work of the professional journalist, or even displace it, but rather inform, interact with, and elevate it.

Time will sort out much of this new relationship. Citizens will bring different strengths to this process, professionals others, and how each of their strengths fit together will be determined by experience, not theory. But the result, if embraced with a practiced eye rather than merely a tribal one, will be better than what came before.

It took some two hundred years for the diffusion of knowledge that began with the discovery of mechanical printing to engender the structural transformation of Western society. This transformation was powered by the spread of knowledge via the printed word, and it enabled the people to become a public sufficiently empowered with knowledge to form a public opinion that could take part in its own social, economic, and political systems. Much of this information came to be distributed to the broad mass of the people by what came to be known as journalism. It was that information that helped them become informed citizens, and it would be in this climate that public opinion would be formed. Public opinion, in turn, made possible the rise of self-government.

In this sense, journalism and democracy were born together. In the first phase of development, the role of the press was simply to provide the people with information about the activities and institutions of power that controlled their lives. Today, when the world is awash in information, the role of the press is different. When information is abundant and available, all the time and everywhere, a new relationship between the press and the public needs to be formed. And just as the values of journalism do not change in this new competitive atmosphere, journalists' role does not change much, either. Where journalism's role once was to simply provide information as a tool of self-governance, it now becomes a role of providing citizens with the tools they need to extract knowledge for themselves from the undifferentiated flood of rumor, propaganda, gossip, fact, assertion, and allegation the communications system now produces. Thus the journalist must not only make sense of the world but also make sense of the flood of information about it as it is being delivered to citizens.

To do this, journalism must first invite the community into the process by which news is produced. That is an ongoing theme in this volume. The community brings diversity of viewpoints, subject expertise, and real-life experience to the news that journalists alone cannot match. Journalists bring skills to the assessment of news, sources inside government, storytelling abilities, and the ability to collate and curate the collective information.

In our chapter on verification (chapter 4), we called on journalists to make a major shift toward transparency, arguing that this concept came closer to the real meaning of objectivity than the more muddled notions connected to neutrality that some journalists have used. We believe that transparency is the first step in the beginning of a new connection between the journalist and the citizen. It allows the public a chance to judge the principles by which the journalists do their work. They are equipped with information that invites them to compare these principles with other choices available. Most important, it gives the public a basis on which to judge whether a particular kind of journalism is the kind they wish to encourage and trust.

The next step involves seeking out members of the community who can help journalists gather the news in ways that are more sophisticated than we imagine. This involves more than creating places for citizens to post and publish. It means approaching them as a new group of sources, organizing their intelligence, and vetting and synthesizing that intelligence into a whole. Minnesota Public Radio did just this in the 1990s when they surveyed their listeners for details on their background and expertise, and organized them into groups to help suggest and vet stories in their particular areas of knowledge. Subsequently MPR could call on specific Native Americans on nearby reservations or on doctors specializing in certain diseases or procedures to help them assign, report, and analyze stories that needed their particular personal knowledge or expertise. This elevates citizens beyond the template of the person on the street, or the person who shot a useful photo.

The third step involves listening when the public reacts to the news. This involvement can come by creating information forums (like those hosted by the *New York Times*, the *Texas Tribune*, and many others), where editors and reporters directly interact with their audience during in-depth discussions of current news trends, including conversations about journalistic ethics and standards.

The more active citizens become in the news, in turn, the more responsibility they begin to bear for it. Consider it the tenth element of journalism, one growing with the advent of new empowering technology.

Citizens, who shape news production by the choices they make, have rights when it comes to news, but they also have responsibilities—even more so as they become producers and editors themselves.

Citizens must set aside prejudice and judge the work of journalists on the basis of whether it contributes to their ability to take an informed part in shaping their society. But the way journalists design their work to engage the public must provide not only the needed content but also an understanding of the principles by which their work is done. In this way, the journalists will determine whether or not the public can become a force for good journalism.

Market demand is clearly the most powerful force shaping society today. It would seem obvious that it is in the interest of journalists to do what they can to create a market for the kind of journalism this book attempts to describe: a journalism that recognizes and applies principles that assist in assuring reliable, timely, proportional, comprehensive news to help citizens make sense of the world and their place in it. The first step in that direction has to be developing a means of letting those who make up that market finally see how the sausage is made–how we do our work and what informs our decisions.

What does this mean to citizens? More precisely, what should we as citizens expect from the news? What should we do if we believe we are not getting it? And what skills are required to be literate citizens, to know how to participate in the news? These questions are important. The elements of journalism belong to citizens as much as they do to journalists for the simple reason, as we said at the beginning, that these principles grow out of the function news plays in people's lives, not out of some professional ethos.

In that sense, the elements of journalism are a citizen's bill of rights as much as they are a journalist's bill of responsibilities. And with rights naturally come responsibilities for citizens as well–responsibilities that in the twenty-first century are growing along with the increased ability of the citizen to interact with the news. Thus, it is useful to enumerate how we as citizens can recognize whether the elements of journalism are evident in the news we receive.

A CITIZEN'S BILL OF RIGHTS AND RESPONSIBILITIES

1 • ON TRUTHFULNESS

We have the right to expect that the evidence of the integrity of the reporting be explicit. This means that the process of verification–

how newspeople made their decisions and why—should be transparent. There should be a clear indication of open-minded examination. We should be able to judge the value and bias of the information for ourselves.

To live up to this responsibility, what elements would such a piece of reporting contain? As we detailed in another of our books, *Blur: How to Know What's True in the Age of Information Overload*, a story should make clear the sources of information and the evidence they offer, or the basis of their knowledge. The story's relevance and implications should be obvious from the way it is presented. Important unanswered questions should be noted. The different sides represented should be given the opportunity to make their best case—even those whose position has less support. If the story raises a point of controversy, we should expect follow-up. Other stories would continue the public discussion over time so that the sorting-out process that leads to truthfulness can take place. News, in other words, should not only engage us but also challenge us and make us think. Not all of these qualities may be found in every piece of content, but they should be expected in the treatment overall.

This, in turn, implies a two-way process. The citizen has an obligation to approach the news with an open mind and not just a desire that the news reinforce existing opinion.

2 • ON LOYALTY TO CITIZENS

We should expect to see evidence that the material has been prepared for our use above all. This means stories should answer our needs as citizens and not just the interests of the players and the political or economic system. It also means that there is a demonstrated effort by journalists to understand the whole community.

Perhaps the best way to judge this is by noting how well the news over time avoids stereotypes. In news, stereotypes are characterizations that may be true in some cases but are not in the specific case being reported. A story about local crime that focuses on only one part of the community when the facts show that crime is spread generally throughout the whole community is an example. Usually, stereotyping is a failure of execution. Stereotypes of this kind can almost always be avoided by more reporting and more specific reporting, both of which should be recognizable in any story carefully done.

We should also expect to see clear cases in which the news provider—whether it is a commercial entity, a political nonprofit, a think tank, or any other source—will at times put its own interests at risk in order to bring us important information through its news, artistic and commercial reviews, and consumer and retail coverage. Katharine Graham did this when she chose to print the Pentagon Papers, but countless others do it every day when they publish a critical review of a restaurant that is also an advertiser, or a tough-minded report on an important local industry. As special interest groups increasingly move into the production of news, the information provided should still be held to the same expectation of integrity. Work that reflects only the point of view and interests of one source should be considered for what it is, a form of propaganda.

Loyalty to citizens also means disclosure of any synergy, connecting partnerships, or conflicts of interest as they relate to a particular story. This would include reporting on a journalist or organization's own lobbying efforts, the organized pressure they put on government that is favorable to their own business interests. We have every reason to expect that our news providers be as transparent in their operations as we expect them to demand other institutions of power to be.

3 • ON INDEPENDENCE

We have a right to expect that commentators, columnists, and journalists of opinion present their material with supporting evidence that demonstrates they are viewing the subject to inspire open public debate, not to further the narrow interests of a faction or a move toward a predetermined outcome. This is no less true of a solitary blogger on the Web than it is of a professional columnist. The voice that demonstrates intellectual independence, that is thinking for itself, is simply more interesting, and adds more value to civic discourse.

This intellectual independence is not to be found in commentaries that are in lockstep with factions or vested interests. Independence implies that we can expect to see Republicans at times criticized by conservative commentators and Democrats at times by liberals. Recalling that the journalist's primary allegiance is to the citizen's needs also implies that while those engaged in journalism need not be neutral, we can expect them not to have divided loyalties. We can expect that they are not writing speeches or secretly counseling those they cover or opine about. Because we look to opinion writers to help us sort through the complex and competing issues confronting citizens, we should expect to see evidence in the body of their writing or reporting that they have examined the ideas of others on the subject.

4 • ON MONITORING POWER

We have a right to expect that journalists monitor and hold to account the most important and difficult centers of power. While this includes government, there are other institutions and individuals in society that wield economic, coercive, social, moral, and persuasive powers equal to or exceeding those of government.

Since this investigatory role vests considerable power in the press itself, we can expect to see great care and discretion in its use. This means that the news organizations have a responsibility to lead–to uncover things that are important and new, and that change community paradigms. We have a right to expect that the watchdog role will demonstrate the news organization's public-interest obligation. This implies that we can expect that that power will not be frittered away on minor or pseudo scandals such as safe levels of bacteria in frozen yogurt or harmless amounts of dirt in hotel bedding. Instead, news organizations should focus their time and resources on major issues, unexpected scoundrels, and new perils. To matter, those who lay claim to the mantle of a free press should also focus on questions that matter.

5 • A PUBLIC FORUM

We should expect our news providers to create several channels through which we may interact with them. Such channels should include not just online forums but also interaction that is direct: answering e-mail and the phone, answering questions online, and despite trends to the contrary, assigning someone inside an institution to act as an ombudsman in some way. These channels should also include regular public appearances in physical public venues, such as forums, civic clubs, PTA meetings, and panel discussions, as well as interactive radio and television appearances.

And as technology continues to make it ever easier, we as citizens should expect to be invited to participate in the production of news, through our photos and our eyewitness testimony, and to be sought out for our experience and expertise to inform the gathering of news.

Through all these contacts, we should, over time, expect to see our views and values reflected in the news coverage and not just those of the most polarized positions on important issues. If the democratic ideal of compromise is to be reached, we should expect the media's public forum to build toward community understanding from which that compromise can be realized.

At the same time, we as citizens have an obligation to approach the news with open minds, willing to accept new facts and examine new points of view as they are presented. We also have a responsibility to show up at these public forums and behave in a way that encourages respect and civility that make the ultimate goal of journalism—community—actually possible.

6 • ON PROPORTIONALITY AND ENGAGEMENT

We have a right to expect journalists to be aware of our basic dilemma as citizens: that we have a need for timely and deep knowledge of important issues and trends at a time when the proliferation of information and outlets has become increasingly unmanageable.

Being aware of this, we have a right to expect journalists to use their unique access to events and information to put the material they gather into a context that will engage our attention and, over time, help us to see these trends and events in proportion to their true significance in our lives. We should not find matters of transitory importance overplayed and distorted for commercial returns.

So that we as citizens may make sound and well-informed decisions about the many issues that touch our lives, we have a right to news reports that reflect the true nature of threats to our community, such as crime, as well as those aspects of community life that are functioning well. Our successes should be as apparent as our failures.

For all this, as the wellspring of information grows, we have a responsibility as citizens not to narrow our focus. We must not simply indulge ourselves in subjects that entertain us or affirm our views. We also must seek out the critical, challenging information that citizens require. The responsibility to focus on what matters, in other words, is ours as well as the journalist's. The challenge of our age—that we not amuse ourselves to death, as Neil Postman warned—is increasingly in our hands.

A close reader will notice two elements of journalism discussed in this book—verification and conscience—missing from this list of citizen's rights. This is because, when restated from the standpoint of how a citizen should recognize these rights, some elements are best understood as part of others. In this context, the journalist's process of verification becomes a hallmark of adherence to a truthful account of the news and is covered under the heading of truthfulness. By the same token, conscience becomes part of the interaction that occurs between citizen and news providers in the public forum function of a news organization and is covered under the heading of a public forum.

What do we do as citizens if these rights are not met? What action, for instance, can and should we take if a newspaper reports on a case of business or political fraud but doesn't follow up on the controversial issues that it raises? First, of course, such contact works best if it comes constructively, as advice and information rather than condemnation. Second, if it is ignored, it should be offered again, perhaps through more than one means. If, for example, an e-mail is not acknowledged, send it again, and then pick up the phone or write a letter, with a copy to the editor in chief. If you want to make other citizens aware of your complaint, keep a public record of your attempts to contact the organization and its reactions on a blog.

What can we do if as citizens we offer this feedback and our contributions, ideas, or criticisms are ignored? Rights mean something only if they are viewed as being nonnegotiable. At the point when these rights of yours are ignored, withhold your business. Stop visiting. Drop the subscription. Delete the app. Stop watching. Most important, write a clear explanation of why you have done so and send it to the management, to media critics, or post it on your own site. The marketplace fails if we as citizens are passive, willing to put up with a diminishing product. It used to be that there was no alternative, but today traditional news organizations don't hold a monopoly on some of the content. They will probably listen and engage in dialogue if we act with a voice and a reason. And if they don't, they have failed their purpose.

In the end it may be that, as TV journalist Carol Marin once put it, "there are no laws of news." But our research and our conversations with journalists and citizens have told us that there are certain enduring ideas about the flow of news and the role of journalism that can be identified. These ideas have ebbed and flowed, and have been misunderstood and abused—usually by those working in their name. Still, they are not artificial creations. The elements of journalism stem from the function that news plays in people's lives, and they have been forged and tempered by three hundred years of experience and testing in the marketplace of competing forms of information. Those who produce journalism must use these elements to steer an ethical course in their work. Time suggests we vary from them at our peril.

The elements of journalism we have outlined here form the basis of the journalism of the new century, a journalism of sense-making based on synthesis, verification, and fierce independence, a journalism that is a collaborative organized intelligence that combines the network, the community, and the unique skills of trained journalists. They also hold the only protection against the force that threatens to destroy journalism and thus weaken democratic society. This is the threat that the press will be subsumed inside the world of commercialized speech or the undifferentiated world of broad communication. The only way to avoid this threat is for those who are committed to journalism to have a clearer and more rigorous understanding of the elements that make journalism a thing of value, a transparent enterprise that creates its own demand by inviting citizens into the process, reconnecting journalism and citizen in a conversation and not a lecture, and that turns journalism into a service that improves people's lives. This shift is not only something citizens and journalists have in their own control; it is something for which both bear some responsibility.

Civilization has produced one idea more powerful than any other: the notion that people can govern themselves. And it has created a largely unarticulated theory of information to sustain that idea, called journalism. The two rise and fall together. This book is an attempt to articulate that theory. Our best hope is not a future that returns to the past, which was never as sweet as people remember it. Our freedom in a digital century depends on not forgetting that past, or the theory of news it produced, in a time when faith in technological and corporate rebirth are surging. We fought two conventional world wars and a largely covert Cold War in the last century against such technological utopianism. We may not survive another.

ACKNOWLEDGMENTS

This book is not ours alone. It is the fruit of the years of work by the Committee of Concerned Journalists and the twelve hundred journalists who gave their names, their time, and their care to its creation. It is also informed by the more than three hundred people who came to our forums to give us their thoughts, by the hundreds who answered our surveys, and by the roughly one hundred more who sat for hours for interviews by our academic partners. Our goal with this book was not to offer an argument of what journalism should be, but to outline the common ground on which journalists already stand. Since journalists are so independent, they have always resisted putting these ideas in one place, or even working through them consciously. But in a time of confusion and doubt about the differences between journalism and all the other forms by which information is communicated, we believe clarity of purpose and professional theory are more crucial than ever before. They are important for journalists who are coming to doubt themselves. It is important to a generation new to the newsroom. It is important to members of the public who express a longing for news they can trust. This was our intention. If we have succeeded in some measure, it is because of their help. If we have failed, it is because we have let them down.

We owe a special debt to some in particular. That list begins on this new edition with Jesse Holcomb, our critic, partner, researcher, and counsel. He is the third wonderful partner to have played this role, each of them different and superb. For the first edition it was Dante Chinni. For the second paperback edition, it was Cristian Lupsa. New colleagues Millie Tran, Kevin Loker, and Jeff Sonderman at the American Press Institute, who are teachers as much as colleagues, added valuable ideas about new tools and new promise. Amy Mitchell was the person most responsible for operating the Committee of Concerned Journalists in its early days, organizing the forums, supervising the survey research, and all of the other activities. This work bears the stamp of her professionalism, organization, and good humor. Tom Avila took over for Amy in shepherding the committee in its next phase and caring for it as if it were his own creation. Carrie Brown-Smith, Wally Dean, Brett Mueller, and a strong cohort of superb journalists served as trainers in newsrooms for the committee's traveling curriculum; their work informed many of the new insights in this edition. In addition, we want to thank Howard Gardner, Mihaly Csikszentmihalyi, and William Damon for sharing their research with us. Damon also became our partner in training journalists. A few key friends played a vital role in encouraging, counseling, editing, and guiding this book, including James Carey, who never failed to elevate our thinking and excite our imagination, Roy Peter Clark, Tom Goldstein, David Halberstam, Richard Harwood, John Kovach, Jim Naughton, Geneva Overholser, Sandra Rowe, Matthew Storin, and Mark Trahant.

The staff of the Project for Excellence in Journalism over years was critical, and that list included many: Nancy Anderson, Jennifer Fimbres, Stacy Forster, Chris Galdieri, Carl Gottlieb, Kenny Olmstead, Mark Jurkowitz, Cheryl Elzey, Dana Page, Monica Anderson, Nancy Vogt, Laura Santhanam, Steve Adams, Hong Ji, Sovini Tan, Heather Brown, Tricia Sartor, Katrina Matsa, Emily Guskin, and Paul Hitlin. We will always owe a debt to the wisdom, humor, and friendship of the late John Mashek. Important help, too, was provided for the original edition by Julie Dempster at the Nieman Fellowship program at Harvard. The steering committee of CCJ played a pivotal role in guiding us along the way. We owe a great thanks to the universities, newspapers, and individuals who cohosted, organized, and in several cases financed our forums, including the Park Foundation. The many hours of conversation with journalists in newsrooms around the country that informed this revision of the book were made possible by a generous grant from the John S. and James L. Knight Foundation, a foundation committed to improving journalism worldwide. We thank our agent, David Black, for his confidence and his passion; Sarah Smith, and our editors at Crown, first Bob Mecoy, then Annik Lafarge, Lindsey Moore, and Derek Reed, for their belief in this project.

None of this would have been possible, too, without the support, both financial and personal, of Rebecca Rimel and Don Kimelman at the Pew Charitable Trusts, who had faith in us to embark on this voyage, and also Eric Newton and Hodding Carter at Knight.

Finally, we owe a debt to those journalists who came before us, who helped create the First Amendment and then gave it its meaning. Their legacy imposes on us the obligation to accept the responsibility of a free and independent press and realize its promise to a self-governing people.

NOTES

PREFACE

1. Melanie Sills, "How to Begin Practicing Open Journalism," Poynter online, http://www.poynter.org/howtos/newsgathering-storytelling/158440/how-to-begin-practicing-open-journalism.

2. State of the News Media 2011, Overview, http://stateofthemedia.org/overview-2011.

INTRODUCTION

1. Michael Schudson, "Theorizing Journalism in Time Fourteen or Fifteen Generations: News as a Cultural Form and Journalism as a Historical Formation," *American Journalism* 30:1 (2013), 29–35. Mitchell Stephens, *A History of News* (Fort Worth, TX: Harcourt Brace College Publishers, 1996), 27. Schudson differs somewhat with Stephens about the strict constancy of news values. We sit in the middle, seeing a consistency among them over time and across cultures, but acknowledge that context, economics, and national mood all influence what is in favor and out of favor in news over time. The *Economist*'s Tom Standage traces the circulation of news through letters and other documents at least as far back as Cicero. Tom Standage, "Writing on the Wall;" available at http://tomstandage.wordpress.com/books/writing-on-the-wall/.

2. Harvey Molotch and Marilyn Lester, "News as Purposive Behavior: On the Strategic Use of Routine Events, Accidents and Scandal," *American Sociological Review* 39 (February 1974), 101–12.

3. Stephens, *History of News,* 12.

4. Ibid.

5. John McCain, with Mark Salter, *Faith of My Fathers* (New York: Random House, 1999), 221.

6. Poynter online, "Deprived of Media, College Students Describe Ordeal," November 14, 2012; available at http://www.poynter.org/latest-news/mediawire/195572/deprived-of-media-college-students-describe-ordeal/.

7. Thomas Cahill, *The Gift of the Jews: How a Tribe of Desert Nomads Changed the Way Everyone Thinks and Feels* (New York: Nan A. Talese/Anchor Books, 1998), 17.

8. Committee of Concerned Journalists (CCJ) and the Pew Research Center for the People & the Press, "Striking the Balance: Audience Interests, Business Pressures and Journalists' Values," March 1999, 79.

9. Pew Research Center for the People & the Press, "Press Widely Criticized, but Trusted More Than Other Information Sources," September 22, 2011; available at http://people-press.org.

10. Pew Research Center for the People & the Press, "In Changing News Landscape, Even Television is Vulnerable." September 27, 2012.

11. Pew Research Center for the People & the Press, "Press Widely Criticized."

12. C. W. Anderson, Emily Bell, and Clay Shirky, *Post-Industrial Journalism: Adapting to the Present* (New York: Columbia Journalism School Centennial, 2012).

CHAPTER 1: WHAT IS JOURNALISM FOR?

1. Anna Semborska, interview by Dante Chinni, January 2000.

2. Thomas Rosenstiel, "TV, VCR's, Fan Fire of Revolution: Technology Served the Cause of Liberation in East Europe," *Los Angeles Times*, January 18, 1990, A1.

3. Maxwell King, at founding meeting of Committee of Concerned Journalists (CCJ), Chicago, June 21, 1997.

4. Tom Brokaw, interview by William Damon, Howard Gardner, and Mihaly Csikszentmihalyi; unpublished interviews conducted for the book *Good Work: When Excellence and Ethics Meet* (New York: Basic Books, 2001).

5. Yuen Ying Chan, interview by William Damon, Howard Gardner, and Mihaly Csikszentmihalyi, ibid.

6. James Carey, *James Carey: A Critical Reader*, ed. Eve Stryker Munson and Catherine A. Warren (Minneapolis and London: University of Minnesota Press, 1997), 235.

7. Jack Fuller, at CCJ Forum, Chicago, November 6, 1997.

8. Omar Wasow, at CCJ Forum, Ann Arbor, MI, February 2, 1998.

9. CCJ and the Pew Research Center for the People & the Press, "Striking the Balance: Audience Interests, Business Pressures and Journalists' Values," March 1999, 79; available at www.journalism.org.

10. William Damon and Howard Gardner, "Reporting the News in an Age of Accelerating Power and Pressure: The Private Quest to Preserve the Public Trust," academic paper, November 6, 1997, 10.

11. In total, all twelve of the ethics codes on file with the American Society of Newspaper Editors that mention purpose describe this as journalism's primary mission. Four of the twenty-four that don't mention purpose include it inside the texts of their ethics codes.

12. Associated Press, report of Pope John Paul II's declaration of the Vatican's Holy

Year Day for Journalists, by Ellen Knickmeyer, June 4, 2000; available at Associated Press Worldstream, via LexisNexis.

13. Mitchell Stephens, *History of News* (Fort Worth, TX: Harcourt Brace College Publishers, 1996), 27.

14. John Hohenberg, *Free Press, Free People: The Best Cause* (New York: Free Press, 1973), 2.

15. Stephens, *History of News*, 53–59. The creation of this government-sponsored daily newspaper was the first formal act of Julius Caesar on becoming consul of Rome, 60 B.C.

16. Hohenberg, *Free Press*, 38. The writers were John Trenchard and William Gordon.

17. Thomas Jefferson, letter to George Washington, September 9, 1792. Retrieved from www.about.com.

18. *New York Times Co. v. United States*, 439 U.S. 713 (1971).

19. Lee Bollinger, at CCJ Forum, Ann Arbor, MI, February 2, 1998.

20. John Seely Brown, expressed to author Rosenstiel at a meeting to discuss the future of journalism curriculum, sponsored by Columbia University Graduate School of Journalism, Menlo Park, CA, June 15–16, 2000.

21. Paul Saffo, expressed to author Rosenstiel, same meeting.

22. Jonathan Stray, "Objectivity and the Decades-Long Shift from 'Just the Facts' to 'What Does it Mean?'" Nieman Journalism Lab, May 22, 2013; available at http://www.niemanlab.org/2013/05/objectivity-and-the-decades-long-shift-from-just-the-facts-to-what-does-it-mean/.

23. C. W. Anderson, Emily Bell, and Clay Shirky, *Post-Industrial Journalism: Adapting to the Present* (New York: Columbia Journalism School Centennial, 2012), 22.

24. Stephen Brook, "News Reporting Faces Web Challenge, Writes New York Times Editor," *Guardian*, November 29, 2007; available at http://www.guardian.co.uk/media/2007/nov/29/pressandpublishing.digitalmedia.

25. CBS News/New York Times poll (October 1994), "Do you happen to know the name of the representative in Congress from your district? (If yes, ask:) What is your representative's name?" Data provided by the Roper Center for Public Opinion Research.

26. This datum refers to the 2012 presidential election. In the 2010 off-year congressional races, only 41 percent voted.

27. The idea that most people get their news from local television is drawn from Nielsen Media Research data; the idea that local television ignores government coverage is drawn from "Project for Excellence in Journalism Local TV Project," *Columbia Journalism Review*, January 1999, November 1999, November 2000; available at www.journalism.org.

28. The percentage of people who read newspapers is from Pew Research Center

for the People & the Press's biennial survey of media consumption, September 2012. The level of knowledge about public life is inferred from work done by Michael Delli Carpini and Scott Keeter for their article "Stability and Change in the U.S. Public's Knowledge of Politics," *Public Opinion Quarterly* (Winter 1991), 583–612.

29. Pew Research Center for the People & the Press, "Public Knowledge of Current Affairs Little Changed by News and Information Revolutions," April 15, 2007; available at http://people-press.org.

30. Walter Lippmann, *The Essential Lippmann*, ed. Clinton Rossiter and James Lare (New York: Random House, 1963), 108.

31. Carey, *A Critical Reader*, 22.

32. John Dewey, review of *Public Opinion* by Walter Lippmann, *New Republic*, May 1922, 286.

33. Two authors have notably made this argument: Carey in *A Critical Reader*, and Christopher Lasch in *The Revolt of the Elites and the Betrayal of Democracy* (New York/London: W. W. Norton, 1995).

34. Lou Urenick, "Newspapers Arrive at Economic Crossroads," *Nieman Reports*, special issue (Summer 1999), 3–20.

35. Several researchers have found this tendency in political coverage over the years. Some recent examples include Joseph N. Cappella and Kathleen Hall Jamieson in *Spiral of Cynicism: The Press and the Public Good*, Thomas E. Patterson in *Out of Order: How the Decline of the Political Parties and the Growing Power of the News Media Undermine the American Way of Electing Presidents*, and the Project for Excellence in Journalism in "In the Public Interest: A Content Study of Early Press Coverage of the 2000 Presidential Campaign," February 2, 2000; available at www .journalism.org.

36. Carey, *A Critical Reader*, 247.

37. David Burgin was Rosenstiel's editor in 1980 and 1982 at the *Peninsula Times Tribune* in Palo Alto, CA, where he taught the author this theory of laying out newspaper pages.

38. Byron Calame, "Turning the Tables: What the Times News Staff Thinks of You," *New York Times*, October 9, 2005; available at www.nytimes.com.

39. C. W. Anderson, *Rebuilding the News: Metropolitan Journalism in the Digital Age* (Philadelphia: Temple University Press, 2013), 164–65.

40. Pew Research Center for the People & the Press, "Broad Support for Renewed Background Checks Bill, Skepticism About Its Chances," May 23, 2013; available at http://people-press.org.

41. Pew Internet & American Life Project, "72% of Online Adults Are Social Networking Site Users," August 5, 2013; available at http://pewinternet.org.

42. Ralf Dahrendorf, *After 1989: Morals, Revolution and Civil Society* (London: Macmillan, in association with St. Antony's College, Oxford, 1997), 98.

43. Pew Research Center, "As Mobile Grows Rapidly, the Pressures on News Intensify," March 18, 2013; available at www.journalism.org.

44. Dan Gillmor, "Google, Please Be a Benevolent Internet Overlord," *Guardian,* May 16, 2013; available at http://www.guardian.co.uk/commentisfree/2013/may/16/google-io-conference-internet-dominance.

45. Rebecca MacKinnon, *Consent of the Networked: The Worldwide Struggle for Internet Freedom* (New York: Basic Books, 2013).

46. Carey made this remark at a CCJ steering committee meeting in Washington, DC, June 19, 2000.

CHAPTER 2: TRUTH: THE FIRST AND MOST CONFUSING PRINCIPLE

1. Hedrick Smith, "U.S. Drops Plans for 1965 Recall of Vietnam Force," *New York Times,* December 21, 1963.

2. Benjamin C. Bradlee, "A Free Press in a Free Society," *Nieman Reports,* special issue (Winter 1990).

3. David Halberstam, "Crucial Point in Vietnam," *New York Times,* December 23, 1963.

4. Bradlee, "A Free Press."

5. CCJ and the Pew Research Center for the People & the Press, "Striking the Balance: Audience Interests, Business Pressures and Journalists' Values," March 1999, 79; available at www.journalism.org and http://people-press.org.

6. Interviews by William Damon, Howard Gardner, and Mihaly Csikszentmihalyi with a number of journalists; unpublished interviews for the book *Good Work: When Excellence and Ethics Meet* (New York: Basic Books, 2001).

7. Patty Calhoun, at CCJ Forum, Chicago, November 6, 1997.

8. Peter Levine, *Living Without Philosophy: On Narrative, Rhetoric, and Morality* (Albany: State University of New York Press, 1998), 169.

9. This concept of image taking precedence over reality is most dramatically portrayed in Joe McGinniss, *The Selling of the President 1968* (New York: Trident Press, 1969).

10. Ron Suskind, "Without a Doubt," *New York Times Magazine,* October 17, 2004; available at www.nytimes.com.

11. Claudette Artwick, "Reporters On Twitter: Product or Service?" *Digital Journalism* 1:2 (2013), 212–28.

12. John Hohenberg, *Free Press, Free People: The Best Cause* (New York: Free Press, 1973), 17.

13. Joseph Ellis, *American Sphinx: The Character of Thomas Jefferson* (New York: Alfred A. Knopf, 1997), 303.

14. Edwin Emery, *The Press in America*, 2nd ed. (Englewood Cliffs, NJ: Prentice-Hall, 1962), 374.

15. Cassandra Tate, "What Do Ombudsmen Do," *Columbia Journalism Review* (May/June 1984), 37.

16. Ibid.

17. David T. Z. Mindich, *Just the Facts: How "Objectivity" Came to Define American Journalism* (New York and London: New York University Press, 1998), 115. Mindich says the first textbook to question objectivity was Curtis MacDougall's *Interpretative Reporting* (New York: Macmillan, 1938).

18. Gordon Wood, "Novel History," *New York Review of Books*, June 27, 1991, 16.

19. Clay Shirky, "Truth Without Scarcity, Ethics Without Force," *The New Ethics of Journalism: Principles for the 21st Century*, ed. Kelly McBride and Tom Rosenstiel (Thousand Oaks, CA: CQ Press, 2013), 10.

20. Richard Harwood, at CCJ Forum, New York City, December 4, 1997.

21. Everette E. Dennis, "Whatever Happened to Marse Robert's Dream?: The Dilemma of American Journalism Education," *Gannett Center Journal* (Spring 1988).

22. Mindich, *Just the Facts*, 6–7. All three of these examples come from this book, but they are representative of statements we have heard from many journalists through the years.

23. Mindich makes this point as well in *Just the Facts*, 141.

24. Bill Keller, at CCJ Forum, New York City, December 4, 1997.

25. Robert D. Leigh, ed., *A Free and Responsible Press* (Chicago: University of Chicago Press, 1947), 23.

26. Jack Fuller, *News Values: Ideas for an Information Age* (Chicago and London: University of Chicago Press, 1996), 194.

27. Carl Bernstein has made this point on several occasions, in speeches, interviews, and conversation with the authors.

28. Eugene Meyer, "The Post's Principles," *Washington Post Deskbook on Style*, 2nd edition (New York: McGraw-Hill, 1989), 7.

29. Wood, "Novel History," 16.

30. Hodding Carter, interview by author Kovach, April 1998.

31. Paul Lewis, "Disproving the Police Account of Tomlinson's Death (How Citizen Journalism Aided Two Major *Guardian* Scoops)," in *Investigative Journalism: Dead or Alive?* ed. John Mair and Richard Lance Keeble (Suffolk, UK: Abramis, 2011).

32. This story is included in Jack Nelson's posthumous memoir, *Scoop: The Evolution of a Southern Reporter*, edited by his widow, Barbara Matusow (Jackson, MS: University Press of Mississippi, 2012), 122–23. The detail about Nelson's use of the double notebooks, not admitted to in the book, came from Gene Roberts, recounting the story at a book event for *Scoop* at the Washington, DC, bookstore Politics & Prose in February 2013.

33. Tom Reiss, "The First Conservative: How Peter Viereck Inspired–and Lost–a Movement," *New Yorker*, October 23, 2005, 42.

34. Variations on this quote have been used by many politicians, writers, and journalists. Mark Twain is often quoted as having said, "A lie can travel halfway around the world while the truth is putting on its shoes."

CHAPTER 3: WHO JOURNALISTS WORK FOR

1. Geneva Overholser, "Editor Inc.," *American Journalism Review* (December 1998), 58.

2. Ibid., 57. A Project on the State of the American Newspaper, a survey of seventy-seven senior newspaper editors, found that 14 percent reported spending more than half their time on business matters, while another 35 percent spent between one-third and one-half of their time on business matters.

3. CCJ and the Pew Research Center for the People & the Press, "Striking the Balance: Audience Interests, Business Pressures and Journalists' Values," March 1999, 79; available at www.journalism.org.

4. Research findings by our academic partners, William Damon, Howard Gardner, and Mihaly Csikszentmihalyi; unpublished interviews for the book *Good Work: When Excellence and Ethics Meet* (New York: Basic Books, 2001).

5. Nick Clooney, interview by William Damon, Howard Gardner, and Mihaly Csikszentmihalyi, ibid.

6. CNN.com, "Top New York Times Editors Quit," March 1, 2004; available at www.cnn.com/2003/US/Northeast/06/05/nytimes.resigns.

7. Don Van Natta Jr., Adam Liptak, and Clifford J. Levy, "The Miller Case: A Notebook, a Cause, a Jail Cell and a Deal," *New York Times*, October 16, 2005.

8. Statement made to author Rosenstiel at a gathering at the Foreign Press Center in Washington, D.C., in July 2013.

9. The Pew Research Center for the People & the Press, "In Changing News Landscape, Even Television Is Vulnerable." September 27, 2012. Available at www.pewresearch.org.

10. Alex Jones and Susan Tifft, *The Trust: The Private and Powerful Family Behind The New York Times* (Boston, New York, London: Little, Brown, 1999), 43.

11. *Washington Post DeskBook on Style*, 2nd ed. (New York: McGraw Hill, 1989).

12. Tom Goldstein, "Wanted: More Outspoken Views," *Columbia Journalism Review* (November/December 2001).

13. Paul Alfred Pratte, *Gods Within the Machine: A History of the American Society of Newspaper Editors, 1923–1993* (Westport, CT: Praeger, 1995), 2.

14. "Dow Jones Code of Conduct," New York: Dow Jones, 2000; see ethics codes at www.journalism.org.

15. "Project for Excellence in Journalism, Local TV Project," focus groups, January 26, 1999, in Atlanta, and January 28, 1999, in Tucson.

16. American Society of Newspaper Editors, "The Newspaper Journalists of the '90s," a study, 1997; available at www.asne.org.

17. Ibid. In 1988, 41 percent said they were less involved than others. In 1996, that number had risen to 55 percent.

18. Tom Rosenstiel, "The Beat Goes On: Clinton's First Year With the Media," Twentieth-Century Fund essay, 30. By 1993, a two-month examination of the front pages of the *New York Times,* the *Los Angeles Times,* and the *Washington Post* showed that only slightly more than half of the stories could be classified as straight news, while nearly 40 percent were analytical or interpretative treatments of news events or trends.

19. Daniel Hallin, "Sound Bite News: Television Coverage of Elections, 1968–1988," *Journal of Communications* 42 (Spring 1992), 6.

20. Ibid., 11.

21. Joseph N. Cappella and Kathleen Hall Jamieson, *Spiral of Cynicism: The Press and the Public Good* (New York: Oxford University Press, 1997), 31.

22. Rosenstiel, "The Beat Goes On," 30.

23. Michael Kelly, "Farmer Al," *Washington Post,* March 24, 1999; available at www .washingtonpost.com.

24. Michael Kelly, "Gore: 'His Wife, His Public Life, It's All Been Too Perfect,'" *Baltimore Sun,* December 13, 1987; available at www.baltimoresun.com.

25. Philip J. Trounstein, at CCJ Forum, Washington, DC, March 27, 1998.

26. Lou Urenick, "Newspapers Arrive at Economic Crossroads," *Nieman Reports,* special issue (Summer 1999), 3–20.

27. Ibid., 6.

28. Ibid., 5. According to figures from the Inland Press Association, these percentages are for the five years ending 1992 and the five years ending 1997. Smaller newspapers were defined as papers of around fifty thousand circulation. Larger were defined as papers of roughly five hundred thousand circulation. Newspaper payroll was cut 8 percent and 15 percent, respectively. Production costs were trimmed 21 percent and 12 percent, respectively. Rather than investing more in product, the newspaper industry invested more in marketing and marketing technology, increased sales staff, and advertising presentations.

29. Based on interviews with television news executives, we believe the practice is equally common for broadcast.

30. Overholser, "Editor Inc.," 54.

31. Thomas Leonard, "The Wall: A Long History," *Columbia Journalism Review* (January 2000), 28.

32. These calculations on revenue are derived by the Poynter Institute's Rick Edmonds, using data from former newspaper analyst Lauren Rich Fine and data from the Newspaper Association of America.

33. Newspaper Association of America.

34. John Sullivan, "PR Industry Fills Vacuum Left by Shrinking Newsrooms," Pro-
     Publica, May 1, 2011; available at www.propublica.org.

35. Peter Goldmark, "Setting the Testbed for Journalistic Values," Fourth Annual
     Aspen Institute Conference on Journalism and Society, August 23, 2000; available
     at www.aspeninstitute.org.

36. An eyewitness to this meeting recounted this moment to the authors. The execu-
     tive, who still works at the network, has requested anonymity for fear of losing his
     or her job, and we have granted it.

37. Joseph N. DiStefano, "Former Knight Ridder Journalists Plan to Nominate Board
     Candidates," *Philadelphia Inquirer*, November 18, 2005; available at www.philly
     .com.

38. Ken Auletta, "The Inheritance," *New Yorker*, December 19, 2005, 76.

39. Tom Johnson, "Excellence in the News: Who Really Decides," speech delivered at
     Paul White Award Dinner, October 2, 1999; Walter Cronkite Award acceptance
     speech, November 12, 1999.

40. Joe Strupp, "Where There's a Wall There's a Way," *Editor & Publisher*, December
     11, 1999, 23.

41. Edward Seaton, at the convention of the American Society of Newspaper Editors,
     April 13–16, 1999; retrieved from proceedings published on the ASNE website;
     available at www.asne.org.

42. Kevin Eck, "Louisville Station Stops Using 'Breaking News,'" *TVSpy*, June 4, 2013.

CHAPTER 4: JOURNALISM OF VERIFICATION

1. Thucydides, *History of the Peloponnesian War*, bks. 1 and 2, trans. C. F. Smith (Cam-
    bridge: Harvard University Press, 1991), 35–39.

2. Walter Lippmann, *Liberty and the News* (New Brunswick, NJ, and London: Trans-
    action Publishers, 1995), 58.

3. *This American Life*, "Retracting 'Mr. Daisey and the Apple Factory,'" http://www
    .thisamericanlife.org/blog/2012/03/retracting-mr-daisey-and-the-apple-factory.

4. Mike Daisey, March 16, 2012, http://mikedaisey.blogspot.com/2012/03/
    statement-on-tal.html

5. Claudia Puig, "Getting Inside the Truth, Filmmakers Accused of Fiddling with
    Facts Cite Dramatic Accuracy," *USA Today*, November 3, 1999; available at www
    .usatoday.com.

6. Dan Gillmor, "The End of Objectivity," *Bayosphere*, January 20, 2005.

7. Michael Schudson, *Discovering the News* (New York: Basic Books, 1978), 6. Schud-
    son's book has a particularly useful analysis of the move away from the naïve
    empiricism of the nineteenth century to the initially more sophisticated idea of
    objectivity.

8.   Walter Lippmann and Charles Merz, "A Test of the News," *New Republic*, August 4, 1920, published in *Killing the Messenger: 100 Years of Media Criticism*, ed. Tom Goldstein (New York: Columbia University Press, 1989), 91.

9.   Walter Lippmann, "The Press and Public Opinion," *Political Science Quarterly* 46 (June 1931), 170. The fact that Lippmann wrote this last passage in 1931, twelve years after his study of the Russian Revolution, is a sign of how the problem continued to dog him.

10. Lippmann, *Liberty and the News*, 74.

11. Ibid., 60.

12. Ibid., 74.

13. Schudson, *Discovering the News*, 155–56.

14. William Damon, to Committee of Concerned Journalists steering committee, February 12, 1999, private meeting.

15. Geneva Overholser, at CCJ Forum, Minneapolis, MN, October 22, 1998.

16. Paul Farhi, "Media Too Quick to Fill In Gaps in Story of School Shooting in Newtown, Conn." *Washington Post*, December 18, 2012; available at www.washington post.com.

17. Robert Parry, "He's No Pinocchio," *Washington Monthly*, April 2000; available from www.washingtonmonthly.com.

18. Ibid.

19. Phil Meyer, at CCJ Forum, St. Petersburg, FL, February 26, 1998.

20. Tom Goldstein, ed., *Killing the Messenger* (New York: Columbia University Press, 1989), 247.

21. Author Rosenstiel was a member with Bradlee of the panel "Why Don't We Trust the News Media? How Can the News Media Recover Public Trust?" Oswego, NY, October 27, 2005.

22. CCJ and the Pew Research Center for the People & the Press, "Striking the Balance: Audience Interests, Business Pressures and Journalists' Values," March 1999 (available at www.journalism.org); Amy Mitchell and Tom Rosenstiel, "Don't Touch That Quote," *Columbia Journalism Review* (January 2000), 34–36.

23. Bill Kovach and Tom Rosenstiel, *Blur: How to Know What's True in the Age of Information Overload* (New York: Bloomsbury USA, 2010).

24. Amy Harmon, "Young, Assured, and Playing Pharmacist to Friends," *New York Times*, November 16, 2005; available at www.nytimes.com.

25. The information is taken from Ron Ostrow's "Case Study: Richard Jewell and the Olympic Bombing," available on www.journalism.org.

26. Walter Lippmann, *Public Opinion* (New York: Free Press, 1965), 226.

27. Jay Mathews, interview by Dante Chinni, September 12, 2000.

28. Felicity Barringer and David Firestone, "On Torturous Route, Sexual Assault Ac-

cusation Against Clinton Resurfaces," *New York Times*, February 24, 1999; available at www.nytimes.com.

29. Michael Oreskes, at CCJ Forum, Washington, DC, October 20, 1998.

30. Jack Fuller, *News Values: Ideas from an Information Age* (Chicago and London: University of Chicago Press, 1996), 350.

31. Laurie Goodstein, at CCJ Forum, Detroit, MI, February 2, 1998.

32. MacCluggage, in an address to regional editors, argued, "Edit more skeptically. If skeptics aren't built into the process right from the start, stories will slide onto page one without the proper scrutiny." Associated Press, "APME President Urges Editors to Challenge Stories for Accuracy," October 15, 1998.

33. Amanda Bennett, interview by author Rosenstiel, April 13, 2000.

34. Sandra Rowe, interview by author Rosenstiel, April 13, 2000.

35. Bennett, interview by author Rosenstiel, April 13, 2000.

36. Pew Research Center for People & the Press, "Public More Critical of Press, but Goodwill Persists," June 26, 2005; available at http://people-press.org.

37. Carol Marin, at CCJ Forum, Chicago, IL, November 6, 1997.

CHAPTER 5: INDEPENDENCE FROM FACTION

1. William Safire, in a note to author Kovach, April 18, 2006. Subsequent quotes attributed to Safire are from the same note.

2. Anthony Lewis, in a note to the authors, October 10, 1999.

3. John Martin, in William L. Rivers, *Writing Opinion: Review* (Ames, IA: Iowa State University Press, 1988), 118.

4. Maggie Gallagher, at CCJ Forum, New York City, December 4, 1997.

5. Maggie Gallagher provided this defense in one of her columns, titled "A Question of Disclosure," January 25, 2005; available at www.uexpress.com.

6. James Carey, *James Carey: A Critical Reader*, ed. Eve Stryker Munson and Catherine A. Warren (Minneapolis and London: University of Minnesota Press, 1997), 233.

7. Carol Emert, "Abortion Rights Dilemma: Why I Didn't March–A Reporter's Struggle with Job and Conscience," *Washington Post*, April 12, 1992; available at www.washingtonpost.com.

8. Jacques Steinberg and Geraldine Fabrikant, "Friendship and Business Blur in the World of a Media Baron," *New York Times*, December 22, 2003; available at www.nytimes.com.

9. Mary McGrory, "Casualty: George Will Finds Being a 'Stablemate to Statesmen' Can Cost," *Washington Post*, July 12, 1983.

10. Howard Kurtz, "Journalists Say Their White House Advice Crossed No Line," *Washington Post*, January 29, 2005; available at www.washingtonpost.com.

11. Elliot Diringer, interview by William Damon, Howard Gardner, and Mihaly Csikszentmihalyi; unpublished interviews for the book *Good Work: When Excellence and Ethics Meet* (New York: Basic Books, 2001).

12. Louis Menand, "Everybody's an Expert," *New Yorker*, December 5, 2005, 98–101.

13. Juan Gonzalez, at CCJ Forum, New York City, December 4, 1997.

14. Richard Harwood, at CCJ Forum, New York City, December 4, 1997.

15. Tom Minnery, at CCJ Forum, Ann Arbor, MI, February 2, 1998.

16. George Washington University and Cicion, "Social Media & Online Usage Study," December 2009. See also Oriella PR Network, "The Influence Game: How News Is Sourced and Managed Today," 2012. The public Twitter usage data comes from the Pew Research Center's Internet & American Life Project, "Twitter Use 2012," May 31, 2012.

17. Pew Research Center for the People & the Press, "Press Widely Criticized, but Trusted More Than Other Information Sources." September 22, 2011.

18. Gonzalez, at CCJ Forum, New York City, December 4, 1997.

19. Peter Bell, at CCJ Forum, Ann Arbor, MI, February 2, 1998.

20. John Hockenberry, at CCJ Forum, Ann Arbor, MI, February 2, 1998.

21. Clarence Page, at CCJ Forum, Ann Arbor, MI, February 2, 1998.

22. Hockenberry, at CCJ Forum, Ann Arbor, MI, February 2, 1998.

23. Monica Guzman, *The New Ethics of Journalism: Principles for the 21st Century*, ed. Kelly McBride, Tom Rosenstiel (Thousand Oaks, CA: CQ Press, 2013), 206.

CHAPTER 6: MONITOR POWER AND OFFER VOICE TO THE VOICELESS

1. John C. Sommerville, *The News Revolution in England: Cultural Dynamics of Daily Information* (New York: Oxford University Press, 1996), 65.

2. Mitchell Stephens, *A History of News* (Fort Worth, TX: Harcourt Brace College Publishers, 1996), 226–27.

3. *Near v. Minnesota*, 283 US 697 (1931).

4. *New York Times Co. v. United States*, 403 US 713 (1971).

5. For a detailed account of Henry Mayhew's work, see Anne Humphreys, *Travels into the Poor Man's Country: The Work of Henry Mayhew* (Athens, GA: University of Georgia Press, 1977).

6. CCJ and the Pew Research Center for the People & the Press, "Striking the Balance: Audience Interests, Business Pressures and Journalists' Values," March 1999, 79; available at www.journalism.org.

7. Pew Research Center's Project for Excellence in Journalism, "News Leaders and the Future," April 12, 2010.

8. James Hamilton, "Subsidizing the Watchdog: What Would It Cost to Support Investigative Journalism at a Large Metropolitan Daily Newspaper?" presented at the Duke Conference on Nonprofit Media, May 4–5, 2009.

9. Pew Research Center for the People & the Press, "Press Widely Criticized, but Trusted More Than Other Information Sources." September 22, 2011.

10. Finley Peter Dunne, in *Bartlett's Familiar Quotations.* Dunne actually put the quote into the mouth of a fictional wag of his creation named Mr. Dooley. The full quote shows Dunne's satirical tone: "The newspaper does everything for us. It runs the police force and the banks, commands the militia, controls the legislature, baptizes the young, marries the foolish, comforts the afflicted and afflicts the comfortable, buries the dead, and roasts them afterward."

11. Emilio Garcia-Ruiz, sports editor of the *St. Paul Pioneer Press,* quoted his executive editor, Walker Lundy, at the annual Premack Journalism Award presentation, Minneapolis, MN, April 10, 2000.

12. Signed in 1798, the Act for the Punishment of Certain Crimes, as the sedition act was known, made it illegal to "write, print, utter or publish ... any false, scandalous, and malicious writing or writings against the government of the United States, or the President of the United States." The law was basically a partisan measure aimed at silencing the opposition to the Federalist Party in the 1800 elections–it had a built-in sunset of 1801. In total there were twenty-five arrests, twelve trials, and eleven convictions under the act.

13. The story that began the *Union-Tribune/*Copley News Service investigation, "Cunningham Defends Deal with Defense Firm's Owner," ran June 12, 2005. It was written by Marcus Stern.

14. *New York Times,* "Class Matters–Social Class in the United States of America," May–June 2005.

15. Robert Samuelson, "Confederacy of Dunces," *Newsweek,* September 23, 1996. Jack Fuller makes a virtually identical argument against "America: What Went Wrong" in *News Values: Ideas for an Information Age* (Chicago: University of Chicago Press, 1996).

16. Arlene Morgan, interview by author Rosenstiel, March 2000.

17. http://shorensteincenter.org/2013/03/natures-prophet-bill-mckibben-as-journalist-public-intellectual-and-activist/.

18. Seymour Hersh, "The Intelligence Gap," *New Yorker,* December 6, 1999, 76.

19. Kirsten Lundberg, "The Anatomy of an Investigation: The Difficult Case(s) of Wen Ho Lee" (1641.0), President and Fellows of Harvard College, 2001.

20. Thomas Patterson, at CCJ Forum, Washington, DC, March 27, 1998.

21. Project for Excellence in Journalism, "Changing Definitions of News: A Look at the Mainstream Press over 20 Years," March 6, 1998, 3; available at www.journalism.org.

22. Marc Gunther, "The Transformation of Network News: How Profitability Has Moved Networks Out of Hard News," *Nieman Reports,* special issue (Summer 1999), 27.

23. Patty Calhoun, at CCJ Forum, Chicago, November 6, 1997.

24. Pew Research Center for the People & the Press, "Press 'Unfair, Inaccurate and Pushy': Fewer Favor Media Scrutiny of Political Leaders," March 21, 1997; available at http://people-press.org.

25. Pew Research Center for the People & the Press, "Public More Critical of Press, but Goodwill Persists," June 26, 2005.

26. "Watchdog Conference: Reporters Wrestle with How to Use Sources," *Nieman Reports* (Fall 1999), 7.

27. Ibid., 8.

28. Rifka Rosenwein, "Why Media Mergers Matter," *Brill's Content,* December 1999–January 2000, 93.

29. Pew Research Center's Project for Excellence in Journalism, "Nonprofit Journalism: A Growing, If Fragile, Part of the U.S. News System," June 10, 2013.

CHAPTER 7: JOURNALISM AS A PUBLIC FORUM

1. *Hardball with Chris Matthews,* CNBC News, transcript, May 11, 1999.

2. Gene Lyons, "Long-Running Farce Plays On," *Arkansas Democrat-Gazette,* May 26, 1999, B9; available in LexisNexis.

3. Cody Shearer, interview by Dante Chinni, June 2000.

4. Robert D. Leigh, *A Free and Responsible Press* (Chicago: University of Chicago Press, 1947), 23.

5. Warren G. Bovée, *Discovering Journalism* (Westport, CT: Greenwood Press, 1999), 154–55.

6. Tom Leonard, *News for All* (New York: Oxford University Press, 1995), 152.

7. Tom Winship, "Obvious Lessons in Hindsight," *Media Studies Journal* (Spring/Summer 1998), 4.

8. These estimates are based on television in Washington, DC, July 10, 2000. The percentage of chat was based on the fact that, on broadcast TV, there were 39.5 hours of news, 27 hours of talk, 3 hours of pseudo-news (*Access Hollywood, Inside Edition*), plus 108 hours of cable news, which was a mix of both talk and news.

9. Michael Crichton, "Mediasaurus," speech delivered to National Press Club, Washington, DC, April 7, 1993.

10. Robert Berdahl, speech delivered to American Society of Newspaper Editors Credibility Think Tank, San Francisco, CA, October 8, 1998.

11. *Crossfire,* CNN, transcript, October 15, 2004.

12. In June 2013, CNN's new president, Jeff Zucker, announced that *Crossfire* would return to the air later that year.

13. Jack Fuller, at CCJ Forum, Chicago, November 6, 1997.

CHAPTER 8: ENGAGEMENT AND RELEVANCE

1. Lara Setrakian, "Single Story Sites Like Syria Deeply Have Lessons to Offer the Rest of the News Business," January 15, 2013, available at www.niemanlab.org, http://www.niemanlab.org/2013/01/lara-setrakian-single-story-sites-like-syria-deeply-have-lessons-to-offer-the-rest-of-the-news-business/.

2. Anajali Mullany, "Syria Deeply Outsmarts the News, Redefines Conflict Coverage," Fast Company, December 3, 2012.

3. Ray Suarez, interview by William Damon, Howard Gardner, and Mihaly Csikszentmihalyi, unpublished interviews conducted for the book *Good Work: When Excellence and Ethics Meet* (New York: Basic Books, 2001).

4. Howard Rheingold, interview by William Damon, Howard Gardner, and Mihaly Csikszentmihalyi, ibid.

5. Project for Excellence in Journalism Local TV Project, *Columbia Journalism Review*: "Local TV News: What Works, What Flops, and Why," January 1999; "Quality Brings Higher Ratings, but Enterprise Is Disappearing," November 1999; "Time of Peril for TV News," November 2000; available at www.journalism.org.

6. Pew Research Center, "Future of Mobile News," October 1, 2012.

7. Andy Smith, "A Touch of Glass," *Providence Journal,* April 14, 2005.

8. Leo Braudy, at CCJ Forum, Los Angeles, March 4, 1998.

9. Tom Rosenstiel, Walter Dean, Marion Just, Dante Chinni, and Todd Belt, *We Interrupt This Newscast* (Cambridge University Press, 2007).

10. Insite Research, Television Audience Survey, October 1999; available from Insite Research, 2156 Rambla Vista, Malibu, CA 90265.

11. News Lab Survey, "Bringing Viewers Back to Local TV News: What Could Reverse Ratings Slide?" September 14, 2000; available at www.newslab.org. People in the survey specifically answered that they got "local news elsewhere," there was "too much crime," "local news is always the same stuff," "too many fluff feature stories instead of real news," and "TV news seldom presents positive things that occur in your community."

12. Insite Research, Television Audience Survey, October 1999; available from Insite Research, 2156 Rambla Vista, Malibu, CA 90265.

13. Mark Bowden, "The Inheritance," Vanity Fair, May 2009; available at http://www.vanityfair.com/politics/features/2009/05/new-york-times200905.

14. Roy Peter Clark, interview by author Rosenstiel, June 2000.

15. Jack Hart described this narrative arc in detail in an October 2004 article in *Above the Fold,* a newsletter on writing and editing published for the employees of the *Minneapolis Star Tribune.*

16. Roy Peter Clark, "Writing and Reporting Advice from 4 of the Washington Post's Best," Poynter Online, May 20, 2013; available at http://www.poynter

.org/how-tos/newsgathering-storytelling/writing-tools/213933/writing-and-reporting-advice-from-4-of-the-washington-posts-best/.

17. William Whitaker, interview by William Damon, Howard Gardner, and Mihaly Csikszentmihalyi.

18. Jim Benning, "Why Journalists Eat Up the Onion: World Media Shedding Tears of Joy Over the Onion," *Online Journalism Review,* May 2, 2000; available at www.ojr.org/ojr/workplace/1017964709.php.

19. Alfred Kazin, "Vietnam: It Was Us vs. Us: Michael Herr's Dispatches: More Than Just the Best Vietnam Book," *Esquire,* March 1, 1978, 120.

20. Doug Marlette, News Lab retreat on storytelling, Washington, DC, April 12 and 14, 2000.

21. Annie Lang, News Lab retreat, Washington, DC, April 12 and 14, 2000.

22. John Larson, News Lab retreat, Washington, DC, April 12 and 14, 2000.

23. *Booknotes,* C-Span, April 29, 1990.

24. Boyd Huppert, News Lab retreat, Washington, DC, April 12 and 14, 2000.

25. http://www.poynter.org/how-tos/newsgathering-storytelling/178038/lets-blow-up-the-news-story-and-build-new-forms-of-journalism/.

CHAPTER 9: MAKE THE NEWS COMPREHENSIVE AND PROPORTIONAL

1. Valerie Crane, interview by author Rosenstiel, June 2000.

2. Project for Excellence in Journalism Local TV Project, "Quality Brings Higher Ratings, but Enterprise Is Disappearing," *Columbia Journalism Review,* November 1999; available at www.journalism.org.

3. Several people have noted this phenomenon. Hess was one of the first, in *The Washington Reporters* (Washington, DC: Brookings Institution, 1981).

4. Various people have made this point, including the authors themselves, local newscasters, and viewers in focus groups and meetings with local broadcasters.

5. Carnegie Corporation of New York, "Use of Sources for News," May 1, 2005. A slide show of the report is available online on the Carnegie Corporation website, www.carnegie.org/pdf/AbandoningTheNews.ppt.

6. John Morton, "When Newspapers Eat Their Seed Corn," *American Journalism Review* (November 1995), 52; available at www.ajr.org.

7. Newspaper Association of America. http://www.naa.org/en/Topics-and-Tools/SenseMakerReports/Multiplatform-Newspaper-Media-Access.aspx.

8. Project for Excellence in Journalism Local TV Project, "Quality Brings Higher Ratings."

9. "Transformation of Network News," *Nieman Reports,* special issue (Summer 1999).

10. The trend has been reflected in data compiled by the Project for Excellence in

Journalism in its annual State of the News Media reports beginning in 2004; available at www.journalism.org.

11. Pew Research Center's Project for Excellence in Journalism, "Coverage of Economy, International News Jump in Year of Big Breaking Stories," March 19, 2012; available at http://stateofthemedia.org/2012/mobile-devices-and-news-consumption-some-good-signs-for-journalism/year-in-2011/.

12. Project for Excellence in Journalism, "State of the News Media 2006," March 2006; available at www.journalism.org.

13. Lucas Graves and John Kelly with Marissa Gluck, "Confusion Online: Faulty Metrics and the Future of Digital Journalism," Tow Center for Digital Journalism, Columbia University Graduate School of Journalism, September 2010.

14. John Carey, interview by author Rosenstiel, June 2000.

15. Ibid.

16. Tom Rosenstiel, Walter Dean, Marion Just, Dante Chinni, and Todd Belt, *We Interrupt This Newscast* (Cambridge University Press, 2007).

17. Tom Rosenstiel and Dave Iverson, "Politics and TV Can Mix," *Los Angeles Times*, October 15, 2002; available at www.latimes.com.

18. Lee Ann Brady, interview by author Rosenstiel, June 2000.

19. Ibid.

20. Leo Bogart, interview by author Rosenstiel, June 2000.

21. Crane, interview by author Rosenstiel, June 2000.

22. Al Tompkins, interview by author Rosenstiel, June 2000.

23. Carey, interview by author Rosenstiel, June 2000.

24. Tim Griggs, speaking at an American Press Institute workshop in New York City, June 11, 2013.

CHAPTER 10: JOURNALISTS HAVE A RESPONSIBILITY TO CONSCIENCE

1. This account comes from interviews with Lichtblau and Berke conducted by author Kovach, March 2006.

2. CNN.com, "Top New York Times Editors Quit," March 1, 2004; available at www.cnn.com/2003/US/Northeast/06/05/NYTimes/resigns/.

3. Carol Marin, at CCJ Forum, Chicago, November 6, 1997.

4. Benjamin Weiser, "Does TV News Go Too Far? A Look Behind the Scenes at NBC's Truck Crash Test," *Washington Post*, February 28, 1993; available at www.washingtonpost.com.

5. Bob Woodward, Nieman Fellows seminar, Harvard University, Fall 1998.

6. Bill Kurtis, interview by William Damon, Howard Gardner, and Mihaly Csikszentmihalyi; unpublished interviews for the book *Good Work: When Excellence and Ethics Meet* (New York: Basic Books, 2001).

7. Jon Katz, interview by William Damon, Howard Gardner, and Mihaly Csikszent-mihalyi, ibid.

8. Tom Brokaw, interview by William Damon, Howard Gardner, and Mihaly Csik-szentmihalyi, ibid.

9. CCJ and the Pew Research Center for the People & the Press, "Striking the Balance: Audience Interests, Business Pressures and Journalists' Values," March 1999, 6; available at www.journalism.org.

10. Marin, at CCJ Forum, Chicago, November 6, 1997.

11. Ibid.

12. Linda Foley, at CCJ Forum, Ann Arbor, MI, February 2, 1998.

13. Donald W. Shriver Jr., "Meaning from the Muddle," *Media Studies Journal* (Spring/Summer 1998), 138.

14. Katharine Graham, *Personal History* (New York: Alfred A. Knopf, 1997), 449.

15. Anthony Lewis, Eleventh Annual Frank E. Gannett Lecture, Capitol Hilton Hotel, Washington, DC, November 28, 1988.

16. Charles Gibson, at CCJ Forum, Ann Arbor, MI, February 2, 1998.

17. David Ashenfelder, at CCJ Forum, Ann Arbor, MI, February 2, 1998.

18. American Society of Newspaper Editors, "1999 Newsroom Census: Minority Employment Inches Up at Daily Newspapers"; available at www.asne.org.

19. Mercedes de Uriarte, at CCJ Forum, St. Petersburg, FL, February 26, 1998.

20. Juan Gonzalez, at CCJ Forum, New York City, December 4, 1997.

21. Tom Bray, at CCJ Forum, Ann Arbor, MI, February 2, 1998.

22. David Halberstam, interview by author Kovach, June 10, 2000.

23. Favre delivered a version of this speech at the Portland *Oregonian*'s annual Fred Stickel Award ceremony in April 2006.

CHAPTER 11: THE RIGHTS AND RESPONSIBILITIES OF CITIZENS

1. Richard Sambrook, "Citizen Journalism and the BBC," *Nieman Reports* (Winter 2005), 13–16; available at www.nieman.harvard.edu/reports/05-4NRwinter/Sambrook.pdf.

2. Ibid.

INDEX

Bill Kovach is the former Washington bureau chief of the *New York Times,* editor of the *Atlanta Journal-Constitution,* and curator of the Nieman Fellowships at Harvard. He was the founding chairman of the Committee of Concerned Journalists, as well as the senior counselor to the Project for Excellence in Journalism. He has won the Elijah Parish Lovejoy Award and the Richard M. Clurman Award for Mentoring. His writing has appeared in the *New York Times Magazine,* the *Washington Post,* the *New Republic,* and many other newspapers and magazines in the United States and abroad.

Tom Rosenstiel is executive director of the American Press Institute in Arlington, Virginia, and previously founder and director of the Project for Excellence in Journalism and vice chairman of the Committee of Concerned Journalists. A former media critic for the *Los Angeles Times* and chief congressional correspondent for *Newsweek,* he is the coeditor of *The New Ethics of Journalism: Principles for the 21st Century,* with Kelly McBride, and *Thinking Clearly: Cases in Journalistic Decision Making* with Amy Mitchell, and author of *Strange Bedfellows: How Television and the Presidential Candidates Changed American Politics* and *We Interrupt This Newscast: How to Improve TV News and Win Ratings, Too.* His writing has appeared in such publications as *Esquire,* the *New Republic,* the *New York Times,* the *Columbia Journalism Review,* and the *Washington Monthly.* A former media critic for MSNBC's *The News with Brian Williams,* he is a frequent commentator on radio and television and in print.

Together, Bill and Tom are also the authors of *Warp Speed: America in the Age of Mixed Media* and *Blur: How to Know What's True in the Age of Information Overload*. Both live in Washington, DC.